What Your Colleagues Are Sayi

Teaching Reading is destined to become "stock-in-trade" for teachers in preparation and practicing teachers who want an updated, easy-to-read, and practical guide for assessing and teaching reading. The modules are predictably organized with practical classroom applications aplenty! The style and tone are accessible for classroom practitioners while communicating the best and most applicable current research evidence available. This new playbook is just the right mix of tactics, strategy, and content to deliver a winning gameplan for teaching reading to all students.

—**D. Ray Reutzel**, Senior Research Fellow, Center for the School of the Future, Utah State University

In their inimitable way Douglas Fisher, Nancy Frey, and Diane Lapp have organized a great deal of practical, evidence-based information into a readable, accessible book! It will become a veritable go-to resource with its comprehensive information.

—**Heidi Anne Mesmer**, Professor of Reading Education, Virginia Polytechnic Institute and State University

Three preeminent literacy scholars, Douglas Fisher, Nancy Frey, and Diane Lapp have done a masterful job of presenting to teachers, preservice and inservice, an actionable guide for implementing the science of reading. *Teaching Reading* is comprehensive coverage of the major competencies required to achieve proficiency in reading. With several unique features that allow readers to take an active role in going from anticipating to understanding to planning and applying the evidence-based strategies presented, this book is a major contribution to the field of literacy education.

—**Timothy Rasinski**, Professor of Literacy Education, Rebecca Tolle and Burton W. Gorman Chair in Educational Leadership, Kent State University

Possibly the most imaginative and informative resource on teaching reading on the market, this book engages readers through thoughtful interactive features that make you reflect, question, and further consider practices as it relates to your daily instruction. These authors and colleagues clearly know classroom instruction, and it shows in their writing. Want to know about the science of reading? This is your resource!

—**Susan B. Neuman**, Professor, Childhood Education and Literacy Development, Steinhardt School of Culture, Education and Human Development, New York University

Wondering how to make sense of all you've been reading about the science of reading? Douglas Fisher, Nancy Frey, and Diane Lapp offer us a text that makes gaining this knowledge our reality. These authors have the unique ability to write professional development books for teachers about current issues exactly at the time they are needed, and this new text reminds us that we must teach skills to children in addition to social and emotional and culturally responsive instruction. This reader-friendly book emphasizes skill development we have neglected to emphasize over the past few years and presents the information in a creative playbook format just right for teachers. Written with evidenced-based practice and thoughtfully organized in a manner that will enable teachers to improve their craft and consequently student achievement, this is a great resource for professional development in schools or as a text for university literacy courses.

—**Lesley Mandel Morrow**, Distinguished Professor, Director of the Center for Literacy Development, Rutgers, the State University of New Jersey

Organized around an expanded adaptation of Scarborough's reading rope, this user-friendly resource expertly translates scientific research findings into a comprehensive guide for reading instruction. Practical Illustrations and classroom examples abound throughout the playbook, allowing research-based recommendations to come to life to foster both word recognition and language comprehension in young learners. This book also encourages teachers to reflect on their own practice at many points and in many ways. A terrific resource!

—**Sonia Q. Cabell**, Associate Professor of Reading Education, School of Teacher Education & Florida Center for Reading Research, Florida State University

Douglas Fisher, Nancy Frey, and Diane Lapp reduce the clamor around the teaching of reading and bring clarity to how to develop strong readers. The authors not only give the *what* and the *why* but, more importantly, also provide interactive examples of the *how* to teach reading—and what our teachers need most is the *how*. The text is broken into neat learning modules that can be used in PLCs or study/book groups. I plan to use *Teaching Reading* as the core text in an interactive professional learning series for our staff. You should too!

—**Michael Rafferty**, Director of Teaching and Learning, Derby Public Schools, Author of *30 Big-Idea Lessons for Small Groups*

Douglas Fisher, Nancy Frey, and Diane Lapp have done the tremendous work of bringing depth and clarity to the foundational skills of reading. They provide a wealth of clear and intentional guidance that will support us [early elementary educators] in providing quality phonemic awareness, phonics instruction, word reading skills, and so on, so that children are confident in their ability to decode and contextualize what they've read.

—**Melissa Black**, Early Childhood Educator and Educational Consultant

Teaching Reading

A PLAYBOOK FOR DEVELOPING SKILLED READERS THROUGH WORD RECOGNITION AND LANGUAGE COMPREHENSION

GRADES PreK–6

DOUGLAS FISHER
NANCY FREY
DIANE LAPP

CORWIN
Fisher & Frey

CORWIN
A SAGE Publishing Company

FOR INFORMATION:

Corwin
A SAGE Company
2455 Teller Road
Thousand Oaks, California 91320
(800) 233-9936
www.corwin.com

SAGE Publications Ltd.
1 Oliver's Yard
55 City Road
London EC1Y 1SP
United Kingdom

SAGE Publications India Pvt. Ltd.
B 1/I 1 Mohan Cooperative Industrial Area
Mathura Road, New Delhi 110 044
India

SAGE Publications Asia-Pacific Pte. Ltd.
18 Cross Street #10-10/11/12
China Square Central
Singapore 048423

President: Mike Soules
Vice President and
Editorial Director: Monica Eckman
Director and Publisher
Corwin Classroom: Lisa Luedeke
Associate Content
Development Editor: Sarah Ross
Editorial Assistant: Nancy Chung
Production Editor: Melanie Birdsall
Copy Editor: Cate Huisman
Typesetter: C&M Digitals (P) Ltd.
Proofreader: Ellen Brink
Indexer: Sheila Hill
Cover Designer: Gail Buschman
Marketing Manager: Megan Naidl

Printed in the United States of America

ISBN 978-1-0718-5053-4

Library of Congress Control Number: 2022943838

This book is printed on acid-free paper.

23 24 25 26 10 9 8 7 6 5 4

Contents

Acknowledgments

This playbook became a reality because of the insights of the many reviewers who offered their expertise throughout its development. Corwin gratefully acknowledges the contributions of the following reviewers:

Melissa J. Black
Elementary Teacher, District of Columbia Public Schools
Washington, DC

Tiffany Coleman
Instructional Coach, Gwinnett County Public Schools
Loganville, GA

Kelly Johnson
Literacy Resource Teacher and Instructional Coach, San Diego Unified School District
San Diego, CA

Hilda Martinez
Early Literacy Resource Teacher, San Diego Unified School District
Chula Vista, CA

Heidi Anne Mesmer
Professor of Reading Education
Virginia Polytechnic Institute and State University

D. Ray Reutzel
Senior Research Fellow, Center for the School of the Future, Utah State University
Professor and Dean Emeritus College of Education, University of Wyoming

Katherine Casey Spengler
Literacy Educator, Author, and Consultant
San Diego, CA

Katherine Stahl
Literacy Consultant
St. Simons Island, GA

Melissa Wood-Glusac
English Teacher, Conejo Valley Unified School District
Thousand Oaks, CA

Introduction

Welcome to the playbook that focuses on teaching reading to every child. This book integrates current research evidence across many aspects of reading instruction. We start Module 1 with an overview of Scarborough's reading rope (2001). You'll learn more about the history of the reading rope and why we use this metaphor for the organization of this information. You'll also learn that we and others have suggested additions to the rope over the past few decades and that new areas of understanding, such as of reading fluency and morphology, have developed.

From there, we focus our attention on the two major bundles of strands of the reading rope: Word recognition and language comprehension. The modules in Part I—word recognition—focus on aspects that include phonemic awareness and phonics as well as fluency and sight word recognition. In Part II, we turn our attention to language comprehension, which includes topics such as vocabulary and background knowledge. In fact, here is a listing of all of the modules in this playbook:

Module 1. How Reading Develops

Part I. Word Recognition

Module 2. Phonological Awareness

Module 3. Alphabetics

Module 4. Phonics and Decoding

Module 5. Sight Word Recognition

Module 6. Reading Fluency

Part II. Language Comprehension

Module 7. Background Knowledge

Module 8. Vocabulary Knowledge

Module 9. Morphological Awareness

Module 10. Text and Language Structures

Module 11. Literacy and Text Knowledge

Module 12. Verbal Reasoning

Module 13. Theory of Mind

Given that this is a playbook, you'll notice several interactive features, including

- An **Anticipation Guide** at the beginning of the module that allows you to consider several statements and determine whether you agree with them or not. We invite you to return to these after reading the module to see if your thinking has been validated or extended.
- **Notice and Wonder**, in which you have an opportunity to reflect on some of the content presented in the module.
- **What's Your Advice?**, a feature that allows you to make recommendations to other teachers based on what you have learned.
- **Find the Mistake**, which requires you to identify errors and determine what you could do to correct those errors.
- **Take Action**, which invites you to apply what you have learned in your own practice.
- A **Text-to-Self Connection** feature that pushes your reflection further and provides you space to scale your level of understanding so that you can keep learning after finishing the module.
- **Takeaways** or key ideas that conclude each of the modules.

Again, this playbook is meant to engage you. Please mark it up and complete the various tasks. The narrative in each module provides current and tested research as well as informed recommendations for practice. And your willingness to engage in the exercises in this playbook demonstrates your commitment to your students and their literacy lives. Happy reading.

online resources

Visit the companion website at
resources.corwin.com/teachingreading
for downloadable resources.

MODULE

1

How Reading Develops

Photo by LinkedIn Sales Solutions on Unsplash

In this module, we will

- Examine reading development through word recognition and language comprehension.
- Discuss the role of constrained and unconstrained reading skills in reading development.
- Review the role of metacognition in reading development.

We'll start with a poem by poet, author, and lecturer Francis Ellen Watkins Harper (1812–1911), who was the first African American woman to publish a short story. Throughout her life she fought for the freedom of equal rights, job opportunities, and education for all.

Very soon the Yankee teachers
Came down and set up school;
But, oh! how the Rebs did hate it,—
It was agin' their rule.

Our masters always tried to hide
Book learning from our eyes;
Knowledge didn't agree with slavery—
'Twould make us all too wise.

But some of us would try to steal
A little from the book,
And put the words together,
And learn by hook or crook.

I remember Uncle Caldwell,
Who took pot-liquor fat
And greased the pages of his book,
And hid it in his hat.

And had his master ever seen
The leaves up on his head,
He'd have thought them greasy papers,
But nothing to be read.

And there was Mr. Turner's Ben,
Who heard the children spell,
And picked the words right up by heart,
And learned to read 'em well.

Well, the Northern folks kept sending
The Yankee teachers down;
And they stood right up and helped us,
Though Rebs did sneer and frown.

And, I longed to read my Bible,
For precious words it said;
But when I begun to learn it,
Folks just shook their heads,

And said there is no use trying,
Oh! Chloe, you're too late;
But as I was rising sixty,
I had no time to wait.

So I got a pair of glasses,
And straight to work I went,
And never stopped till I could read
The hymns and Testament.

Then I got a little cabin—
A place to call my own—
And I felt as independent
As the queen upon her throne.

Source: Watkins Harper (n.d.)

What happened for you as your eyes processed the words? Did you have an emotional reaction? Did you make connections and see faces of students you've taught? Did you think about all the processes that occurred in your brain that allowed you to take those little squiggly lines from the page and make meaning of them? That's reading. It's an impressive set of skills that you just mobilized to make sense of the message.

You weren't born reading. Your brain was taught to read, just like every other brain that reads. Unfortunately, there is no reading gene that is passed from one generation to the next. Experimental psychologist Steven Pinker notes that while "children are wired for sound[,] . . . print is an optional accessory that must be bolted on" (Pinker, 1999, p. ix).

Every brain needs to be taught to read.

Every brain needs to be taught to read. And over the past 100+ years, there have been hundreds of thousands of studies that together compose a science of reading. As Pearson and Tierney (2021) noted, there are waves of research as educators and researchers strive to understand this complex cognitive skill that serves as a gateway to all other learning.

Read each statement and mark **T** if you think the statement is true and **F** if you think the statement is false. As you read through the module, you might change your responses. Be prepared to explain your responses and use the text for evidence.

Before Reading	Statements	After Reading
T F	1. Word recognition skills must be mastered before language comprehension can be effectively taught.	T F
Why did you indicate true or false?		Has your thinking changed after reading?
T F	2. Constrained reading skills are easier to assess because they have a finite ceiling.	T F
Why did you indicate true or false?		Has your thinking changed after reading?
T F	3. Metacognition is an important skill for strategic readers to master.	T F
Why did you indicate true or false?		Has your thinking changed after reading?

"The Reading Rope"

Hollis Scarborough, a cognitive developmental psychologist who cheerfully reminds people that "I never taught anybody to read," worked throughout the 1980s on a longitudinal study of preschoolers who were at risk for later reading difficulties. As a researcher, one of her responsibilities was to disseminate results to the field. In preparation for professional meetings, she conducted a review of the research on reading and drew a visual for her audiences to capture the existing research (see Figure 1.1). True to her developmental orientation, she also wanted to portray how reading changes over time. The "reading rope," as it is affectionately known, began its life in 1991 as a handout!

The reading rope should not be misinterpreted as either a curriculum or an instructional framework.

As Scarborough (2001) noted, there are strands that are each important and are represented within the two major skill bundles of language comprehension and word recognition. (See Figure 1.2 for our adaptation of the rope; italicized labels on the left indicate where we propose adding new strands.) It's important to note that strands within each bundle are intertwined to illustrate the increasing consolidation of skills needed for strategic and automatic processes to support children becoming skilled readers. To accomplish this, a future reader must develop all strands and mobilize them together. Importantly, one strand is not more important than the others, and the strands themselves do not represent a developmental sequence. In other words, the reading rope should not be misinterpreted as either a curriculum or an instructional framework. Rather, it is a visual metaphor to represent the theoretical research on reading.

Figure 1.1 *Scarborough's Reading Rope*

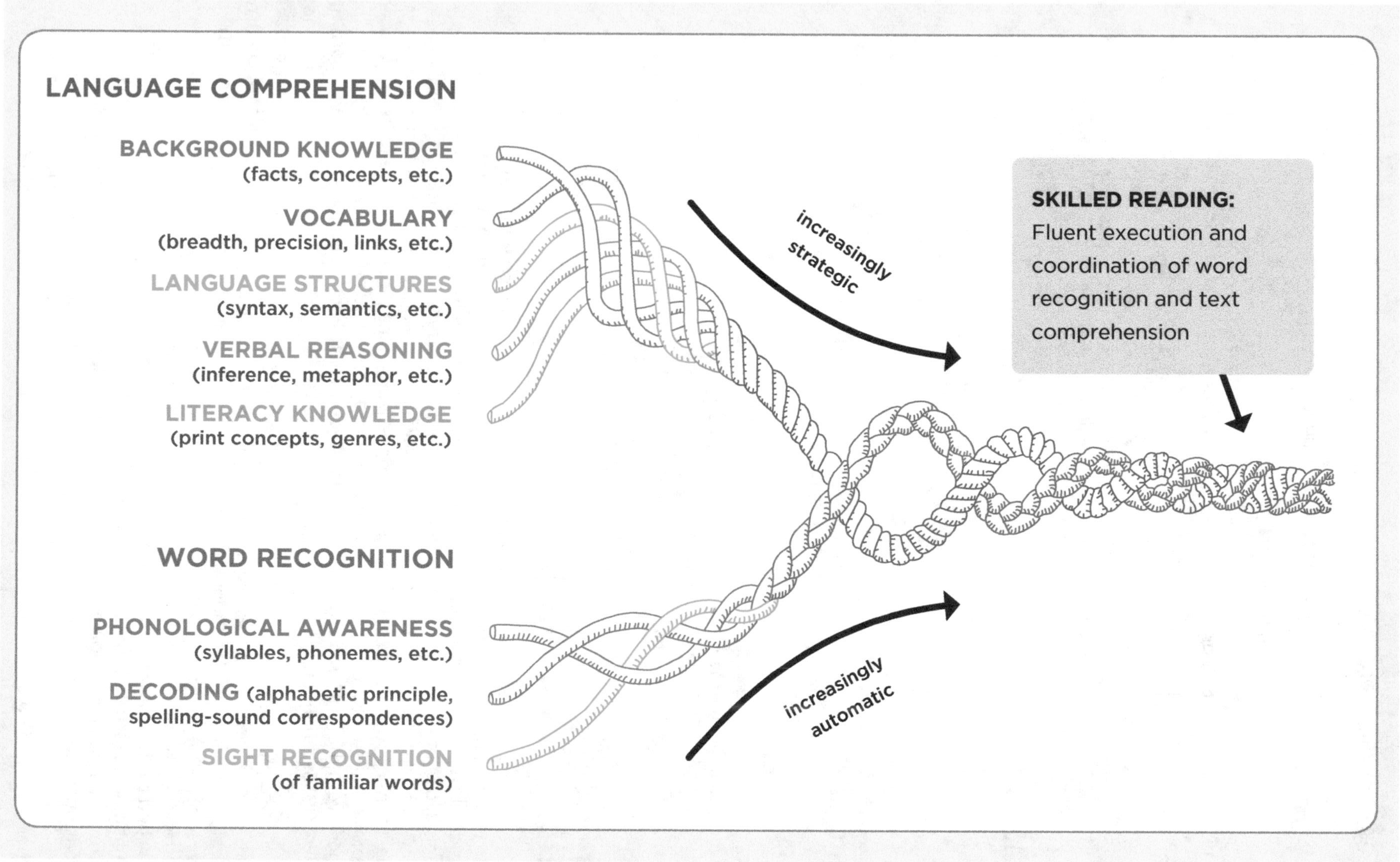

Source: Scarborough, H. S. (2001). Connecting early language and literacy to later reading (dis)abilities: Evidence, theory, and practice. In S. Neuman & D. Dickinson (Eds.), *Handbook for research in early literacy* (pp. 97–110). Guilford Press.

Figure 1.2 Suggested Modifications of the Reading Rope

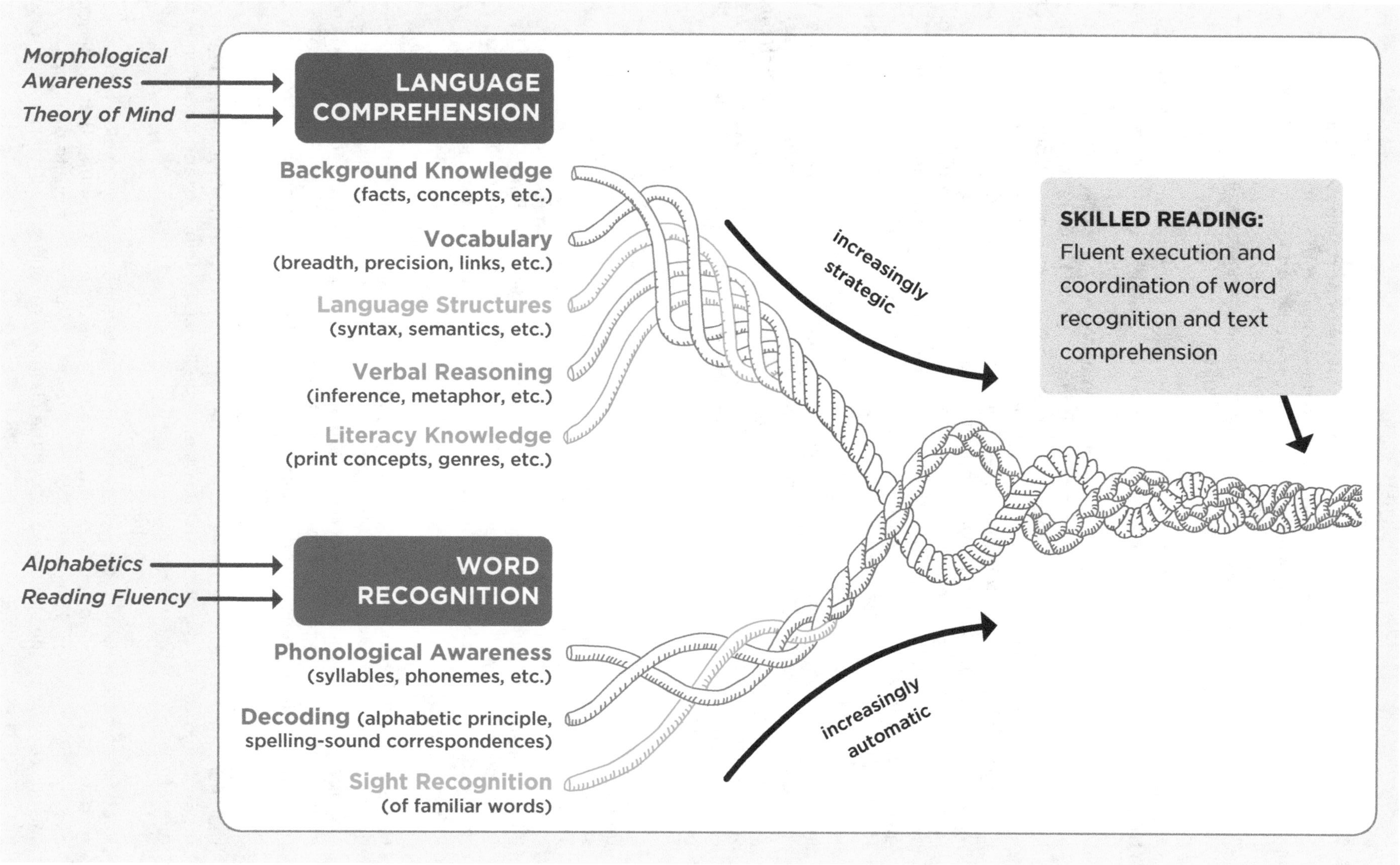

Source: Adapted from Scarborough, H. S. (2001). Connecting early language and literacy to later reading (dis)abilities: Evidence, theory, and practice. In S. Neuman & D. Dickinson (Eds.), *Handbook for research in early literacy* (pp. 97–110). Guilford Press.

As Scarborough noted in the interview,

> Being strong on the lower strands affords more opportunities to acquire knowledge of the upper strands, and being strong on the upper strands has been shown to enable faster and more accurate decoding of unfamiliar words. Therefore, if any of the strands gets frayed, it can hold back development of the other strands and by extension can eventually weaken the entire rope. (University of Florida Literacy Institute, 2020)

Although we appreciate what this visual infographic accomplishes in its attempt to convey the complexities of reading, it doesn't fully reflect the waves of reading research that have continued since its publication two decades ago. Our adaptation to the original rope offers an expansion on Scarborough's work. First, we added *alphabetics*. It was previously part of decoding, and certainly recognizing letters is an important aspect of decoding. But our collective knowledge about alphabetics has grown, and readers need to understand so much about this that we elevated it. This is especially true for English learners who use other writing systems, such as those of Arabic, Georgian, or Mandarin. In addition, we have added *reading fluency* and included it in the word recognition bundle, because the goal of fluency instruction is to increase automaticity. The volume of research on fluency has grown considerably since the original publication of the reading rope and demands further attention.

In terms of language comprehension, we have added *morphological awareness* given the significant amount of research on this topic that has been conducted in the past 20 years. We have also included *theory of mind*, a newer area of literacy research that suggests readers need to develop an understanding of others' mental states, such as beliefs, intents, desires, emotions, and knowledge, if they are to deeply understand the texts they read.

Language comprehension is the focus of the upper bundle. Readers use their understanding of print concepts and their background knowledge, vocabulary, language structures, verbal reasoning, and literacy knowledge to read and understand the text. These language comprehension skills become increasingly *strategic* through instruction, experience, and practice. In the lower bundle, the focus is on word recognition. This involves a student's understanding and use of phonological awareness, alphabetics, and decoding, as well as their recognition of sight words and fluency. These word recognition skills become increasingly *automatic* through instruction, experience, and practice.

However, we must address the shortcomings that this visual infographic, albeit updated to reflect newer research, still holds. It can be tempting to view the rope as a recipe of ingredients. Wexler (2022) notes that it can lull educators into a sense of complacency, failing to fully challenge current instructional practices. The point of reading is to understand. Word recognition is crucial and cannot be minimized. But for reading to be fully realized, there must be a relentless focus on comprehension, not as a mere collection of ingredients but as a series of chemical reactions. The chemistry of reading comprehension requires building background knowledge (not just activating it), motivation (not just the hope that it will emerge), analytic thinking, and persistence to move forward when the text gets hard.

Reading comprehension is a science, and one that requires skill to develop among readers. We encourage you to read deeply and reflect on the modules that highlight each of these strands. They are not discrete items in a grocery store to be either selected or left on the shelf. Appreciate the chemical reactions that happen as a result of ingredients coming in contact with one another.

NOTICE AND WONDER

Review our adaptation of the reading rope. Note that each strand is one component of reading and that the strands combine into two bundles that are braided together into the rope.

What are you noticing about the various strands?

____

____

____

Which strands are strong in your classroom?

____

____

____

Which strands need more attention or are not yet clear to you?

____

____

____

Untangling *Skill*, *Skilled*, and *Strategic*

Look at the reading rope visual again. There are two arrows intended to represent change over time. The lower one is labeled "increasingly strategic" while the upper one is labeled "increasingly automatic." The latter is more straightforward in that there is widespread and consistent usage of the term *automaticity*. Automaticity refers to smooth and effortless word recognition and was described by LaBerge and Samuels (1974) as the way print is processed in the brain. The braiding of the word recognition strands of the reading rope reflects the notion that the skills of phonological awareness, alphabetics, decoding, and sight recognition work together in increasingly efficient ways to make this dimension of reading more fluent. It is an essential part of the journey to becoming a *skilled* reader.

The goal is to develop *skilled* readers—those who deploy the strategies they have learned with great automaticity.

However, the second term, *strategic*, is more problematic. Educators often informally use the terms *skill* and *strategy* interchangeably. Afflerbach et al. (2008) took on this topic and noted that

> Reading *strategies* are deliberate, goal-directed attempts to control and modify the reader's efforts to decode text, understand words, and construct meanings of text. Reading *skills* are automatic actions that result in decoding and comprehension with speed, efficiency, and fluency and usually occur without awareness of the components or control involved. (p. 368; emphasis added)

As reading develops, the ability to be strategic (solve problems) while moving smoothly and accurately through text (automatic) consolidate into a tight process. To our thinking, the goal is to develop *skilled* readers—those who deploy the strategies they have learned with great automaticity. In other words, they have developed habits they use almost without thinking about them. And, when texts are complex, they revert to known strategies to regain meaning. Our desired outcome is the development of skilled readers. In order to accomplish this, we teach reading skills such that a reader can use them strategically when reading is a challenge.

WHAT'S YOUR ADVICE?

How might you respond to a colleague who says that literacy develops naturally in children or that there is no need to teach students to map sounds onto letters?

____

____

____

Constrained and Unconstrained Reading Skills

Now let's go more deeply into a discussion of reading skills. Reading researcher Scott Paris (2005) described a variety of reading skills across a continuum from *constrained* to *unconstrained*. Constrained reading skills are those that have boundaries or upper limits. Some reading skills, such as phonemic awareness, alphabetics, grapheme-phoneme correspondences, basic print concepts, and oral reading fluency, are constrained reading skills, because they have a finite point at which they are learned. For instance, there are 44 phonemes in English and 26 letters. As well, there is a finite number of letter combinations that represent the sounds. And there is a limit as to the rate of reading one can sustain without sacrificing accuracy and meaning. Because these skills are constrained, we can count them, and as such they are more easily measured. There also are some of foundational reading skills that readers must acquire.

Keep Scarborough's reminder in mind: Strength in one bundle (language comprehension or word recognition) influences and acts upon the other bundle.

However, mastery of these reading skills alone is not the final destination. If it were, we wouldn't need to provide much instruction beyond elementary school. But true reading is much more than accurate word identification. All of us spend a lifetime acquiring what Paris calls the unconstrained reading skills of background knowledge, vocabulary, and comprehension. Unlike constrained skills, unconstrained skills have no endpoint. Your vocabulary is more expansive today than it was five years ago, and your reading comprehension of many topics will be greater and deeper five years from now if you keep reading and learning. As you read and experience life, you're continually adding to your background knowledge, which influences both your vocabulary and your comprehension of text. Notice the continuum of constraints described by Stahl (2011) in Figure 1.3.

Figure 1.3 **Continuum of Constraint**

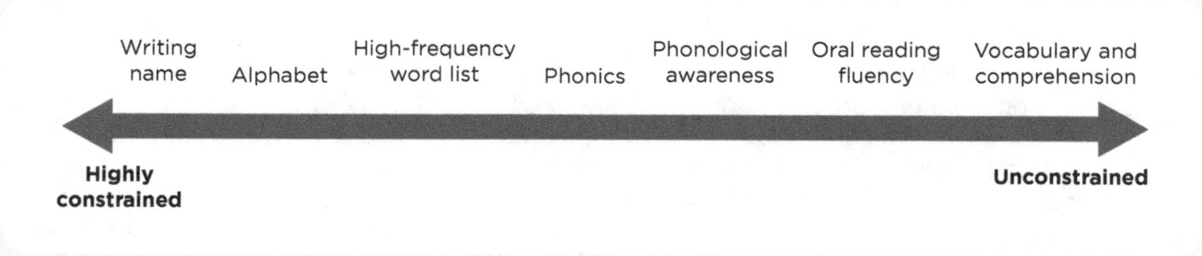

Source: Stahl (2011).

So effective reading instruction involves both constrained and unconstrained skills development. No responsible teacher would limit attention to constrained skills while ignoring vocabulary and reading comprehension. But once the constrained skills are learned, there is no additional benefit to continuing to teach them. Therefore, attention to constrained skills instruction fades as students acquire them. Unfortunately, there are older students who have yet to automate these constrained skills and continue to require instruction to build the skills needed to read texts that are appropriate for them. As students master the constrained skills, vocabulary and reading comprehension take an even more dominant role. However, keep Scarborough's reminder in mind: Strength in one bundle (language comprehension or word recognition) influences and acts upon the other bundle.

FIND THE MISTAKE

A list of constrained and unconstrained skills was developed, but there are errors in it. Identify which of the following should not be in each column.

Constrained Skills	Unconstrained Skills
• Letter recognition	• Vocabulary
• Print concepts	• Comprehension
• Oral language	• Syntax
• Phoneme awareness	• Morphology
• Grapheme-phoneme correspondences	• Background knowledge
• Verbal reasoning	• Critical analysis
• Sight word recognition	• Inference
	• Author's craft

Which errors did you identify? ______________________________

____

Why are these incorrect? ______________________________

____

Metacognitive Strategy Use in Reading

We can't leave this opening module on skilled reading without discussing the importance of metacognition in reading. Metacognition is evidenced through reflection and decision-making about the strategies deployed by a reader, such as pausing to reflect, being aware of their personal perspectives, or engaging in retrospection by looking backward at past events in the story. The ability to reflect upon and think about one's thinking and monitor one's thinking are essential for learning (e.g., Flavell, 1979).

The ability to reflect upon and think about one's thinking and monitor one's thinking are essential for learning.

The term *metacognition* means "above cognition" and works in parallel to the skills and knowledge (cognition) needed to complete complex tasks. And reading for understanding, to be sure, is a complex task. A reader with a high degree of metacognitive awareness approaches reading as a conscious act and recognizes that they are in command of their own understanding. Metacognitive readers don't view the act of reading as simply moving their eyes down line after line of the text. They reflect, monitor their thoughts and understanding, summarize along the way, generate questions and images, and so on. They notice when they have lost meaning and manage their strategies to recover meaning. Much like a master craftsperson, these readers not only have a full toolbox, but they are also able to select the right tool to accomplish the goal.

Importantly, strategy use is not limited to older students or only for comprehension. Imagine the young child who is trying to blend sounds or chunk word parts to decode text. They must be taught strategies and then use those strategies. Students learn strategies to predict long versus short vowels, for example. Again, it's the repeated application of the strategies that is so important.

TAKE ACTION

Consider the following strategies of highly effective readers, and then analyze the reading behaviors of your students. Which of these need to be further developed in students? Do you have a plan to model these for students? Do you have a way to monitor students' progress in developing metacognition? In the modules of the language comprehension bundle, we'll explore these strategies further.

Strategy	Definition
Activating	"Priming the cognitive pump" in order to recall relevant prior knowledge and experiences from long-term memory in order to extract and construct meaning from text
Inferring	Bringing together what is spoken (written) in the text, what is unspoken (unwritten) in the text, and what is already known by the reader in order to extract and construct meaning from the text
Monitoring-Clarifying	Thinking about how and what one is reading, both during and after the act of reading, for purposes of determining if one is comprehending the text combined with the ability to clarify and fix up any mix-ups

Strategy	Definition
Questioning	Engaging in learning dialogues with text (authors), peers, and teachers through self-questioning, question generation, and question answering
Searching-Selecting	Searching a variety of sources in order to select appropriate information to answer questions, define words and terms, clarify misunderstandings, solve problems, or gather information
Summarizing	Restating the meaning of text in one's own words—different words from those used in the original text
Visualizing-Organizing	Constructing a mental image or graphic organizer for the purpose of extracting and constructing meaning from the text

Source: McEwan (2007).

TEXT-TO-SELF CONNECTION

Now consider your own knowledge of reading development as it applies to your students. What in this module was confirming for you? What new information did you add to your conceptual understanding of reading development? Fill in the table below to record your top two confirmations and top two instances of new knowledge gained from this module.

Confirming Knowledge in the Reading
1.
2.
New Knowledge From the Reading
1.
2.

The subsequent modules are organized broadly around the reading rope, as it serves as a great visual metaphor to discuss the literacy field's continuously deepening knowledge base of how to teach children to become skilled readers. Before moving forward, take a few minutes to reflect on your current practices in reading instruction. The next five modules will focus on the word recognition bundle, while the subsequent seven modules will discuss dimensions of the language comprehension bundle. How would you describe your level of confidence in your knowledge of instructional practices for each of these topics? Use your reflection as a guide for your playbook plan.

(Continued)

(Continued)

Using the traffic light scale, with red being not confident, yellow being somewhat confident, and green indicating very confident, how confident are you in your ability to teach toward these topics?	
Word Recognition Strands	
Module 2: Phonological Awareness	
Module 3: Alphabetics	
Module 4: Phonics and Decoding	
Module 5: Sight Word Recognition	
Module 6: Reading Fluency	
Language Comprehension Strands	
Module 7: Background Knowledge	
Module 8: Vocabulary Knowledge	
Module 9: Morphological Awareness	
Module 10: Text and Language Structures	
Module 11: Literacy and Text Knowledge	
Module 12: Verbal Reasoning	
Module 13: Theory of Mind	

Takeaways

- Reading is a complex process, and each brain needs to be taught to read, because there is no reading gene that is passed down from one generation to the next.
- Readers need to develop their automatic and strategic processes.
- There are two major bundles of strands, word recognition and language comprehension, that are braided together to develop skilled readers.
- Some skills have a ceiling, meaning that there isn't more to learn once the content is mastered. There are other skills that continue to develop across the life span.

PS: The answers to the anticipation guide are F, T, T.

PART

I

Word Recognition

Think about yourself as a reader. Whether you are reading fiction or fact, or reading for pleasure or information discovery, or to complete a work task or a personal task, as a proficient reader you effortlessly and instantly recognize the majority of the words you encounter. You may not know the meaning of all of them, and while you may even be reading in an unfamiliar context, there is high probability that you will be able to effortlessly pronounce every word in the text (Stanovich et al., 1985). This happens because your brain recognizes the *orthography*. You are aware of the familiar spelling patterns, and your brain also adds the phonology or pronunciation to the word even before adding the meaning (Forster, 2012; Perfetti, 2011).

This matching occurs because you have a large vocabulary of words with familiar meanings that have become your sight vocabulary, and this is combined with efficient decoding skills (van den Broeck & Geudens, 2012). You can use a word's grapheme-phoneme correspondences and morphology to identify the word even when it is contextless. However, when you meet an unfamiliar word, you most likely have both the language comprehension and word recognition skills needed to sound it out and then use the context to recognize its meaning (Cunnings & Clashen, 2007; Frost, 1998).

The end goal of reading instruction is understanding.

The end goal of reading instruction is understanding. To ensure that every student becomes the proficient reader we just described, one who has the language and skills needed to comprehend a wide array of texts, each needs to be exposed to a growing base of language through interaction with many topics and texts. In addition, each must be taught the skills needed to decode and instantly encode or recode written information.

In **Part I** we address the **word recognition skills** needed to ensure that every student becomes a proficient reader. These skills include

- Phonological/phonemic awareness
- Print letter recognition or alphabetics
- Phonics and decoding skills
- Sight word recognition
- Reading fluency

Early reading instruction occurs as children are introduced to the letter names of the alphabet. This begins their entree into an understanding of the alphabetic principle, which is that there is a relationship between letters of the alphabet and the spoken sounds of language. Once children know the names and shapes of the letters, they can be taught the letter sounds and how they are used to spell words. There are many instructional activities that support the sequence of learning letter names, their shapes, and their sounds. In many homes very young children and their caregivers sing the alphabet song, which supports their early learning of the names of the letters. They also play with letter blocks and magnetic letters while identifying the first letters of their names.

As children are learning to name and identify letters, they should also have opportunities to write them. Their writing may include uppercase and lowercase letters or a mixture of both. The goal at this early stage is to ensure that children are beginning to develop the alphabetic principle, which will grow stronger through instruction that continually introduces and reinforces the idea that the sounds of their spoken language are represented in written language.

In this set of modules on word recognition, we also share instructional activities that support children learning letter-sound relationships and opportunities to practice these relationships orally and in writing and reading experiences. In addition to exposure, children need extensive opportunities to apply their growing letter-sound knowledge. Children will acquire an understanding of the alphabetic principle at different rates because they enter school with different home experiences that have provided different foundational supports. Early instructional differentiation must ensure that all children develop an understanding of the alphabetic principle, which is foundational to becoming a proficient reader (Blachman, 2000).

Also shared in the word recognition modules are discussions about phonological awareness and phonics teaching, with the goal of ensuring that children become skilled readers whose knowledge of written words is bonded in memory. When this bonding occurs, there is no longer a need to decode each word by sounding out and sequentially blending letters (Ehri, 2020). Rather, as children become skilled readers, they can map words into their permanent memory and store thousands of words that are then recognizable instantly and effortlessly by sight. In doing so, with instruction and practice, students develop their reading fluency.

MODULE

2

Phonological Awareness

Photo by iStock.com/FatCamera

In this module, we will

- **Explore both phonological awareness and phonemic awareness.**
- **Consider the relationship between phonological awareness and learning to read.**
- **Identify the relationship between language and phonological awareness.**
- **Review instructional practices that promote phonological awareness.**
- **Consider assessments that inform our instructional practice.**

Look at the children in the picture. Imagine the teacher is saying a word, and then she and the children are clapping the sounds they hear in the word. Each time she says a word like *bat*, *ham*, or *bit,* she asks the children to repeat the word and echo it back to her. Then, together, they repeat the word, and this time clap the letter sounds they hear, such as /b/ /a/ /t/ or /h/ /a/ /m/. Did you notice that this activity did not require the children to know the letter names of the sounds they were hearing?

They only needed to be aware of how many discrete sounds they were hearing in each word and be able to repeat them. The children and the teacher were segmenting the sounds they were hearing in each spoken word. Being able to segment the letter sounds, or phonemes, heard in a spoken word is an early literacy skill that should be developed during preschool, kindergarten,

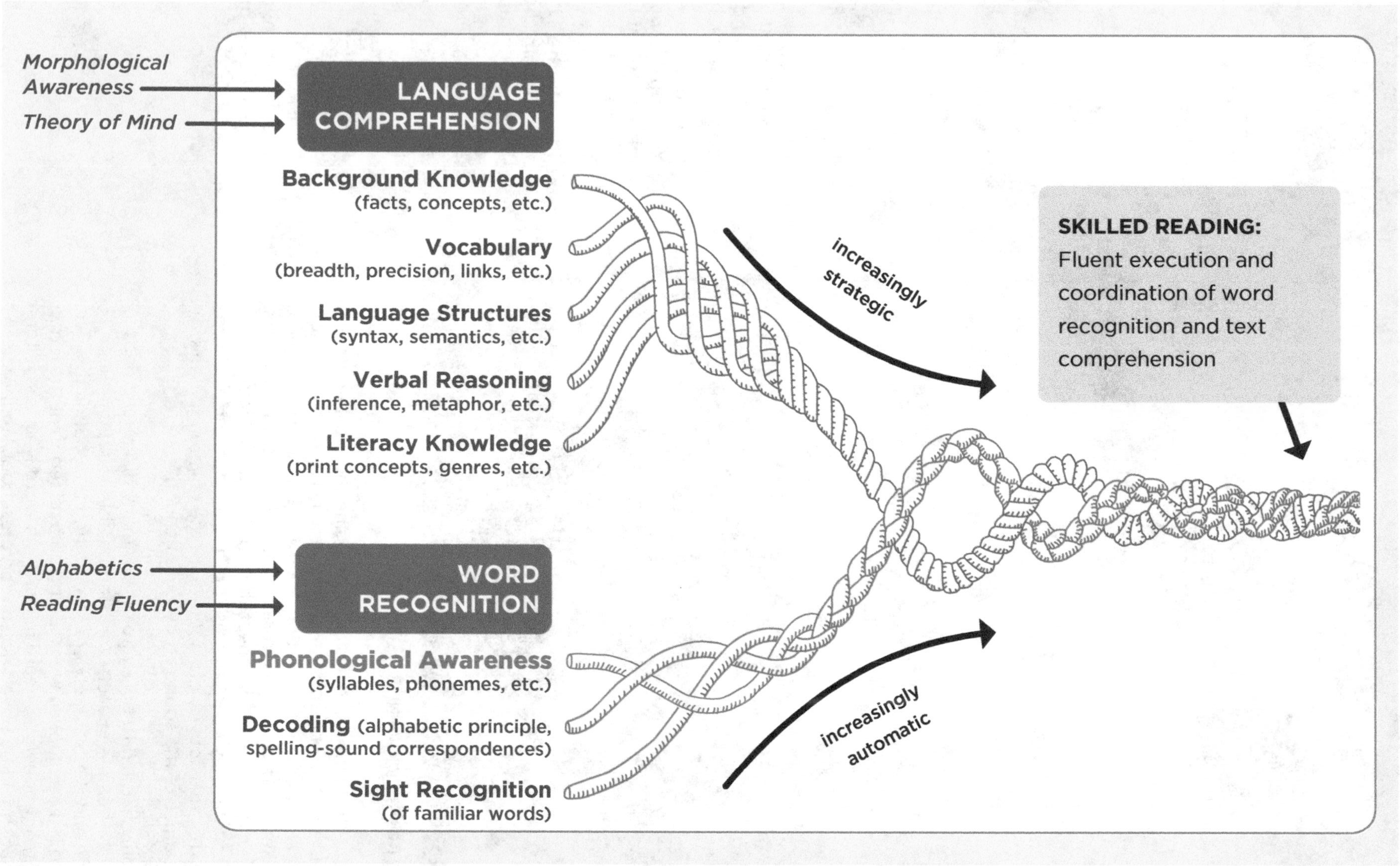

Source: Adapted from Scarborough, H. S. (2001). Connecting early language and literacy to later reading (dis)abilities: Evidence, theory, and practice. In S. Neuman & D. Dickinson (Eds.), *Handbook for research in early literacy* (pp. 97–110). Guilford Press.

and first grade. Being able to do so indicates that the children are developing phonemic awareness, which is the ability to identify the phonemes or sounds they are hearing in words.

Prior to having the children identify by clapping that they were hearing three sounds in each word, this teacher first had the children identify the initial sounds (phonemes) they were hearing in words. For example, she would say the word *bat* and ask the children to repeat the initial sound of /b/. Other phonemic awareness skills involve blending, deleting, and substituting letter sounds in words. These skills involve an awareness of words at a phoneme/letter or sound level. They are all skills associated with phonological awareness, which includes both letter-sound awareness and awareness of larger chunks of words, such as syllables.

Being able to segment the letter sounds, or phonemes, is an early literacy skill that should be developed during preschool, kindergarten, and first grade.

Read each statement and mark **T** if the statement is true and **F** if the statement is false. As you read through the module, you might change your responses. Be prepared to explain your responses and use the text for evidence.

<table>
<tr><th>Before Reading</th><th colspan="2">Statements</th><th>After Reading</th></tr>
<tr><td>T F</td><td colspan="2">1. Phonemic awareness is primarily developed through rhyming.</td><td>T F</td></tr>
<tr><td colspan="2">Why did you indicate true or false?</td><td colspan="2">Has your thinking changed after reading?</td></tr>
<tr><td>T F</td><td colspan="2">2. Most children have developed phonemic awareness by the end of kindergarten.</td><td>T F</td></tr>
<tr><td colspan="2">Why did you indicate true or false?</td><td colspan="2">Has your thinking changed after reading?</td></tr>
<tr><td>T F</td><td colspan="2">3. Early phonemic awareness activities are primarily taught and practiced orally.</td><td>T F</td></tr>
<tr><td colspan="2">Why did you indicate true or false?</td><td colspan="2">Has your thinking changed after reading?</td></tr>
<tr><td>T F</td><td colspan="2">4. Phonemic awareness supports writing and spelling as well as reading.</td><td>T F</td></tr>
<tr><td colspan="2">Why did you indicate true or false?</td><td colspan="2">Has your thinking changed after reading?</td></tr>
</table>

Untangling Phonological Awareness and Phonemic Awareness

Phonological awareness is an overarching term that describes a person's sensitivity to the parts of speech—syllables, rhymes, and phonemes. A person who is phonologically aware can identify and manipulate units of oral language such as words, syllables, and onsets and rimes. A subset of phonological awareness is referred to as *phonemic awareness,* which more narrowly addresses the specific ability to focus on and manipulate individual sounds (**phonemes**) within a spoken word. Specifically, phonemic awareness, one of the best early predictors of the success a student will have in learning to read (Ehri & Nunes, 2002; National Reading Panel, 2000), involves development of the understanding that there are discrete sounds within spoken words. The International Literacy Association (2019) defines phonemic awareness as "the ability to detect and manipulate the smallest units (i.e., phonemes) of spoken language." For example, recognition that the word *moon* includes three distinct sounds or phonemes is one dimension of phonemic awareness. Individuals with phonemic awareness can blend phonemes to form spoken words, segment spoken words into their constituent phonemes, delete phonemes from spoken words, add phonemes, and substitute phonemes. (See Figure 2.1 for a visual representation of the relationship between phonological and phonemic awareness.)

Phonemic awareness is one of the best early predictors of the success a student will have in learning to read.

Figure 2.1 The Relationship Between Phonological and Phonemic Awareness

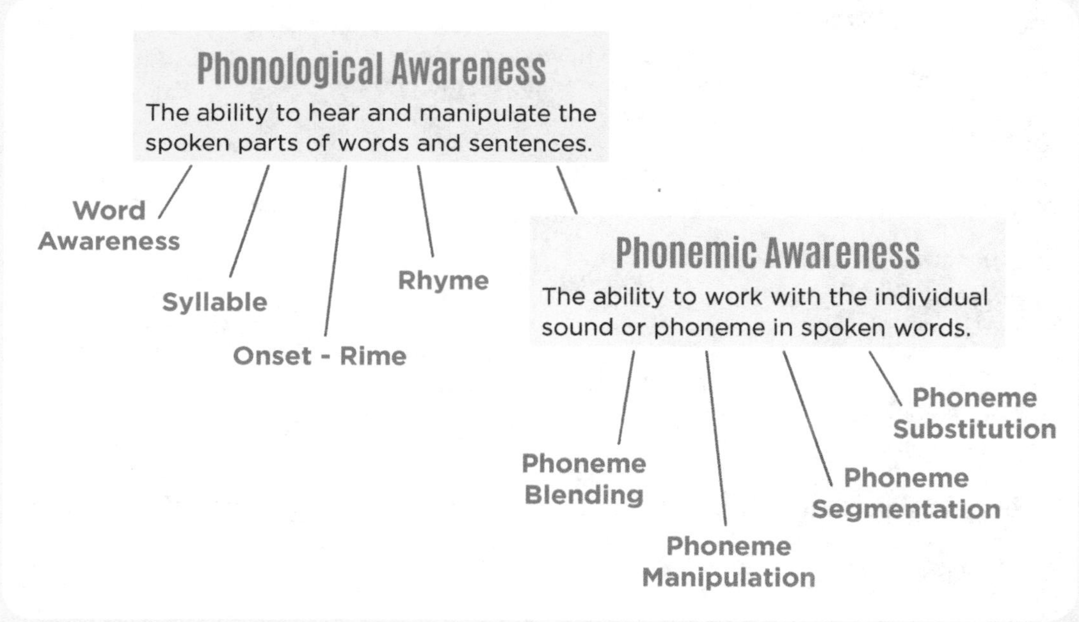

Source: © Hanging Around in Primary (2017).

As this definition suggests, being phonologically aware means that one is attuned to how sounds work in words. Phonemic awareness is a crucial dimension of phonological awareness, which specifically focuses on individual sounds. These are constrained skills, meaning that they have a finite number of components. In practice, phonological and phonemic awareness are taught in relation to one another. We don't announce to five-year-olds that "it's phonological awareness time, and later this morning, we'll have phonemic awareness centers!" Rather, lessons often encompass elements of each.

NOTICE AND WONDER

Review Figure 2.1. Did you notice the differences between phonological awareness and phonemic awareness? What implications for instruction might these differences hold?

The research evidence on work with rhymes and alliteration is less compelling than the findings on the importance of developing phonemic awareness in young readers. The National Early Literacy Panel (2008) noted as much when it reported its meta-analysis on the practice. Its results found that work on rhyming, syllable, and alliteration work alone did not have a great degree of impact, compared to work on segmenting and manipulating phonemes. In his review of early literacy research, Reutzel (2015) noted that there are nuances to this finding, stating,

> This is not to suggest, however, that early childhood educators totally abandon rhyme and alliteration activities; rather, it is to point out the transitory value of these activities in relation to the more sustained outcomes associated with phonemic awareness instruction focused on phoneme-level activities. (p. 16)

With that in mind, let's turn our attention to rhyming and alliteration before attending to a deeper exploration of phonemic awareness.

NOTES

Phonological Awareness Instruction

Instruction in phonological awareness of syllables and rhymes can be developed quite naturally for most children through word play activities such as singing songs and chanting poems with rhymes (O'Connor & Vadasy, 2011). During these activities, students' attention can be directed to the idea that if they change the sounds they are saying, they will be changing the words. Other tasks include clapping the sounds of the syllables they hear, tapping the number of words they hear in a spoken sentence, and tongue twisters.

For other ideas useful in teaching these elements of phonological awareness, see the Florida Center for Reading Research's website of other activities at https://www.fcrr.org/student-center-activities.

Phonological awareness can also be developed by reading aloud books with rhymes and alliterations and talking with children about the rhymes they hear. Three such books that are truly enjoyed by children are *How Do Dinosaurs Say Goodnight*? by Jane Yolen and Mark Teague, *There's a Wocket in My Pocket* by Dr. Seuss, and *Brown Bear, Brown Bear* by Bill Martin Jr. and Eric Carle.

The evidence suggests that reading develops best when teachers begin with familiar words and then systematically focus students' attention on smaller and smaller sound segments in these words (e.g., Gillon, 2017):

1. Teachers begin with spoken sentences and focus on the different words within the sentence and then note that some words can be broken into smaller words.

2. Students practice identifying the unique words in sentences as well as the components of compound words.

3. Teachers then turn their attention to syllables and teach students how to identify syllables.

4. Students practice identifying and manipulating syllables in familiar words.

5. Once students can identify the syllables in words, teachers can focus on smaller units within words, which are the onsets and rimes.

   - **Rhyming** involves saying two or more words that have the same ending rimes, such as *bat, rat, cat, mat,* and *flat;* or *see, me*, and *flea*. These rhymes are determined by the sound, not the spelling pattern.
   - **Syllable awareness.** Teacher says words having two or more syllables and asks the children to clap the number of syllables they hear. For instance, children hearing the spoken word *rainbow* clap twice as they say the word.
   - **Syllable blending.** Teacher separately says the syllables in a multisyllable word and asks the children to put the syllables together to make a word. Teacher says *vid-e-o* and asks the children to blend these syllables into one word. Children respond, *video.*
   - **Syllable deletion.** Teacher says the word *dancing* and asks the children to repeat the word without a second syllable. Children respond *dance*. Children asked to omit the sound of *rain* in *rainbow* can answer back *bow*. Other examples: *backpack* repeat without the word *pack* (back); *refinement* repeat without *-ment (refine).*

NOTICE AND WONDER

Notice that the task difficulty level increases when children are asked to blend and delete syllables. Being engaged in syllable awareness and deletion activities with multisyllabic words expands children's spelling skills. Did you notice that working with syllables is important?

Can your students complete these tasks?

____

____

How might you develop these skills with your students?

____

____

First-grade teacher Alexandria Washington uses several techniques to help her students develop awareness of multisyllabic words. To support students developing this awareness, she stresses that every syllable has a vowel sound. To ensure children understand this, she incorporates additional sound pattern practices that involve a tactile dimension.

Chin Drops. The first practice is called *Chin Drops*. (Your chin drops when you utter a vowel sound. Try it.) She tells her students to hear each syllable in a word. After reminding them that every syllable has a vowel sound, she models how her chin drops down each time she says the vowel sound in a word. Then, inviting them to place their hands under their chins, she says, "Let's say and touch the syllables in some words." Together, they each place one hand under their chin and say a few words: *kite, candy, kitten, swimming, November.* After saying a word, they discuss how many times their chins dropped and how many corresponding syllables the word contains. This tactile activity provides children with a more concrete way to hear and touch the syllables.

The Syllable Jump. A second tactile activity, called *The Syllable Jump,* also concretizes children's understanding that words have sounds and syllables. As the children stand in line for a visit to the library, go to recess, or go home, Ms. Washington asks them questions and invites them to jump their responses. For example, she might ask, "Where are we going?" Children might respond by saying "library" while jumping three times. Another time, the children might say "recess" while jumping two times, and at the end of the school day, the children respond "home" and jump once.

Humming. A third activity Ms. Washington presents involves inviting children to hum a word and to be aware of how often their hum is chunked. "Remember" she says, "each hum represents a syllable in the word, and each syllable has a vowel sound. Let's hum the word *alligator.*" She then invites them to hum a few additional words like *sunshine, dinosaur,* and *caterpillar* to reinforce the concept of hearing syllables.

Not all students need the same amount of practice to grasp this concept, but by using these activities, Ms. Washington is able to ensure that all the students will have time to learn these important concepts.

Phonemic Awareness

Phonemic awareness is a subcomponent of the broader umbrella that is phonological awareness. Readers who possess a full degree of phonemic awareness are able to discern and manipulate the 44 phonemes in the English language. These manipulations of the sounds range from segmentation and isolation of individual sounds to reversals. Young children typically learn to attend first to the initial phoneme in a word, recognizing that *map, moose*, and *Megan* all begin with the same sound. Final sounds follow shortly thereafter, such as when a student accurately identifies that *lamb*, *Mom*, and *time* end with the same sound. Medial sounds are the most challenging, as students must listen for the middle sound, such as short /o/ in the words *pot, mop, dog*, and *sock*.

Phonemic awareness should not be confused with grapheme-phoneme correspondences, which involve the relationship between the sounds and the written letters in words (Vadasy & Sanders, 2021). Sometimes a sound is associated with a single letter, and other times multiple letters make a sound. Consider the /k/ sound which can be made with the letters -c, -k, or -ck as in *cat, kite*, and *dock*. Phonemic awareness involves the individual sound, whereas grapheme-phoneme correspondence involves mapping the sound onto the letters or letter combinations.

There are different facets of phonemic awareness instruction that deepen a child's ability to discern and manipulate the sounds of the language more ably. Further, there is strong evidence about why phonemic awareness development should not be left to chance. Ehri and colleagues' 2001 meta-analysis of 52 studies, performed as part of the National Reading Panel's deliberations, found that phonemic awareness instruction had a significant impact on reading and spelling. Additionally, phonemic awareness instruction is essential for English learners and students in dual immersion programs, because the phonemes of one language do not completely map onto another language (Brown & Copple, 2018). As an example of range, Spanish has 24 phonemes, while !Xóõ (pronounced /kō/ in English), spoken primarily in Botswana, has 112 phonemes.

Being able to notice and manipulate single phonemic sound structures in spoken language indicates early phonemic awareness skills. These skills, primarily developed from preschool through first grade, serve as foundational knowledge for phonics decoding and spelling. Dimensions of phonemic awareness include the following:

- **Sound blending** involves hearing parts of a word and being able to repeat them as a whole word: hearing the phonemes /b/ /a/ /t/ and putting them together as *bat*.
- **Sound segmenting** involves hearing a word as a whole and being able to separate it into its represented phonemes: hearing *bat* and repeating it as /b/ /a/ /t/.
- **Sound deleting** involves being able to hear a word and then repeating it without one of the sounds: hearing *bat* and deleting the phoneme /b/ and saying *at*.
- **Sound substituting** involves hearing a word but, before repeating, changing one phoneme for another: Hearing *bat* but substituting for /b/ with /c/ and saying *cat*.

In sum, the goal of phonemic awareness instruction is to increase children's ability to discriminate between the sounds that compose the words they speak and read. This provides a foundation for them to manipulate these sounds into new spoken words.

TAKE ACTION

The *Yopp-Singer Test of Phonemic Segmentation* (Appendix A) is one assessment that—in addition to being reliable—is easy to administer, score, and analyze. The test should be administered to one child at a time. It takes between 5 and 10 minutes to administer to an individual child. Using the assessment tool found in Appendix A, assess your students and determine the areas of needed instruction.

What does the *Yopp-Singer Test of Phonemic Segmentation* tell you about your students and what might be the next steps in learning for them?

Strengths:

Areas of Focus:

NOTES

Using Elkonin Boxes for Phonemic Segmenting

Elkonin boxes, often called sound boxes, allow learners to isolate the sounds within a word. Sound boxes are squares drawn on paper or a board. There is one square for each sound or phoneme heard in a particular word. The purpose is to slow down the analysis process a bit as the child moves an item, such as a chip or coin, into the space in a box (see Figure 2.2 for an example of sound boxes). As McCarthy (2008) notes, Elkonin boxes "teach the student how to hear the phonemes in words in sequence by connecting the slow verbal stretching of a word's sounds to the simultaneous pushing of tokens into boxes, one for each sound as it is heard" (p. 346). Ross and Joseph (2019) noted in their review of research that the use of these boxes positively impacts students' early reading performance.

As an example, the spoken word *den* requires three squares to represent the three phonemes heard. There may not be a direct correspondence between letters and sounds. For instance, the word /goat/ has three phonemes (/g/oa/t) but four letters. Although commonly used for phonemic awareness, sound boxes can also be used to develop grapheme-phoneme correspondences and spelling knowledge. (At that point they are called word boxes; Keesey et al., 2015).

The children in Jeff Ryan's kindergarten class are using Elkonin boxes and plastic tokens to segment the sounds in the words they speak and hear. Mr. Ryan calls these "sound boxes" with his students to reinforce the concept that spoken words are made up of sounds. Remember, in this lesson, the teacher is focusing only on the phonemes, not the letters that represent those phonemes.

He begins the lesson by sharing with children what they will be doing and explaining why. "Today we're going to pull apart the words we speak so we can hear each sound. Let me show you how."

The children listen to Mr. Ryan slowly pronounce the word *hit.* He repeats it several times, now stretching the sound of the word so that each phoneme can be heard: /h/ /i/ /t/. As he does so, he taps his arm from shoulder to wrist in correspondence with all the sounds they are hearing; one tap to represent each sound. "I'm hearing three sounds, so I know I need three sound boxes," he says, drawing them in the document camera. Once he has drawn, he repeats the sounds as he moves the tokens into a box.

Figure 2.2 A Sound Box for a Three-Phoneme Word

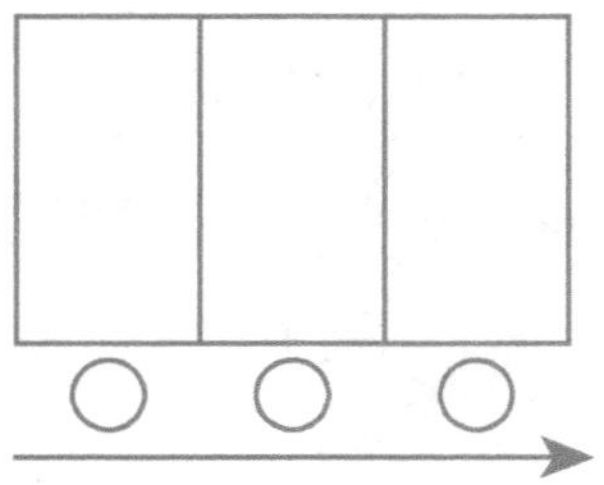

"Now let's try this all together. Listen carefully. I'll again say a word; and then together, at the same time, we'll say the word; and then we'll tap on our arms each sound we hear in the word. Our word is *sit.* Say it with me." Mr. Ryan and his students repeat the word several times, tapping the sounds they hear on their arms. Next, he asks them to tell their elbow partners how many sounds they heard and what those sounds were. Now Mr. Ryan asks the children, using their own sound boxes and tokens, to demonstrate how they move each chip as they repeat the sounds in the word *sit*. Finally, he asks one child to share and demonstrate for the whole class. They practice together a few additional words (*mitt, fit,* and *bit*).

Using sound boxes and tokens helps children see the number of sounds they are saying and hearing in each word. This visual element emphasizes that separate sounds are heard in a spoken word. Mr. Ryan uses this strategy with the whole class when he discusses a new pattern and then continues using it with small groups and individuals until all have mastered a particular sound pattern. When children are working alone, Mr. Ryan encourages them to tap a sound pattern on their arm, which helps them identify how many sounds they are hearing. As they become more proficient in recognizing sound patterns, he moves from one-syllable to multisyllable words. Students should have the auditory skill to recognize sound patterns in multisyllable words by the end of kindergarten (Anthony et al., 2002).

Using Elkonin boxes helps children see the number of sounds they are saying and hearing in each word.

WHAT'S YOUR ADVICE?

Your colleague is using sound boxes to develop students' phonemic awareness. This person projects the word on the whiteboard while reading it aloud. The boxes at students' desks have magnetic letters in the squares, such as the following:

b	u	g

s	u	n

h	u	t

You note that this has moved into a phonics lesson.

What questions might you ask to determine how this colleague has developed students' phonemic awareness?

What data would you recommend be considered to determine students' readiness for this task?

Phoneme Blending

We blend sounds together to form spoken words. And we need to learn when words start, when they end, and how to recognize the short pauses between them. The blending part requires that children learn to push together the sounds in words, in sequence, to create the word. Blending will come in handy when students are learning to read words and encounter words they do not know. As Al Otaiba et al. (2016) noted, blending supports the overall understanding of the ways words work and can be used to support students through whole-class and small-group instruction.

Rosa Blanco taught her kindergarten students the skill of blending, which involves combining the individual sounds of letters together to make a word. Blending helps children develop their phonemic awareness, but it may be more challenging for multilingual learners, since it requires holding one or more sounds in mind while adding the sounds together in a word. Like Mr. Ryan, Ms. Blanco used Elkonin boxes to teach word blending, and she also used rubber bands to give children a visual for the concept of stretching as they say a word. The rubber band helped them see just how far a word needs to be stretched to hear all its sounds.

Ms. Blanco began by sharing the purpose. "Today we are going to think about words and the sounds we need to put together or blend together to make each word. I am going to show you how to put together or blend separate sounds to make words. I will tap my arm each time I change the sound. Listen to these sounds /f/ /a/ /t/. Then say /ffffaaat/. The word I said was *fat*. I tapped three sounds that I said." She modeled several words until the students understood that she was blending sounds to make words.

As a warm-up, Ms. Blanco began with two-letter words (*at, is, it*) and then progressed to consonant-vowel-consonant (CVC) (fan, man) words. She also chose words that started with consonant sounds that were easy to stretch out, so children would have time to hear each discrete sound (/f/, /l/, /m/). Once children were having success with stretch consonants, she shared words that had stop sounds as initial consonants (*bat, bug, pit*).

When children were demonstrating success, she moved on to blends. She moved from modeling for the children, to having children join her in saying the word using their rubber bands to stretch the word to hear each sound ("say it slowly"), to tapping each sound on their arms, and finally to blending the sounds together ("say it fast"). When she felt that children were beginning to understand the concept of blending sounds to make a word, she had them independently do so while she observed. She encouraged children having trouble tapping while blending to instead raise one finger each time they said a sound. If children needed more practice, she repeated the same words multiple times to provide children the opportunity to hear each sound she was asking them to blend into a word.

FIND THE MISTAKES

Review a student's blended words. The first column is the sounds the teacher made. The words in italics are what the student said.

/b/ /i/ /l/	*bell*
/h/ /a/ /t/	*hat*
/p/ /i/ /t/	*pet*
/s/ /a/ /d/	*sad*
/p/ /i/ /g/	*peg*
/r/ /a/ /g/	*rag*

What error is the student making as they blend words? ______________________________

____

What could be the next step in their learning? ______________________________

____

NOTES

Phoneme Deletion

Deleting phonemes helps students deepen their phonemic awareness as they learn to isolate sounds by removing some of them within a word. If this is initially too difficult for students, they can start by deleting syllables in compound words so that they develop an understanding of the task. Phoneme deletion requires that students develop an understanding that sounds can be deleted from a word and when that happens, the remainder of the sounds within the word all remain in place (Rauth & Stuart, 2008).

For some children it is easier to grasp the concept of deletion by introducing compound words and taking away one of the words.

Deletion tasks are more difficult than other phonemic awareness tasks because they require the manipulation of the phonemes in a word. Lewkowicz (1980) suggested that sound deletion activities should not be taught until children can segment and should only include initial and final phoneme sounds in a word. For some children it is easier to grasp the concept of deletion by introducing compound words and taking away one of the words. "I can say *hotdog*. If I take away *dog*, my new word is *hot*." Continue with additional compound words (*baseball, shoelace, zigzag*) until you assess that the children have grasped the concept of deletion. Remember that to get proficient at phonemic awareness activities, children need direct and explicit instruction with lots of repetitions.

In most kindergarten classes, children learn to make new words from ones previously used when blending and substituting phonemes. Teachers like Mr. Ryan and Ms. Blanco offer precise directions to share both the learning intention and the process when they say, "Today we are going to make new words by removing some letters and their sounds in words we already know. I'll show you how. I will say a word, then I will take away or delete a letter and its sound so I can make a new word. You listen to see if you can tell me which sound I deleted. My word is *mat.* It has three sounds, /m/a/t/. When I delete the /m/ sound, my new word is *at.*"

Next, they practice a few additional words with the children to be sure they understand the practice of sound deletion (*cat, bit, fan*). Once they are secure that the children understand the concept of deletion, they offer the next direction.

"Now it is your turn. I'll say a word. Then together we will say its sounds. I will tell you which sound to take away, and then we'll say the new word together. Say *pit,* /p/i/t/. Take away the /p/ sound. What is the word? *It.*"

They then practice several additional words with the children. Elkonin boxes can be used to help children visualize phoneme deletion.

You'll also want to explain to the children that while some of the words might be nonsense words because they are not real words we use when we speak, write, or spell, it is okay to create new real and nonsense words by deleting letters and their sounds. Begin by sharing a few words, and with the children delete the first letter and sound (e.g., *bug, jug, dug*). You may want to initially try words with similar phonemic patterns, like *tip, nip, dip*, and *flip,* since phoneme deletion may be initially difficult for some children. Also have children delete the initial letter first, as in *sock* and *rock,* before trying ending sounds. "Say the word *fort.* Now say it without the first /f/ sound." The task of phonemic deleting is often easier if it is presented as a sound-take-away-game. "I can say the sounds in *rat,* /r/a/t. If I take away the sound /r/, I have the word *at.* I can say the word *meat*, m/ea/t. If I take away the first sound of /m/, I have *eat.*" Continue to try whole-class and small-group tasks as needed.

Phoneme Manipulation

Being able to manipulate phonemes is a skill that includes the ability to modify, change, or move the individual sounds in a word. Students play around with the sounds in a word to make a new word. And it turns out that their ability to do so is predictive of later reading and writing development (Savage & Carless, 2005). Being able to manipulate phonemes in spoken words is a prerequisite to visually manipulating letters or combinations of letters to eventually read and write. When teaching phoneme manipulation, start by sharing with children what you are going to be doing and why.

"Today we are going to make new words by manipulating or changing some letters and their sounds in words we already know so that we can make new words that are a little different."

Begin to make new words from ones that children have previously used when blending, segmenting, and deleting. Say to the children, "I will say a word; then I will change a sound so I can make a new word. You listen to see if you can tell me which sound changed. My word is *at.* I will put a /b/ sound before /at/. What word do you now hear? Let's add sounds before /at/ to make new words."

Continue sharing additional words and then manipulating the initial phoneme. "I can say the word *at.* What other new words can we make by changing the first sound?" (Continue the pattern using the letters *b, f, h, p, r,* and *s.*)

Continue further by saying additional first sound manipulations. "My word is *un.* If I add /s/, what word do you hear?"

Continue the pattern. What other sounds can you add before *un* to make new words?" (Continue the pattern with *g, n, r,* and *s.*) Note that it's harder to change middle sounds (e.g., *bag, beg, big, bug, bog*). Songs like "Apples and Bananas" provide children with opportunities to change long and short vowel sounds at the beginning, middle, and end of words:

- I like to ate, ate, ate apples and bananas. (long and short *a*)
- I like to eat, eat, eat, eeples and benenes. (long and short *e*)
- I like to ite, ite, ite, ipples and bininis. (long and short *i*)
- I like to oat, oat, oat, opples and bononos. (long and short *o*)
- I like to ute, ute, ute, upples and bununus. (long and short *u*)

TEXT-TO-SELF CONNECTION

How is phonological awareness taught in your classroom?

____

____

____

Using the traffic light scale, with red being not confident, yellow being somewhat confident, and green indicating very confident, how confident are you in your ability to

- Teach phonological awareness instruction in your classroom?

- Use Elkonin boxes, or sound boxes?

- Teach phoneme segmenting and blending?

- Teach phoneme deletion and phoneme manipulation?

Takeaways

- Phonological awareness starts with students' ability to recognize words in sentences, syllables in words, and then sounds within those words.
- Phonemic awareness is an important aspect of word recognition. As Adams (1990) noted, children who lack the skills of phonemic awareness are "severely handicapped in their abilities to master print" (p. 412).
- The sound units (phonemes) in English are not obvious. The 26 letters make about 44 phonemes, and sounds are represented in 250 different spellings.
- Students need to practice focusing on the sounds in words, substituting, deleting, and manipulating those sounds.

PS: Answers to the anticipation guide are F, F, T, T.

MODULE

3

Alphabetics

In this module, we will

- Examine the relationship between learning letters and sounds and reading.
- Realize that the spoken sounds in language are graphically represented by letters that compose the words we read and write.
- Identify quality alphabet instruction.

Photo by iStock.com/FatCamera

If this photo had sound, we would hear a teacher giving precise instruction to support these young children naming the letters of the alphabet. An introduction to this knowledge often begins well before children come to school with caregivers teaching the letter names and sometimes a corresponding sound. These early home lessons are usually based on a child's name. Therefore, Kevin may be very familiar with the visual and sound representation of the letter *k*, while Yolanda knows quite a bit about *y*. As young children enter formal schooling, exposure to letters and their sounds becomes more systematic. When

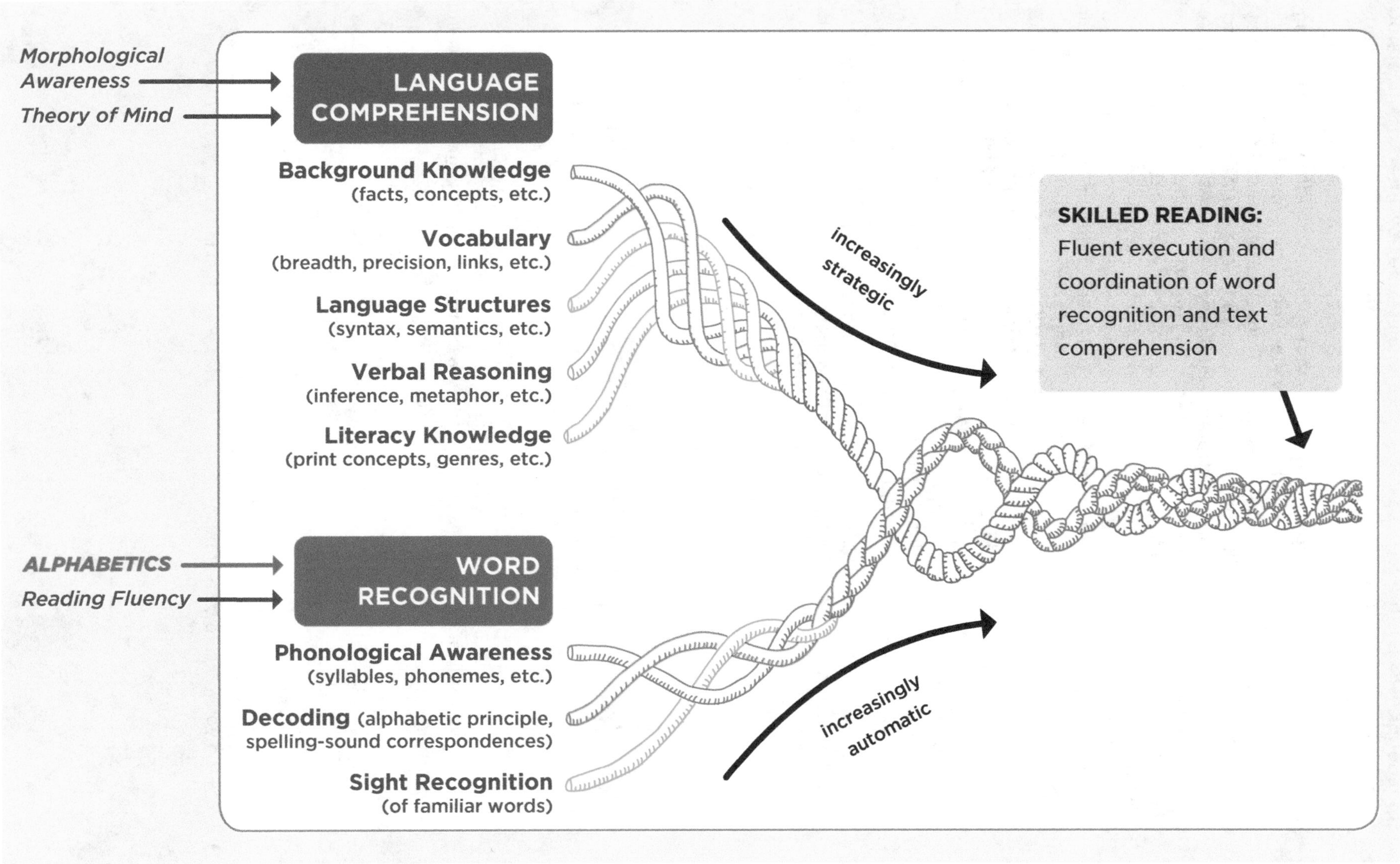

Source: Adapted from Scarborough, H. S. (2001). Connecting early language and literacy to later reading (dis)abilities: Evidence, theory, and practice. In S. Neuman & D. Dickinson (Eds.), *Handbook for research in early literacy* (pp. 97–110). Guilford Press.

alphabetics, which is the representation of spoken sounds by letters, is understood by children, they will have mastered the **alphabetic principle**, which is key to early reading development.

While you may agree that explicit instruction that supports children in developing the alphabetic principle is a must in early literacy learning, let's remember that it wasn't so long ago that the contrary was true. McGill-Franzen et al. (2002) reported that children in the publicly funded preschools they visited were not being exposed to the alphabet or any type of alphabet instruction until they were considered "ready" for this type of instruction. This raises questions regarding equity that must be considered, since these researchers also found that children in private preschools with more affluent families were receiving instructional exposure to the alphabet, which certainly enhanced their readiness. Children with a firm grasp of alphabetics are positioned to make gains in reading, as the identification of letters and their associated sounds are good predictors of early reading success (Adams, 1990; Chall, 1996; Piasta & Wagner, 2010). The National Early Literacy Panel (2008) goes even further, citing alphabet knowledge as the single best predictor of later reading success. Alphabetic knowledge has another crucial effect, and that is the promotion of transcription fluency—the ability to quickly and accurately write. Transcription fluency promotes better composition and notetaking skills. For this reason, alphabetics instruction is often coupled with handwriting instruction; this module will focus on the relationship between alphabet knowledge and learning to read.

Read each statement and mark **T** if the statement is true and **F** if the statement is false. As you read through the module, you might change your responses. Be prepared to explain your responses and use the text for evidence,

Before Reading	Statements	After Reading
T **F**	1. Learning letter names generally helps children learn letter sounds.	**T** **F**
Why did you indicate true or false?		Has your thinking changed after reading?
T **F**	2. Children usually learn the letters in their names first.	**T** **F**
Why did you indicate true or false?		Has your thinking changed after reading?

Before Reading	Statements	After Reading
T F	3. Alphabet instruction that contrasts letter shapes is often confusing.	T F
Why did you indicate true or false?	Has your thinking changed after reading?	
T F	4. Letters that look alike may be harder to learn and need more instruction.	T F
Why did you indicate true or false?	Has your thinking changed after reading?	

NOTES

What Is Alphabetics?

Alphabet recognition is the ability to recognize uppercase and lowercase letters of the alphabet. These are the graphemes of the language. As children are learning to write their names, they are also often experiencing the writing of their first letters (Bloodgood, 1999). This knowledge is expanded, and by the end of kindergarten most children know how to write their names in a form that is recognizable.

English is an alphabetic language, which means that sounds are represented by letters (graphemes). These sounds compose some of the phonemes of the language. Therefore, these letter-sound relationships are more correctly called grapheme-phoneme correspondences.

Students must be taught that the sounds in the words they speak are represented by the letters in the alphabet.

In addition to understanding these grapheme-phoneme correspondences, children must be able to recognize both upper- and lowercase letters and eventually read them in manuscript and cursive writing and in different fonts. Some letters are more difficult to recognize because they look similar to other letters, such as *b* and *d*. When looking at and naming letters with children, it's important to help the children distinguish visual differences by talking about these similarities of appearance. The positioning of lines, how tall the letters are, how big they are, and whether they have curved lines are all similarities that should be discussed. Examples include the curves of the letter *S*, the vertical lines of *T* and *V*, the horizontal lines of *E* and *B*, and the letters *H* and *X*, which have both vertical and horizontal lines *H* and *X*. Learning the alphabet is a complex task.

There is widespread agreement that the outdated letter-of-the-week approach, with its march through the alphabet from A to Z, is not effective.

NOTES

Learning Order in Alphabetics

While the specific order of letters taught differs, there is widespread agreement that the outdated letter-of-the-week approach, with its march through the alphabet from A to Z, is not effective (Reutzel & Cooter, 1992). Much research has been conducted regarding alphabetics, which Reutzel synthesized as six principles for learning order (see Figure 3.1).

Figure 3.1* *Learning Order for the Alphabet

1. **Own-Name Effect:** Children often first learn the letters of their first name, and particularly the initial letter of their name. Capitalize on this knowledge by associating letters taught with the names of children in the class.
2. **Alphabetic-Order Effect:** The letters near the beginning and end of the alphabet are typically learned before the middle section of the alphabet. Take this into consideration when parceling time necessary to teach a letter. Because of the variance, an arbitrary one week for each letter doesn't make much sense.
3. **Letter-Frequency Effect:** Letters that occur more frequently in print will be learned more quickly due to relative exposure. Keep this in mind with low-frequency letters such as *q, u,* and *v,* as they require more intentional encounters.
4. **Letter-Name Effect:** A letter that has a corresponding sound similar to its name (such as *a, b, o, s,* and *t*), will be learned more quickly than a letter that does not (e.g., *h, w, y*).
5. **Consonant Phoneme Acquisition Effect:** Children learn consonant letters that are voiced more earlier and therefore more frequently. This has a developmental component, as early consonant speech sounds of infants, such as /m/, /b/, and /p/, emerge around 18 months of age. Later speech sounds, such as /j/ and /v/, don't emerge until around age 4. Letter recognition appears to follow a similar trajectory, with those early consonants learned more readily than later consonants mastered in speech later (Justice et al., 2006).
6. **Distinctive Visual Features Letter-Writing Effect:** Children who learn the distinctive marks that are components of written letters (e.g., curved, straight, diagonal, and intersecting line) before learning how to write the alphabet will acquire transcription fluency more quickly.

Remember, acquiring an understanding of alphabetics is no simple task. It involves visual and auditory discrimination and memory. Children must learn and be able to recognize how each letter is formed, how to pronounce each letter, what sounds represent each letter, how to write each letter, and eventually how to read combinations of letters in words and combine them into words. Developing these skills of recognition and discrimination involves significant amounts of practice.

NOTICE AND WONDER

Review Figure 3.1. What did you notice about the order of letter learning? Many students enter school already knowing how to write some, or all, of the letters of their names. But some do not.

What will you do so support students who do not yet know all of the letters in their names?

As learning the alphabet progresses, how will you organize and teach the letters?

Why do you believe that the letter-of-the-week approach would be ineffective?

NOTES

Uppercase, Lowercase, or Both?

There doesn't seem to be a clear answer to whether it is best to teach uppercase first, lowercase first, or to teach them in tandem. Each has a certain logic to it. For example, many children enter school with some knowledge of some uppercase letters. So, might it be useful to leverage what they know and teach from that perspective? Perhaps, and there's additional reasoning that uppercase letters, with more starting points, are easier for young children, who are developing fine motor skills, to write. On the other hand, wouldn't it make sense to teach them lowercase letters first? After all, 95% of the letters they see in print are in their lowercase form.

Others have argued that teaching both as pairs makes sense, in order to reinforce the sound properties held in common. (Some teachers talk about Mama Letters and Baby Letters that match.) To be sure, some letter pairs are identical except for size (*Cc, Oo, Ss, Uu, Vv, Ww, Xx, Zz*), and others are visually similar (*Ff, Ii, Jj, Kk, Ll, Mm, Pp, Tt, Yy*). Still others are quite different (*Aa, Bb, Dd, Ee, Gg, Hh, Nn, Qq, Rr*). When upper- and lowercase letters are very different, students have more demand on their attention and require more repetitions to make the connection.

In light of these many factors, we recommend using a hybrid approach. From the beginning, children should learn that letters have two forms. Early alphabetic learning should include pairs when they are identical. Subsequent cycles can introduce those that are similar but not identical. Later cycles can add those pairs that are visually dissimilar. In reality, some letters take longer to learn than others.

WHAT'S YOUR ADVICE?

When peers ask you about teaching upper- and lowercase letters, what advice do you give?

How would you recommend that peers can know that students are learning their letters?

Instruction in Alphabetics

Instruction in alphabetics is often multidimensional, accompanied by embedded opportunities to learn the letters' sounds, shapes, and presence in words. Rather than a letter-of-the-week approach, which fails to capture what is known about learning order, early literacy researchers recommend a letter-of-the-day approach that provides a deeper dive that anchors this knowledge in reading, writing, speaking, and listening (Jones et al., 2012). These researchers caution that children's learning of letters is not a one-and-done proposition, but rather should be reviewed in cycles to ensure that children maintain the knowledge they are acquiring. Instead of taking 26 weeks to teach the letters, a letter-of-the-day schedule allows for seven or so repeating cycles throughout the school year. (Each cycle takes about six weeks to move through each letter.) Later cycles can drop out the most readily learned ones, such as *Oo,* in favor of integrating visually similar (*Tt*) and then visually dissimilar (*Gg*) letter pairs. The use of cycles provides more timely opportunities to gauge who isn't making adequate progress and with whom additional small-group supplemental instruction might be needed.

The targeted letter of the day should always include both the upper- and lowercase versions.

Many children come to school with some knowledge of the letters of the alphabet and their associated sounds. However, while a caregiver may proudly say that the child "knows all their letters," in practice the child may have only rudimentary knowledge. For instance, they can sing the alphabet song (a home favorite), but it may be recitational only, without a clear understanding of the distinctions between each letter. Relatively few children know lowercase letters, as practice at home often is usually exclusively on uppercase ones. For these reasons, the targeted letter of the day should always include both the upper- and lowercase versions.

Your instruction will likely need to be differentiated. Piasta (2014) studied alphabet alphabet knowledge among kindergarteners. The range of knowledge proved to be between 1 and 52 upper- and lowercase letters, due to variance in prior letter instruction. Having said that, they all require intentional and systematic instruction that is engaging and fun rather than scripted and lockstep for all (National Early Literacy Panel, 2008).

Children learn the alphabetic principle by being actively engaged in activities that promote this awareness (Bear et al., 1996). Such activities include singing letter songs while pointing to each letter or making the shape with their bodies, writing one's name and talking about its spelling, and matching pictures cards to the letter that represents the first sound heard in the name of the picture. Each letter name, shape, and sound can be taught to mastery using picture cards, movable letters, and whiteboards for writing practice. It's important to vary the activities and songs so that children don't become bored or view this important learning as a drill.

TAKE ACTION

Appendix B contains a letter recognition assessment. In most cases, these assessments include the names of the letters as well as the sounds that they make. Letter recognition assessments are useful in determining what students already know and what they still need to learn. These assessments are administered individually, and then instructional and grouping decisions can be made. Assess your students, and identify which letters still need to be learned. There are a number of free letter lists (like the one in Appendix B) that include both uppercase and lowercase letters. On the tool in the appendix:

- Check in the "N" column for the correct letter name.
- Check in the "S" column for correct letter-sound response.
- If the student says a word with or for the letter, record that word in the "Word" column for word response.
- Record any incorrect responses in the "I.R." column.

NOTES

Providing Opportunities for Children to Read and Practice Alphabetics

Let's now consider a few additional instructional activities that support children in learning the letters and sounds of the alphabet.

Personalize It. One engaging activity that supports alphabet learning is to have children build alphabet rings or personal alphabet books of their design that contain pictures they have selected that begin with the same initial consonant or vowel. The first letter on the ring can be the letter *A*, which is followed by pictures of an apple, apron, and ant. Blank cards follow the picture cards to allow children the opportunity to write and draw additional words that begin with the same first letter, including their names and the names of their classmates.

Collect old magazines because these are perfect for children to browse and then cut and paste selected pictures into their alphabet books or rings on the page containing the target letter. Each of the word cards should also include the spelling of the word. As these rings are built, they can be shared with peers and referred to when writing.

Once several letters and letter cards have been added to the rings, you can invite class members to hold up a particular card, identify the letter, and tell another word that begins with the same letter. While the words on the cards will initially be recognized by the picture, after multiple exposures you can cover the picture, hold up the initial letter, and ask the children to say a word and other words that begin with the same letter. This allows you to assess children's letter recognition, and also to eventually determine whether the children can identify words that begin with the targeted letter. This activity can also be done efficiently with small groups of students who have knowledge gaps in the alphabet.

Use Fast-Paced Games. Letter-of-the-day lessons are short in duration (10–12 minutes) but packed with lots of opportunities to practice the sounds, visual characteristics, and letter formations needed.

- **Use mnemonic cards** that contain drawings or pictures of something that contains the target letter. An example is an *S* embedded in a picture of a snake, an *a* embedded in the shape of an apple, or an *e* embedded into the shape of an egg. Scaffolds such as these should be included as needed early in alphabet learning but should be faded as quickly as possible to ensure that children do not become dependent on them.
- **Match uppercase and lowercase letter pairs** to strengthen these associations.
- **Sort uppercase letters into one pile and lowercase letters into another.** Then have children write them on their whiteboards.
- **Cut apart letters in words and reassemble them** to encourage learning of left-to-right directionality. Both sorting and matching activities require the child to look carefully at all dimensions of the letters and visually discriminate among their similarities and differences.
- **Find the letter** using a photocopied page from a book your class has been reading. Give children highlighters to mark all the examples of the target letter they can find. Make sure that the text you select contains words with the target letter in medial and final positions, too, not just initial letters.
- **Have children write the targeted letter** on paper or whiteboards, in the air, on the carpet, or with their feet or an elbow to reinforce the shape of the letter.

A quick assessment of children's growing knowledge of letters can occur each morning as children sign in on a sign-in sheet before taking their seats. They can be asked to write the letter of the day in both uppercase and lowercase representations.

This accomplishes the dual purpose of taking attendance while also recording their progress as an assessment of their developing motor control and visual discrimination.

Read Alphabet Books. Shared readings with alphabet books allow you to direct children's attention to the visual formation of the letters as well as the sounds of the letters. When sharing these, point out that the letters have names and sounds. Engage children in saying and practicing these. After seeing and naming the letter, children can draw pictures or just partner share words they know that start with the target sound.

Make a Class Alphabet Book. Create a class alphabet book to add to throughout the year. Begin with pages that contain each child's name with the appropriate initial letter. For example, begin the book with the letter Aa. Then follow the letter with names of students that begin with the letter, like Angelina and Antonio. Through each six-week cycle, add new words that correspond to the targeted letters, both uppercase and lowercase, such that Omar, octopus, out, and Orlando, for instance, are profiled.

Link Instruction With Assessment and Grouping. Children may initially know the names and/or sounds of various letters and how to write them, especially the ones in their names. This information can serve as a baseline to help you know where to start your instruction. In small groups, children can be asked to complete the following tasks. These will illustrate to you when regrouping and supplemental instruction should occur. Possible tasks can include the following:

- Asking a child to name a letter you are showing. "Can you tell me the name of this letter?"
- Sharing a few visually different letter configurations and asking the child to identify a particular one. "Look at each of these letters and tell me which one is ______?" (*B, T, O*)
- Sharing a few visually similar letters and asking the child to identify a particular one. "Look at each of these letters and tell me which one is ______?" (*b, d, p,* or *M, N, W*)
- Asking a child to produce a sound when a letter is shown. "Can you tell me a sound this letter makes?"

The responses of the children can help you form needs-based small groups that will benefit from supplemental instruction. Small-group instruction adds value over one-on-one instruction, because children learn from the feedback being offered their peers and also from listening to their peers naming and sounding letters (Piasta & Wagner, 2010). Additionally, young children are better able to maintain their focus for shorter periods of time as they work with peers in smaller groups.

FIND THE MISTAKES

Greutman (2017) identified seven mistakes to avoid when teaching the alphabet, including the following:

- Mistake 1—Too many worksheets
- Mistake 2—Not enough hands-on learning
- Mistake 3—Not enough variety
- Mistake 4—Expecting kids to write their letters before they're ready
- Mistake 5—Insisting a child finish an activity the way you expect it to be done
- Mistake 6—No flexibility (meaning not responding to the learning of students and adjusting lessons)
- Mistake 7—Forgetting to read and talk about books

From this list of mistakes, inventory your classroom and talk with your colleagues. Are there mistakes that you could correct to increase students' alphabetic knowledge?

Into the Classroom

Carolyn Rogers is surrounded by her kindergarten children on the reading rug. Her targeted letter of the day is *b.* They have just finished sharing the book, *The Baby Bee Bird* by Diane Redfield Massie and Steven Kellogg. They talk about the sound the baby bird was making that was annoying the other animals. An important concept in the reading and discussion that followed is that the annoying sound was the same as one made by the letter *b.* Ms. Rogers then leads them into a round of *Mamma Went to Market,* a familiar game to the children. Ms. Rogers starts the game by holding up a letter card of the lowercase letter *b* and saying, "Today let's think about all the things Mamma could buy at the market that start with the letter *b.*" On the rug in front of the children are other cards that contain pictures and words of items such as *banana, bat, boat, bed, bug, bee, bell, boat, balloon, bread*, and *butter.*

Ms. Rogers hands the letter card to the first child in the circle and says, "What did Mamma buy at the market that begins with the letter *b*?" Nicky picks up a picture card of butter and says, "butter." Ms. Rogers replies, "Yes, butter begins with the letter *b*, but let's remember to use our sentences." Nicky, making a second attempt, says, "Mamma went to the market, and she bought butter."

After Ms. Rogers and the other children agree that Nicky has correctly said a word that begins with the letter *b,* the letter card is passed to Daniella, who selects another picture card and says, "Mamma went to the market, and she bought butter and bread." The card is next passed to Omar, who, holding the letter *b* card says, "Mamma went to the market, and she bought butter, bread, and bananas." The game continues with children repeating and adding to the pattern. When there are no remaining picture cards, Ms. Rogers asks if there are any other items Mamma could buy at the market that begin with the letter *b.* Everyone agrees when Jesse says bubblegum, and everyone laughs when Daniel says bacon.

Ms. Rogers confirms that everything Mamma bought at the market began with the letter *b.* She then asks the children to look at her lips as she says the sound of *b* in the initial consonant position. She invites the children to say it too. Then together they sing along with a video of a song featuring words beginning with *b.* She follows their singing by asking them to again look at a few word and picture cards and to say the word on the card while listening for the beginning sound of *b.* She writes the letter b on a whiteboard and with the children says the names of a few of the items that begin with the letter *b* that Mamma bought at the market.

NOTES

A Teacher's Rationale During Whole-Group Instruction

During this instruction Ms. Rogers was focusing on the lowercase letter *b,* because the children had previously learned the uppercase letter *B.* She always teaches the uppercase letter first, because she has found that children are better able to learn the lowercase letter after the uppercase of the same letter has already been mastered (Pence Turnbull et al., 2010). She feels this is possibly true because some uppercase letters seem to have more distinctive features that, other than size, are similar in appearance in both their uppercase and lowercase forms, for example, *Cc, Kk, Oo, Ww, Vv,* and *Zz.*

However, since the uppercase and lowercase formations of the letter *Bb* are not the same, Ms. Rogers had previously targeted the uppercase *B* with explicit instruction that involved the children first looking at the letter both on a letter card and in the posted classroom alphabet. While looking, they talked about its formation. Then they made the formation in the air, then on their arms, and finally on their whiteboards, with Ms. Rogers writing it first and the children modeling her formation. Ms. Rogers was simultaneously saying the sound of *B,* which the children also mimicked while forming the letter *B.* Bernardo and Badra each excitedly said their names started with *B* and then immediately wrote the letter B on their whiteboards.

Today the focus is on the lowercase *b.* The work being done by Ms. Rogers and her students with the lowercase *b* mirrors their previous work with the uppercase *B.* Abdullah was able to find b in his name, as was Aubrey. Together, they found additional words in the story that contained the lowercase *b* within words. The instruction concludes with children writing the letter *b* on their whiteboards.

NOTES

A Teacher's Rationale During Small-Group Instruction

Jeramiah DeMarcus teaches in the classroom next door to Ms. Rogers. He and Ms. Rogers jointly plan instruction that occurs primarily with children working in small groups at centers with one center allowing for direct instruction from the teacher. Their instruction is grounded in the beliefs that

- **Learning** the alphabet and becoming phonemically aware involves quantity and quality exposure and practice.
- **Instruction** should involve children seeing, talking, and writing about letters in isolation and in words.
- **Assessment** must be continuous and differentiated to recognize when a child has learned to identify a certain letter by name and sound.

The learning in Mr. DeMarcus's classroom primarily occurs in configurations similar to those in Ms. Rogers's classroom, with heterogeneous groups of children working on certain activities, while groups of children with similar knowledge needs work with him. Like the instruction occurring in Ms. Rogers's classroom, his is also based on research-supported tenets.

As part of their alphabetics instruction, students work in five small groups at tables on various tasks that all involve gaining competency with identifying the look and sound of letters. These include matching and comparing activities done as partners, writing that involves tracing the letters of the alphabet, viewing alphabet books, and singing, listening, and moving to alphabet songs. Mr. DeMarcus moves among the students to observe their performance. As the children work together, he has the opportunity to provide support to individual children or even to assemble a group with similar skills to work together with him. This is a perfect time for him to observe student performance and then to provide appropriate instructional scaffolds to ensure that each of the children is becoming proficient in learning the letters of the alphabet. More specifically, here are the learning tasks in which the children are engaged:

- **Table 1:** Four children are seated at this table, working as pairs. They are looking at a stack of cards of words and letters. Their task is to sort them into piles of letters and words and then to partner read as many as possible. This task supports their visual discrimination of letters and words.
- **Table 2:** Six children are writing their names, cutting them up into separate letters, and then rearranging them to make a new name to share with table members. Many of the rearranged names cause the children to laugh. They may only rearrange two letters (initial and final letters); Sam becomes Mas, for example; Mario becomes Oarim; Sarah becomes Haras; Chuck becomes Khucc. This task supports their discrimination of letters and sounds as they make their names into new words.
- **Table 3:** Five children are working with the teacher and are tasked to write their names, say the letters, and then look at each other's whiteboards to identify

whose names begin with the same letter. As they look at each other's names, they are deciding

  - who has the longest name and how many letters it contains.
  - the shortest name and how many letters it contains,
  - which pairs or sets of names start with the same letter, end with the same letter, or have a similar middle letter

- **Table 4:** Five children are looking at alphabet books with a peer and talking about the book. Some of the books at the table are *Dr. Seuss's ABC: An Amazing Alphabet Board Book*, *There Was an Old Lady Who Swallowed the ABCs* by Lucille Colandro and illustrator Jared Lee, and *The Alphabet's Alphabet* by Chris Harris.
- **Table 5:** Four children are listening to *See It, Say It, Sign It* by Jack Hartman (https://www.youtube.com/watch?v=WP1blVh1ZQM) and whisper singing into plastic play microphones. Next, they listen and move to *Get Your Alpha Grove On* from GoNoodle (https://www.youtube.com/watch?v=BrGnv8AxRYI). Finally they have fun saying the alphabet backward with *The CBAs* from GoNoodle (https://www.gonoodle.com/videos/NXQ6G2/the-cbas) As they listen to others say the letters of the alphabet, they are practicing the names and letter formations with their body movements.

All students, whether working with Mr. DeMarcus or at one of the other independent group tasks, are engaged in learning to identify the letters of the alphabet.

TEXT-TO-SELF CONNECTION

What are the key reasons for teaching children the alphabet?

Using the traffic light scale, with red being not confident, yellow being somewhat confident, and green indicating very confident, how confident are you in your ability to

- Teach the alphabet?

- Develop students' alphabetic knowledge?

Takeaways

- Knowledge of letter shapes and names is a strong predictor of success in learning to read.
- There is no prescribed sequence to learning letters, but letter of the week is not an effective approach. It's more effective to start with letters that occur in students' names and letters that occur frequently, to follow these with letters that look similar, and to end with those that are harder to learn.
- Letters have names and sounds, and both should be taught. Without strong alphabetics, students are likely to have difficulty with grapheme-phoneme correspondences and learning to read.

PS: The anticipation guide answers are T, T, F, T.

online resources

Visit the companion website at
resources.corwin.com/teachingreading
for this module's downloadable resources.

MODULE

4

Phonics and Decoding

Photo by iStock.com/FatCamera

Look at the child and the teacher in the picture. Together, they are saying the word and then the sounds represented by each letter to create the word. Because the student is so young, the teacher is expanding their phonological awareness skills to learn that speech comprises identifiable sounds that together compose spoken words, syllables, and letter sounds. The teacher is sharing both uppercase and lowercase letters in the word *hat* and its grapheme-phoneme correspondences. Lessons like these provide the teacher with opportunities to explicitly teach students to associate speech sounds with print.

In this module, we will

- **Learn the role of phonics and its impact on reading, spelling, and writing.**
- **Realize that the spoken sounds in language are graphically represented by letters that compose the words we read and write.**
- **Identify sequential instruction that develops phonics skills for reading and writing.**

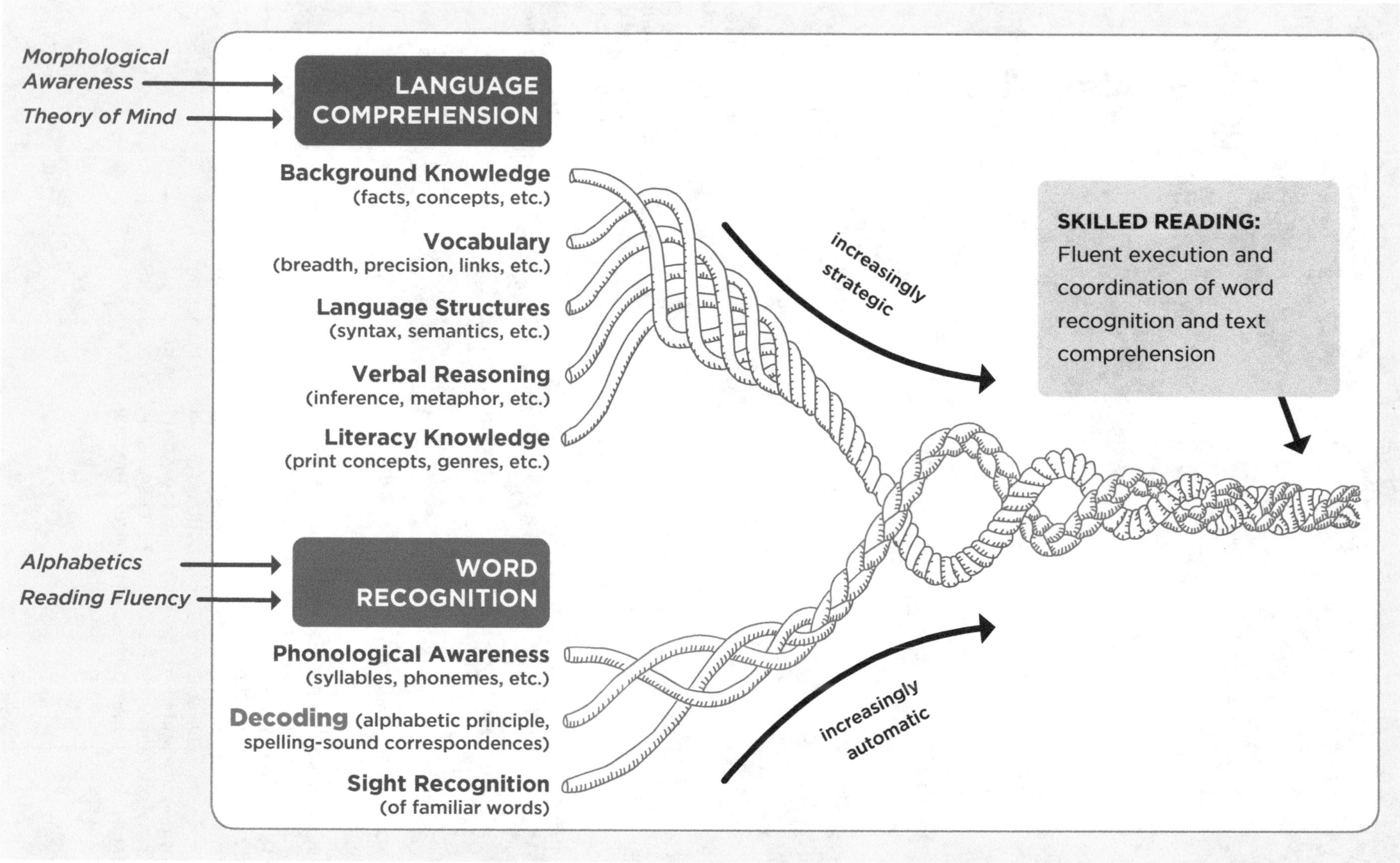

Source: Adapted from Scarborough, H. S. (2001). Connecting early language and literacy to later reading (dis)abilities: Evidence, theory, and practice. In S. Neuman & D. Dickinson (Eds.), *Handbook for research in early literacy* (pp. 97–110). Guilford Press.

Intentional, intensive, and systematic phonics instruction is crucial for young readers, who must bolt the sounds of the language onto its graphemes. These grapheme-phoneme correspondences are key to decoding the patterns of written language, beginning with the alphabetic principle that written words are composed of the sounds of spoken language, which are represented by the letters of the alphabet. This understanding is essential to initial decoding, which becomes automatic and supports the accumulation of one's expanding sight vocabulary, which we define as words recognized instantly without being sounded out. Application of children's understanding of the alphabetic principle should include instruction that extends their knowledge to the consonant-vowel pattern level, such as being able to accurately decode CVC (*mat*), CVCe (*mate*), and CVV words (*due*). (*C* is for consonant, *V* is for vowel, and *e* is silent.) A third level of phonics instruction is at the meaning level, as students learn about prefixes and suffixes. At this third level, children are able to focus less attention on sounding out the individual letter sounds and are able to focus on how letter-sound combinations such as prefixes and suffixes affect the spelling, reading, and meaning of words (Ehri, 2004; Moats, 1995). These skills are key for reading, of course, but also for spelling and writing. We will discuss this third level in the morphology module.

Read each statement and mark **T** if the statement is true and **F** if the statement is false. As you read through the module, you might change your responses. Be prepared to explain your responses and use the text for evidence.

Before Reading	Statements	After Reading
T **F**	1. When students can't decode, they rely on environmental clues (such as logos) to make meaning.	**T** **F**
Why did you indicate true or false?	Has your thinking changed after reading?	
T **F**	2. Phonemic awareness is an important prerequisite to phonics instruction, and both impact reading, writing, and spelling.	**T** **F**
Why did you indicate true or false?	Has your thinking changed after reading?	
T **F**	3. Phonics should be taught systematically as a part of daily reading instruction.	**T** **F**
Why did you indicate true or false?	Has your thinking changed after reading?	

(Continued)

(Continued)

Before Reading	Statements	After Reading
T F	4. Modeling and thinking aloud allow students to see how phonics knowledge supports reading, spelling, and writing.	T F
Why did you indicate true or false?		Has your thinking changed after reading?

What Is Phonics?

Although the conversation continues about how to best teach young children to read, there is a deep body of research that confirms that phonemic awareness and phonics instruction benefit children learning to read (National Reading Panel, 2000). Further, when these processes are combined, students progress more rapidly in learning to read (Erhi, 2020) and achieve the goal of phonics instruction, which is to "develop automatic, error-free word recognition during reading" (Mesmer, 2019).

As we noted in Module 2, phonemic awareness instruction should begin early in a child's life, with targeted instruction and practice using word games, songs, and chants. As children become phonemically aware, this knowledge can be mobilized for phonics instruction that supports their spelling, reading, and writing. Using their growing grapheme-phoneme correspondence knowledge, children get better at looking at an unknown word—one that has not become a part of their instantly recognized words—and associate the sounds with the letters to accurately decode the word.

NOTES

Stages of Phonics Development

Students in the early grades are rapidly developing the ability to make grapheme-phoneme correspondences and to blend the sounds in order to accurately decode words. Chall (1983) described this as part of a progression of development in learning to read. Subsequent stages include vocabulary and comprehension development and knowledge building. Because this module focuses on phonics instruction, we will confine our discussion to stages 0–2, when children acquire the prereading and phonics skills needed to become fluent readers.

- **Stage 0: Prereading.** Prereading occurs before most children enter school. Before they enter kindergarten, many children are aware of the existence of some alphabetic letters and that these letters have sounds. This is a significant stage in which children develop and learn language and basic concepts about language (Kupetz, 1993). They begin to understand that the print in the environment around them carries meaning. They are becoming phonemically aware, meaning they understand that words they speak are made up of discrete sounds represented by letters and that manipulation of these sounds, and eventually the associated letters, change the words.
- **Stage 1: Initial Reading and Decoding.** For most children, this stage begins in kindergarten and lasts through the end of grade 1; for some it extends into grade 2. During this stage children are learning the sound patterns they need to decode. The focus of instruction is on learning phonics skills and using them to read connected text.
- **Stage 2: Confirmation, Fluency, and Ungluing From Print.** Most children in grades 2 and 3 are at this stage of reading development. Their phonics skills are so well practiced that they can now automatically apply these to new unfamiliar words, which—once read without being consciously sounded out—become a part of their sight vocabularies. This is referred to as the *amalgamation theory,* "when written words have become familiar and their identities have bonded together in memory. The words are no longer decoded by sounding out and blending letters sequentially" (Ehri, 2020, p. 49). Rather, all properties (orthographic, phonological, and semantic) are automatically activated as soon as an unfamiliar word is seen (Ehri & Wilce, 1985).

ALPHABETIC PRINCIPLE AND BLENDING

The alphabetic principle, which was the focus of the previous module, drives the decoding skills of early readers. Children who understand this principle recognize that there is a steady and predictable relationship between the sounds of the language and its written form. They further realize that while the texts or the print font may change, the representation of the word remains the same.

Directionality is also crucial for students to learn to blend represented sounds. Children need to be taught that if they do not instantly read a word they see in print (sight words), they must use a left-to-right sequence through the word until it is decoded and recognized. We want students to engage in successive blending, such as writing the letters of a word, running a finger underneath each letter, and blending the sounds together several times, each one more rapid than the last (Blevins, 2017). It is for this reason that children should be taught to read using texts that contain both familiar words and words they will be attempting to sound out. Since all children do not come to school with the same base of language, texts that are first read aloud by the teacher can provide opportunities to apply decoding skills within a familiar context (Stigler & Hiebert, 1999).

Once a student has developed the requisite skills of grapheme-phoneme correspondence and can blend these sounds together, they are more easily able to sound out, pronounce, and recognize unfamiliar words. Their increasing automaticity in decoding one-syllable words and units of letters (e.g., *-ate, -ing, -able*) contributes to their growing reading fluency. By the end of second grade, children are developing the ability to recognize whole words, which allows them to get to other unknown words. This process, called *unitization*, allows them to more efficiently decode words like *skate*, *skating*, and *skateable* (Harn et al., 2008). Many struggling readers are unable to sound out unfamiliar words because they have limited phonics skills. This lack of independence when encountering a new word subsequently slows down their reading and interferes with comprehension.

"When a new skill is introduced, it should be systematically and purposefully reviewed for the next four to six weeks" (Blevins, 2017, p. 203).

NOTES

Principles of Phonics Instruction

Phonics instruction should include teaching students

1. Grapheme-phoneme correspondences
2. How to blend and pronounce spelling patterns in words being read
3. How to use this knowledge to decode less-familiar words

We also believe that phonics skills should be developed through a well-planned sequence that is explicitly taught daily until children can fluently read the learned patterns in words. Importantly, review and repetition are key. Blevins (2017) notes that a common error in phonics instruction happens when the focus is on exposure rather than mastery. He notes that "when a new skill is introduced, it should be systematically and purposefully reviewed for the next four to six weeks" (p. 203).

The instructional plan should contain specified learning targets and lessons that support teachers engaging children in instruction that ensures accomplishing the goals (Templeton, 2015). For example, an early lesson might focus on teaching the individual sound /b/ that the letter *b* makes in the words *bed, baby,* and *ball.* This could be followed by additional, more sophisticated lessons focused on teaching /b/ as an initial first or onset sound that can be followed by various rimes (the letters that follow) to make many *b* words, such as /b/ /a/ t/, /b/ /i/ /t/, /b/ /e/ /t/, and /b/ /u/ /t/.

Many similar iterations illustrating this direct grapheme-phoneme connection may be needed before all children own the concept that the /b/ sound is represented by the *b* letter in words that begin with *b.* Notice that an implicit approach would involve less direct instruction, because it would involve showing children the words *bug, bat, bit* and asking what is similar in each word. Children would offer responses until they identified that all three words begin with the /b/ sound and the letter *b.* Discovery is appropriate for some learning tasks, but we believe that, in the early stages of reading, many young children do not have the phonemic awareness skills needed to hear only the first letter in these three words and also make the connection that the sound they are hearing is the letter *b* and that it is represented by the /b/ sound they are hearing. We encourage you to provide all the explicit instruction a child needs to master these grapheme-phoneme correspondences and be able to use them to write and read. We, however, also encourage you to consider that not all children need the same amount of instruction to become fluent at recognizing letters and reading words (Jones et al., 2013) and that teaching smaller groups of children with similar needs allows teachers to provide the instruction each child needs.

We encourage you to provide all the explicit instruction a child needs to master grapheme-phoneme correspondences.

Once teachers have explicitly taught grapheme-phoneme correspondences such as these and assessed students to ensure that the correspondences have been learned, practice activities such as word sorts and word building that engage students in more implicit exploration are appropriate for reinforcement and mastery (Ehri, 2005; Lonigan & Shanahan, 2008; Muter et al., 1998). All the while this systematic instruction is occurring, children should be being introduced to texts containing these words and being supported to read them independently.

FIND THE MISTAKE

Blevins, as part of his master class on phonics instruction, noted that there are at least 10 mistakes educators make in this area. His list includes

Mistake 1—Inadequate or nonexistent review and repetition cycle

Mistake 2—Lack of application to real reading and writing experiences

Mistake 3—Inappropriate reading materials for practicing skills

Mistake 4—Ineffective use of the gradual release model

Mistake 5—Too much time lost during transition

Mistake 6—Limited teacher knowledge of research-based phonics routines and linguistics

Mistake 7—Inappropriate pacing of lessons

Mistake 8—No comprehensive or cumulative mastery assessment tools

Mistake 9—Transitioning to multisyllabic words too late

Mistake 10—Overdoing it (especially isolated skill work) (Blevins, 2022)

Which of these common mistakes are happening in your class or school? What can you do about this?

NOTES

Systematic Instruction in Phonics and Decoding

A systematic plan for phonics instruction includes a developmental sequence similar to the one shown in Figure 4.1. This phonics sequence is grounded in the work of Jones and Reutzel (2012) and is featured in many states' standards for reading. You can use this staircase to create a phonics skills progression that identifies a sequence from learning short vowels and consonants in the vowel-consonant (VC) words *at* and *it* to the consonant-vowel-consonant (CVC) words *bat*, *bit*, and *but* through multisyllable words. However, the findings from Kearns (2020) suggest the need to closely monitor the progression of implementation. This monitoring should be grounded in a continuous noticing of the growth of knowledge and utility being exhibited by students as they apply this sound sequence to the reading of words.

Do you know your phonics progression? Phonics instruction in the early grades should align with the instructional materials selected by your school or district. Familiarize yourself with the scope and sequence of your phonics program, and note whether there are sufficient opportunities for your students to reach mastery (four to six weeks) rather than just to have exposure (a new phonics skill every week, with little rehearsal and repetition). You may wish to add additional books, but when you do so, be sure they align with the strengths of the readers and promote their growth. Keep in mind that effective phonics instruction is not solely delivered to the whole group. Frequently during early learning, instruction occurs with small groups of students who have been assessed by you as having similar language and literacy strengths and are therefore ready for instruction that will advance their skill levels. The goal is to make phonics instruction precise, efficient, and effective for each learner.

The goal is to make phonics instruction precise, efficient, and effective for each learner.

NOTICE AND WONDER

Review the learning progression for phonics skills. Are there any surprises?____________

____

How do your instructional materials align with the progress of skill development?______

____

Are your students on track with this progression? ____________ If not, where do you need to focus your efforts? ____

If you teach older readers, have they mastered the skills noted on the progression?

____

Figure 4.1 Progression of Phonics Skills

								Multisyllabic words (syllable types)
							Multisyllabic words (prefix/ suffix)	
						r-controlled vowels, variants, dipthongs		
					Long vowels			
				Final *e*				
			Short vowels and digraphs					
		Short vowels and blends						
	Short vowels and consonants							
ABCs								

|KINDERGARTEN _|

|Grade 1 ______|

| Grade 2 ______|

Link Phonics Instruction to Practice

The goal of reading instruction is to ensure that children have the skills they need to read connected text independently (Adams, 1990). To learn any skill, learners need explicit instruction that is followed by supported, deliberate practice until the skill is mastered and can be used independently without support from the teacher. It is for this reason that children who are learning phonics skills should have the opportunity to practice a newly learned target skill in a decodable text that contains repeated patterns that they can quickly learn to read.

To learn any skill, learners need explicit instruction that is followed by supported, deliberate practice until the skill is mastered.

Teachers often invite the reading and rereading of a decodable text to provide students the opportunity to practice. For example, if the long /e/ sound spelled as *ee* and *ea* in words like *bee* and *beat* has been the focus of phonics instruction, the decodable text selected for practice should contain words with this long /e/ pattern and also high-frequency words such as *the, and, a* that are familiar to the children and support their practice. Decodable texts should not be selected to support the deepening of reading comprehension, because the simple language used to support decoding is generally not sophisticated enough to also promote comprehension beyond a very literal level. The goal of using decodable text should be to get the orthographic skill learned well enough so that the reader can apply it automatically when reading more authentic texts.

Shanahan (2019) cautions us "to use decodable, predictable texts as a temporary crutch to practice phonics in a favorable text environment—an environment in which there aren't likely to be many words that can't be figured out easily." Like us, he emphasizes the words *temporary* and *practice*. Controlled, predictable texts used for practice are not the only texts emerging readers should be experiencing. Children need to also be exposed to authentic texts with support from their teacher during shared reading and read-aloud experiences, with the goal being to expand their listening comprehension, vocabulary, sense of story, background knowledge, and comprehension by engaging in conversation and retelling. However, in providing these experiences, teachers can also engage in print referencing and invite students to notice various aspects of the text, including letters and words (Zucker et al., 2011). For example, a teacher may ask students how many words are on a page, to identify the words that start with a specific letter, or to notice and read specific words.

TAKE ACTION

Record yourself in a read-aloud or shared reading lesson. Analyze how many times you reference the text to develop students' text knowledge. Use the checklist provided by Zucker et al. (2011) to analyze the learning experience (see Figure 4.2). Depending on the needs of your students and their ages, you may be focused on print concepts (which will be explored in Module 10), alphabetics (which was the focus of Module 3), or decoding and phonics.

Figure 4.2 Print Targets Addressed Through Print-Reference Read-Alouds in Early Childhood Settings

Print Targets	Definition/Examples
Print Meaning Domain	
Print Function	The function of print is to carry meaning; some special typefaces convey meaning. Sometimes print appears in illustrations (e.g., visible sound). • These are fox's words—he's talking." • "These words are red because he's angry."
Environmental Print	Words present in the environment are portrayed in illustrations (e.g., signs, labels, lists, calendars, recipes, etc.). • "This jar has the word *Cookies* on it." • "Let's read these traffic signs."
Concept of Reading	The function of reading is to convey information or tell a story. There are many things we do when we read. • "If I want to find out how they solve this problem I will have to keep reading." • "Who can tell me some things we do when we read?"
Book and Print Organization Domain	
Page Order	The order in which book pages are read (i.e., the physical act of manipulating a book). • "I read this page first and this page next." • "Where is the front of the book?"
Title of Book	The role of the title as a label and to convey meaning. • "This is the half title page. It tells us the name of the book again." • "The title page tells us this was published in New York."
Top and Bottom of Page	Reading in English occurs from top of the page to the bottom of the page. • "This is the top of the page. The writing starts here." • (move finger down page) "I will read this top line, then this line, and then this last line."
Print Direction	Reading in English must occur from left to right. Some text is printed with unusual orientations or shapes to convey meaning. • (sweep finger under print) "When I read I go this way." • "These words are printed at an angle so they'll look like they're splashing into the water."

Print Targets	Definition/Examples
Book and Print Organization Domain	
Author's Role	The role of the author(s)/illustrator(s). • "The author is the person who wrote the words in this book." • "The author wrote a dedication to his mother."
Letters Domain	
Names of Letters	There are names for all 26 letters. • "I see a word on this page that starts with an *R*!" • "Who can find a letter *S*?"
Concept of Letter	The purpose of letters in forming words. The same letters can be used in many ways. • "I see the same letter in these two words." • "There are three letters in the word *cat*."
Upper- and Lowercase Letters	Letters come in two forms. • "This is a capital *D*. Damian has a capital *D* in his name." • "Uppercase *S* is the same shape as lowercase *s*."
Words Domain	
Concept of Word in Print	Words are distinct units of print and are different from letters. • "Let's count the words on this page." • "Who can show me just one word?"
Short vs. Long Words	Words have different structures. Some words are short, others are long. • "*Dinosaur* is a long word. It has lots of letters." • "Which word is longer—*vegetable* or *soup*?"
Letters vs. Words	Letters make up words. • "This is the letter *G*. It is in the word *grow* and *garden*." • "This is the word *sun*. S-*u*-*n* spells sun."
Word Identification	Some familiar or meaningful words can be identified. • "This is a picture of a tomato. The word *tomato* is written beside it." • "This is the word *the*. It's in this book a lot!"

Source: Justice et al. (2006); Zucker et al (2011).

What did you notice about your print referencing?

What needs do your students have that could be addressed through print referencing?

Controlled, predictable texts used for practice are not the only texts emerging readers should be experiencing.

In addition to practicing reading newly learned patterns while reading decodable text, children also need to have opportunities to use these patterns in their writing. Word work activities such as word card sorting and creating word journals provide opportunities for both practice and extension of newly learned letter-sound patterns (Stanovich & Cunningham, 1992; McCandliss & Posner, 2003). Children will need to be introduced to word work activities with an initial teacher-modeled lesson (Bear et al., 2008; Williams et al., 2009) that is followed throughout the week with time for small-group and individual practice. During the initial teacher modeling and subsequent student practice, be sure children are becoming aware that their focus should be on how each word looks and sounds, rather than on memorizing words. Word sorting activities that invite children to work as partners to sort words with similar patterns invites conversation about the reasons why words are being placed in a particular pile. As newly learned words are transferred into word journals, children can view all the language they are learning, practice reading the words alone and with a buddy, and use their words when writing a larger piece.

NOTES

Word Building

Teaching grapheme-phoneme correspondences involves focusing on rules and patterns and providing students sufficient practice such that they internalize the idea and knowledge. As we have noted earlier in this playbook, students must learn that there are sounds associated with letters and letter combinations. For example, the sound /s/ can be found in *seat*, *city*, or *pass* and thus can be represented by the letters *s*, *c*, or *ss*. Understanding these grapheme-phoneme correspondence rules helps students recognize words and impacts their overall reading fluency. If readers have to use their working memory to assign sounds to symbols, they slow down.

> Readers who have not yet achieved automaticity in word recognition (fluency) must apply a significant amount of their finite cognitive energies to consciously decode the words they encounter while reading. Cognitive attention or energy that must be applied to the low-level decoding task of reading is cognitive energy that is taken away from the more important task of comprehending the text. Hence, comprehension is negatively affected by a reader's lack of fluency. (LaBerge & Samuels, 1974, p. 22)

When readers automate that process, reading rates and accuracy increase. Experiences with decoding are aligned with the letter recognition skills and the phonological awareness that students have developed.

NOTES

Providing Opportunities to Read and Practice Learned Phonics Patterns in Skills-Aligned Texts

Deliberate practice is an important part of the learning process (Ericsson et al., 1993). This is a special type of practice that is purposeful and systematic.

For example, second-grade teacher Jamison Carter is teaching his students about diphthongs, which are gliding vowels that often appear in clusters. His students have previously mastered the following:

- /i/,/y/, /igh/—diphthongs that form the sound similar to *eye*: *hi, cry, my, light, bright*
- /ey/, /ay/, /ai/—diphthongs that form sounds similar to *great*: *they, stay, strain*

They are currently learning about the diphthongs of /ou/ and /ow/ that form the sound similar to *ouch*. Mr. Carter's whole-group lesson is designed to address the needs of students who are at the beginning and the advanced levels. He uses a routine across his lessons that begins with a warm-up. He first identifies the diphthong pattern they are focusing on, and he provides examples that are at first minimally, and then more overtly, different from one another. In addition, he brings in *r*-controlled vowel word patterns that they have learned more recently and are still practicing. (See lines 5 and 6 in the table that follows). This method, pioneered by Blevins (2017), provides students with a predictable routine.

Line 1 (minimal contrasts—new to known)	shot-shout moth-mouth fund-found
Line 2 (focus on one spelling)	cow now, down town, brown drown clown crown
Line 3 (focus on other spelling)	out, round sound, south, mouth, mouse house
Line 4 (mixed set, target skill)	couch ground how frown about growl
Line 5 (review words for mastery)	stir verb born burn sports serve
Line 6 (review words for mastery)	roar porch third thorn thirst fork
Line 7 (challenge words)	downtown campground doghouse dropout somehow thundercloud
Line 8 (connected text)	How do I drive to the next town?
Line 9 (connected text)	My house is south of this town.

Source: Blevins (2017, p. 77).

The words Mr. Carter shares have high utility, because children will see these often as they read longer passages in texts he carefully selects that support alignment with the skills he is addressing at the time. Also, once these new words are added to their word journals, children will have them to use when writing.

Sound Walls

As many including Bottari (2021) and Bruyère and Rusk-Carter (2022) note, *word walls* are print-to-speech organizing tools that contain words that are categorized by the initial letter of the word. Under the letter K, you would find the words *knot, knife,* and *kitten* because these word spellings all begin with the letter *k.* This listing would work well for students who already know how to spell these words. But what about students who only know the sound of the phoneme they are hearing at the beginning of these words? They would probably fare better using a *sound wall,* where the words are categorized by the sounds of the initial phonemes rather than by the initial alphabet letter. Thus, in a sound wall the words *knife* and *knot* would appear under the letter *N,* since the /n/ sound is the initial phoneme sound one hears at the onset of each of these words. The sound wall, unlike the word wall, is a speech sound-to-print support that is organized by the sounds made by the initial phonemes in a word.

Both word walls and sound walls support early literacy development, but here's how they differ.

Word Wall	Sound Wall
Organized alphabetically by the letters A to Z	Organized by the initial speech sound(s) (phonemes) heard when the word is spoken (speech-to-sound pattern)
Moves from print to speech sound	Bridges readers moving from speech sounds to a visual representation of a printed word
Dependent upon teacher support	Builds reader independence
Involves the matching of letters to the initial sounds heard in a word	Involves hearing the sound(s) of the initial phoneme(s) when a word is spoken and categorizing it by its sound pattern
Focuses on identifying one word at a time	Focuses on the transfer of sounds to multiple words with the same initial phonemes

Source: Bruyère and Rusk-Carter (2022).

Think about the words *know, ghost, photo, our,* and *hour.* Where would you place these on your sight word wall? Did you place them alphabetically? Or did you make a column of these irregular words and tell children that they should just memorize them because these words have an irregular pattern? If you asked that they just be memorized, think about it. That means you were asking students to memorize many words without any sound supports to help them with later retrieval.

Instead of being organized from print to sound, sound walls are organized by the phonemes children hear when they articulate a word. Under which letters on a traditional word wall would you place the words *gnat, not*, and *know*? Likely under *g*, *n*, and *k,* respectively. On a sound wall you would find these three words under the sound made by the letter *n,* because children are using their sound-to-grapheme knowledge to place and later to locate the word. Although not much research exists on the efficiency of sound walls, they do seem to make sense, since they are built to support children moving from speech sound to visual recognition.

A sound wall can be developed one sound at a time instead of one letter at a time, which is how most word walls are developed. When introducing a new phoneme, ask the students to think about the sound and about the placement of their tongue as they say a few words sharing the phoneme. After sharing a few words that contain the initial phoneme, place them on the sound wall. For the phoneme /f/, you may introduce words such as *find, for, four, fun,* and *photo.* You may want to have one key word with a picture next to the letter (e.g., *fan*) to remind students of how the initial graphemes having similar phonemes sound. The initial sound of a word is not the only categorization for sound walls. Let's consider the sound /z/—It can be spelled *z* as in *zip*; *zz* as in *fuzz*; *s* as in *is/has*, *se* as in *lose*, or *ze* as in *prize*. So, under the sound /z/ on a sound wall, all of these spelling alternatives could be listed as options to represent the sound /z/ in varying positions of a spoken word.

A sound wall can be developed one sound at a time instead of one letter at a time.

Leah Jenkins has two sound walls: One focuses on consonants and the other on vowels. In English, there are five (and sometimes six) vowel patterns that represent 18 different vowel sounds. For example, the long *i* sounds, as in *ice*, can be made using *I ,e, ie, igh, -y,* or *i.* Having taught the word *fight*, Ms. Jenkins placed the word in the long *i* area on the vowel wall and in the *f* section of the consonant wall under the fricatives with a picture of air going through the lips. Ms. Jenkins has taught her students that there are specific ways that we make sounds for letters (see Figure 4.3).

Figure 4.3 Manners of Articulation

Phonetic Term	Brief Description	Sample IPA Symbols
Nasal (Stop)	Soft palate is lowered so that air flows through the nose; complete closure of the oral cavity	/m n η/
(Oral) Stop	Soft palate is raised, forming a velic closure; complete closure of articulators in the oral cavity	/p b t/
Fricative	Narrowing of two articulators to produce a turbulent airstream	/f v θ/
Approximant	Approximation of two articulators without producing a turbulent airstream	/w j l ɹ/
Trill	An articulator set in vibration by the airstream	/r R/
Tap or Flap	A rapid stop articulation. Caused by a single motion so that one articulator is thrown against another	/ɾ/
Lateral Consonant	With a central obstruction, so that air passes along side (or sides) of the tongue	/l/
Central Consonant	Articulated so that air passes across the center of the mouth	GAE consonants except /l/

Source: Katz (n.d.).

The students in Ms. Jenkins's class know how to use the sound wall. They play several games with the words on the wall and add new words that they encounter in their reading. When they are reading or writing and get stuck on a word, they know that they can use the sound wall to help them. For example, Hugo was writing and wanted to use the word *could*. He forgot how to spell it but knew that it started with the /k/ sound. He used the sound wall to remind himself and practiced it several times. Jayla was reading and encountered the word *light*. The word was not on either wall, but the word *flight* and *right* were. Using this, she said to her group, I think that this word is *light*, and then she finished the sentence.

Using Encoding to Support Decoding

While decoding is the act of interpreting the letters of a word with its associated sounds, encoding involves the reverse, as students formulate a word and commit in writing as they think about each letter and sound. Dictation begins in kindergarten with the teacher saying a particular sound and children writing the related letter. Over time, dictation activities involve the teacher saying targeted words that the students write. Dictation occurs as a part of the daily instruction. This supports children both hearing and practicing letter-sound relationships as they write and spell during this focused, guided practice activity (Stahl & Miller, 1989). Consistent with other dimensions of phonics instruction, dictation should be systematic and explicit. The dictated routine can also include the writing of sentences as students develop their skills.

Dictation begins in kindergarten with the teacher saying a particular sound and children writing the related letter.

Second-grade teacher Yvette Hebert has been working with her students on the digraphs /ch/, /sh/, and /th/ for the past few weeks, and her students are learning to consolidate these phonics skills. Her students are equipped with whiteboards and dry erase markers so that they can make corrections more easily.

"We're going to write some sentences that have words using the digraphs we have been learning," Ms. Hebert begins. She conducts a brief review of the targeted digraphs using letter cards, as students repeat the sounds of each with her.

"That's great. You're ready to write! Listen to my word and repeat it with me. *Chip*. He ate a *chip* before dinner. *Chip*."

As the children write, Ms. Hebert circulates to see how each is doing. She notices that Nayeli has written *cip*. "Let's stretch out the sounds: *ch-i-p*," Ms. Hebert says. Nayeli and her teacher each move their hand down one of their arms as they slowly repeat the word in unison. This movement allows Nayeli to both visually and verbally stretch the word. If Nayeli had not mastered the word after this attempt, Ms. Hebert would then have used one finger to tap the three sounds heard in *chip* on her arm. By adding this multisensory approach, children can hear each sound as it is associated with the tap. Nayeli heard her error and then made the correction on her whiteboard. Continuing, Ms. Hebert then asks the children to hold their whiteboards up. She repeats this routine several times, featuring the words *thin, shop, show, chin*, and *three*. The teacher layers instruction throughout, as this is not a spelling test but rather practice for students to encode words. As she reviews, she encourages her students to make the changes they need to any errors, in order to build the habit of self-correction.

"Now's our challenge sentence! Go ahead and clear your boards so we can put some of these words together. Ready? *The shop has three chips*." She reminds her students as she repeats it, "Make sure you hear all the sounds, because one of those words has an ending that is different."

Again, Ms. Hebert circulates among the children offering individual help as needed. If she had noticed that many children were making similar errors she would have stopped, regrouped, and retaught the targeted information. A few of the students make other mechanical errors, such as failing to capitalize the first letter or forgetting to end the sentence with a period. To address this, she gently prompts them to always check their work before sharing.

When asked about this instruction, she said, "Dictation is really about consolidating a whole constellation of skills, including phonics knowledge, word recognition, handwriting, and composition," She then added, "Daily dictation practice gives students the opportunity to bring lots of skills together." As shown in this lesson example, dictation was used to support guided practice of newly learned information. Ms. Hebert had introduced her students to a new digraph. She was using dictation to initiate guided practice opportunities for the children to practice writing words containing digraphs. As they did so, she shared additional supports as needed.

WHAT'S YOUR ADVICE?

A colleague asks you about the use of dictation in your classroom, saying that it seems like you're just giving a spelling test. What do you see as the differences between a weekly spelling test and daily dictation practice?

Which words are used to assess spelling and which words are used for dictation as part of phonics instruction?

NOTES

Routines That Allow Students to Practice and Use Their Knowledge of Learned Phonics Patterns

To ensure that students gain automaticity with letter-sound relationships that can support their reading and writing, they need focused practice through intentionally designed instructional routines such as the following.

WORD SORTING

Sorting words involves reading and categorizing a set of words into identified categories. Being able to correctly sort indicates that the reader can read the words and also understand the relationships among the words (Barnes, 1989; Zutell, 1998):

- **Closed sorts** involve the sorting of 5 to 20 terms into categories that have been preset by the teacher. These may be more appropriate for young children who are just learning orthographic patterns.
- **Open sorts** are similar, but the categories are identified by the students as they engage with the words.

In the early grades the focus could be on predictable word patterns, such as words that end with *at* versus *ar.* This purposeful focus on an identified pattern in a word allows students to become orthographic experts.

WORD SORTING ROUTINE

1. Identify the words that contain the orthographic pattern you will ask the students to sort for.
2. Create word card sets that can be used for the sort. Have enough sets to accommodate all the individuals or pairs who will be doing the sort. You may want to conduct the sorts within a guided reading group if your students have a wide variance of either phonics or word knowledge.
3. Introduce students to the word sorting routine. You may want to use closed sorts until the children master the concept. Explain that the words should be placed in either the pile that **Does** contain the targeted feature or that **Does Not** contain it. For example, the targeted feature might be all words that end with the letter *t,* that begin with the letter *b,* or that contain the /ick/ pattern and sound.
4. Model a closed sort for the children. While doing so say, "This word (name the word) goes in the **Does** pile because . . . ," or "this word (name the word) goes in the **Does Not** pile because. . . ."

(Continued)

(Continued)

5. Provide ample time for the students to complete the sort. As they do so, watch them closely, and ask them why they are choosing and not choosing to put words into either pile. This is a perfect time to assess what your students have learned about the orthographic features you have taught.
6. When students finish the sort, have them write the words in the **Does** pile on whiteboards, or better yet, provide each child with a notebook for recording words they know. They can write the words in their word notebooks. You can also make word notebooks with students.
7. Once students have mastered the routine of closed sorts, introduce them to open sorts. Make packets of cards that include all their newly learned patterns, or of words that have become a part of their sight vocabulary, and invite students to sort and then to share the categories they used for their sorts. As you listen to their rationales, you will be able to assess how well they have learned the word and phonics patterns you've taught. This information will help you to identify individuals or groups who need scaffolds to help them acquire previously shared information and those children who are ready to move forward.

WORD BUILDING

Ensure that your students develop the cognitive flexibility they need to use known patterns and words to get to unknown ones. This routine includes a dictation process to ensure they can also encode and use their familiar patterns to learn additional words having the same patterns. For example, being able to read the word *it* becomes the base for reading, writing, and spelling many words (*kit, fit, hit, pit, sit*). Be careful not to teach this bank of words too quickly. Watch the children to be sure they are comparing and learning the pattern of each word being added.

This same routine can be used for more complex phonics skills, such as using consonant blends (such as /tr/, /fl/, /sm/), consonant digraphs (/wh/, /sh/, /ph/, for example) and vowel digraphs (/ay/, /ai/, and /ey/ that all make the same sound). Encourage second-grade students to use word parts they know to get to decodable multisyllabic words they don't know, such as *airline*, *outline*, *everything*, and *something*. Cunningham and Stanovich (1998) encourage that word building should include supporting students to build multisyllable words, because when they appear in text, they often carry the major content of the information or message. Additionally, they note that students who are taught to look for patterns in words not only become better decoders but also better writers.

WORD BUILDING ROUTINE

1. Prepare enough sets of word cards for the number of children in the group. If you are teaching words that contain the rime /it/, you should have word slips containing this word. Again, you will introduce only one word at a time until you are sure the children understand the orthographic pattern.
2. Model reading the word and one of the additional words (*it, fit*).
3. Cover the first letter *f* and read the remaining word *it*.

4. Uncover the initial letter, and show the word again as a whole word. Read it and point to the /it/ sound in *fit*, and explain that the sound of the word *it* is the same sound of the /it/ they hear and see in the word *fit.* Read the word together. Invite them to practice separating and blending the word parts.
5. If you assess that they need more practice, you may again repeat this modeling, or you can cut the word into two chunks, /f/ and /it/. Model putting the two chunks back together, starting with the chunk they know, /it/.
6. As their knowledge grows, cut the three letters apart and have the children reassemble them.
7. Then, have them write the word on whiteboards and finally in their word books.
8. After you have repeated this pattern with additional words, scramble all the initial letters, and have the children reassemble the words and write each one on their whiteboards.
9. Finally, say each word and ask the children to write the word from memory. This allows you to assess if they have mastered the word. If you notice that a child is unable to successfully spell one of the words, be sure to again have them practice looking at it, comparing it to the phonogram in focus, and correcting it.

TEXT-TO-SELF CONNECTION

What are the key reasons for teaching students phonics and decoding using a systematic an explicit approach?

____

____

Using the traffic light scale, with red being not confident, yellow being somewhat confident, and green indicating very confident, how confident are you in your ability to

- Teach decoding and phonics systematically?
- Explain the various aspects of phonics, such as blends, digraphs, and dipthongs?
- Select skills-aligned decodable texts?
- Engage students in dictation activities?

Takeaways

- Phonics instruction must be planned and systematic. You should consider the development of phonics skills as you select instructional materials.
- Spiral phonics instruction to include previously taught patterns. This provides additional maintenance of skills as students acquire new knowledge. Remember, a common error in phonics instruction is an emphasis on acquisition at the expense of mastery. Students typically need four to six weeks of systematic instruction to move to mastery, so give them lots of opportunities to practice.
- Develop instructional resources, such as sound walls, that support students' learning of phonics and decoding.
- Use encoding to support decoding.
- Engage students in tasks such as word sorting and word building that require that they use their phonics knowledge.

PS: The answers to the anticipation guide are T, T, T, T.

online resources

Visit the companion website at
resources.corwin.com/teachingreading
for this module's downloadable resources.

MODULE

5

Sight Word Recognition

Photo by iStock.com/GlobalMoments

In this module, we will

- **Identify the difference between high-frequency words and sight words.**
- **Explore orthographic mapping as a process for developing students' sight word recognition.**
- **Explain how sight word vocabularies expand with instruction and practice.**

If you could read along with the student in this picture, you would notice that she reads some words effortlessly, while others cause a bit of a pause. In all likelihood, some of the words the reader recognizes by sight. And it is likely that this child relies on decoding skills for other words in the text. Over time, with instruction and practice, more words are recognized instantly. That's why sight word recognition is part of the increasingly automatic aspect of reading. When a reader can read words automatically and without effort, they no longer need to focus attention on sounding them out. Instead, their attention while reading can increasingly shift to comprehending what the text says (Kilpatrick, 2015; LaBerge & Samuels, 1974).

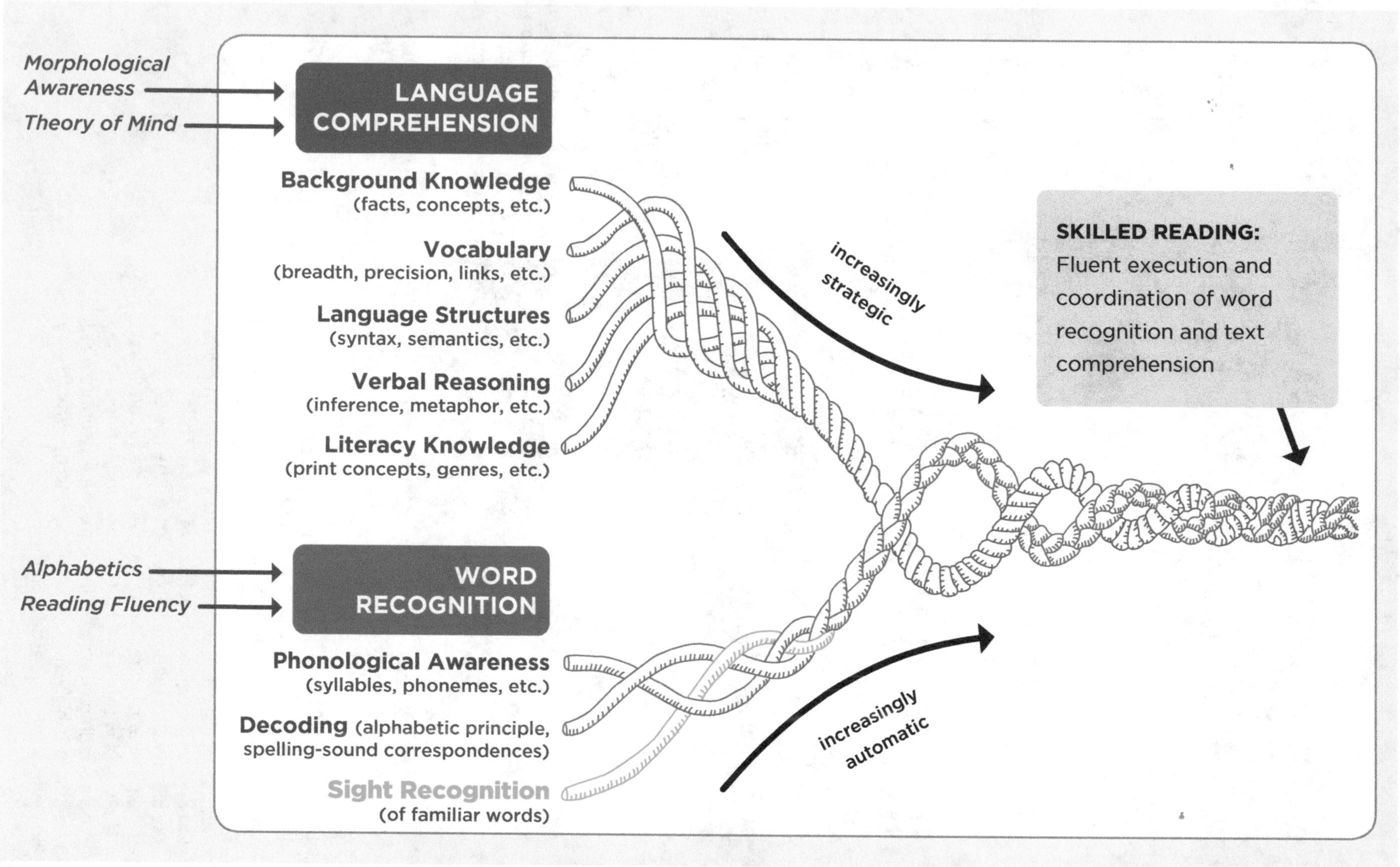

Source: Adapted from Scarborough, H. S. (2001). Connecting early language and literacy to later reading (dis)abilities: Evidence, theory, and practice. In S. Neuman & D. Dickinson (Eds.), *Handbook for research in early literacy* (pp. 97–110). Guilford Press.

It's important to clarify: Words that appear often or with high frequency in texts may be members of one's sight vocabulary. In addition, there are other words in one's sight vocabulary that aren't high-frequency words. They have become words that the reader recognizes instantly and effortlessly when seen. They too, become members over time of the reader's sight vocabulary. Ehri (2014) referred to these as "*sight words*, because sight of the word immediately activates its pronunciation and meaning in memory" (p. 6). In other words, readers can recognize and read the word without having to sound it out or break the word into parts. Breaking the word into parts and sounding it out require decoding, which was the focus of the previous module.

Read each statement and mark **T** if the statement is true and **F** if the statement is false. As you read through the module, you might change your responses. Be prepared to explain your responses and use the text for evidence.

Before Reading	Statements	After Reading
T **F**	1. The terms *high-frequency words* and *sight words* mean about the same thing.	**T** **F**
Why did you indicate true or false?	Has your thinking changed after reading?	
T **F**	2. Words that are instantly and effortlessly recognized when reading become sight words.	**T** **F**
Why did you indicate true or false?	Has your thinking changed after reading?	
T **F**	3. Reading ensures that students develop sufficient sight word vocabularies.	**T** **F**
Why did you indicate true or false?	Has your thinking changed after reading?	
T **F**	4. In many words that are irregular, there are patterns within the word that can be taught and decoded.	**T** **F**
Why did you indicate true or false?	Has your thinking changed after reading?	

What Is Sight Word Recognition?

Students must learn to recognize words by sight if they are to become skilled readers. Simply said, we cannot spend all our energy decoding each word. It would slow us down considerably and interfere with deeper comprehension of texts. As Ehri (2005) noted, eventually all words that readers immediately recognize are added to the category of sight words. Sight words become members of the reader's sight vocabulary and can be retrieved effortlessly and instantly at a speed of around 300 words a minute (Farrall, 2018). Such automaticity supports, rather than hinders, comprehension.

The process of increasing sight word vocabularies relies on orthographic mapping. This is the phenomenon that allows readers to recognize the visual outline of a word, recognize the letters that make the word, and then use the word without having to sound it out. Phonemic awareness, letter-sound knowledge, and phonological long-term memory are used together to store the words we have learned. Essentially, orthographic (written) sequences of letters are attached to pronunciations of words that are stored in our long-term memory. As Kilpatrick explained, "Orthographic mapping proposes that we use the pronunciations of words that are already stored in long-term memory as the anchoring points for the orthographic sequences (letters) used to represent those pronunciations" (2015, p. 97). Torgesen (2004) noted at the time that orthographic mapping is "the most current theory of how children form sight word representations" (p. 36) and it remains so today (e.g., Kilpatrick, 2016).

Often a child's first sight words are also high-frequency words, or words that appear frequently in texts, regardless of the content or grade level. These are words like *the, of, and, a, to, in, is, you, that, it, he, for, was* and yes, even *like.* Reading researchers have analyzed texts and identified commonly occurring words (e.g., Dolch, 1936; Fry, 2004). For example, Dolch created his list by examining common words in children's books. The list contains 220 words that are tools for language, as they are used in writing across subject areas. However, the Dolch list of words contains no nouns. There is a separate list of common nouns that occur frequently, but these have received less attention compared with the words that Dolch considered tools. Edward Fry first created his list of the 1,000 most common words in 1957 and then updated it in 1980. Of course, there are commonalities between these lists. The high-frequency words shown in Figure 5.1 are the 100 most frequently appearing words in texts. The first 25 high-frequency words account for about 33% of all the words in print (Fry, 2004). Teaching children to read and recognize these words prepares them to read 90% of the single-syllable words in their texts (Solity & Vousden, 2009).

Figure 5.1 100 Most Frequently Appearing Words in Texts

Top 100 High-Frequency Words									
1	the	21	be	41	which	61	into	81	made
2	of	22	this	42	their	62	has	82	over
3	and	23	from	43	said	63	more	83	did
4	a	24	I	44	if	64	her	84	down
5	to	25	have	45	do	65	two	85	only
6	in	26	or	46	will	66	like	86	way
7	is	27	by	47	each	67	him	87	find
8	you	28	one	48	about	68	see	88	use
9	that	29	had	49	how	69	time	89	may
10	it	30	not	50	up	70	could	90	water
11	he	31	but	51	out	71	no	91	long
12	for	32	what	52	them	72	make	92	little
13	was	33	all	53	then	73	than	93	very
14	on	34	were	54	she	74	first	94	after
15	are	35	when	55	many	75	been	95	words
16	as	36	we	56	some	76	its	96	called
17	with	37	there	57	so	77	who	97	just
18	his	38	can	58	these	78	now	98	where
19	they	39	an	59	would	79	people	99	most
20	at	40	your	60	other	80	my	100	know

Source: Adapted from Adams (1990), Carroll et al. (1971), and Fry (2004).

NOTICE AND WONDER

What do you notice about these words? What are some of the common characteristics that they share?

Did you notice a number of pronouns? Which ones? ______________________________

____

Did you notice articles and connectors? Which ones? ____________________________

____

Did you notice function words? Which ones? __________________________________

____

Some of the high-frequency words need to be recognized by sight, as they are difficult to decode. The most common word in printed text is *the*. Most students will get it wrong when they first encounter this word and try to read it. But the *th-* can be taught, as in *that*, *this*, *there*, *their*, *them*, *then*, *these*, and *than*, and then parts need to be remembered when they are not regular (the -e ending of *the*). One approach for doing this is called *heart words*, which we will discuss later in this module.

Once students know the letter names, a small number of high-frequency words can be taught. These might include *the*, *a*, *I*, *to*, *and*, *was*, *for*, *you*, *is*, *are*, *said*, or *of*. Knowing 10 to 15 words by sight that are not decodable when the short vowel patterns VC and CVC are taught helps students read short texts and write sentences with the decodable words that they have learned. These words are suggestions that teachers can modify based on their knowledge of their students and the instructional materials that will be used. We can assess students' mastery of these words by having them

- find the word in a list of other words,
- find the word in a text,
- read the word from a card, or
- spell the word.

Although learned high-frequency words can become members of a reader's sight word list, don't confuse the words that appear frequently in texts with sight words. Sight words are those that can be read without the reader having to pause to sound them out. If sight words were limited to high-frequency words, then there would only be a couple hundred words recognized by sight. A reader's sight vocabulary likely includes high-frequency words but is not limited to these. For example, many readers can automatically read words such as *frequent*, *molecule*, *dollar*, and *pageant* as well as *there*, *with*, *his*, *by*, and *most*. It is highly probable that most of the words you will read in this text are a part of your sight word vocabulary, even though many—like *comprehension* and *phonics*, do not occur with high frequency across grade-level and content texts. Your physician likely has *acetabulum* as a sight word, and an engineer likely has *permittivity* as a sight word, even though you need to read and decode those words more carefully. The doctor and engineer have likely encountered those words many times and have developed automatic letter-sound associations and know the orthographic pattern of the words.

Now let's consider how to develop students' sight word vocabularies. Remember, when these words can be read automatically, they become members of the reader's sight word list, because there is no pausing to match letters and sounds. The reader instead is using all their grapheme-phoneme knowledge to automatically read the word (Ehri, 2005).

Instruction in Sight Word Recognition

INTRODUCING SIGHT WORDS

Much like phonics acquisition, sight word acquisition requires systematic instruction. Students must be introduced to specific sight words and then provided opportunities to practice them. It is unlikely that students will develop sophisticated sight word vocabularies from reading alone, although reading allows students to practice recognizing the sight words they have been taught. Be careful not to teach words that are visually similar or easily confused (such as *no* and *on* or *will* and *well*) at the same time. There is a free word list generator called Phinder (https://devinkearns.com/phinder) that allows you to select patterns, and it will generate words that you can then teach. Many of the high-frequency words we profiled earlier in this module are phonetically decodable and can be taught as part of the phonics lessons and then practiced so that students can read them "in a flash" as Farrell et al. (2019) suggest. These "flash words" should be grouped by spelling pattern so that students are more likely to generalize their knowledge to new words. Other words are irregularly spelled, and part of the word must be learned by heart ("heart words"). A simple process for introducing sight words includes the following steps:

It is unlikely that students will develop sophisticated sight word vocabularies from reading alone.

See and Say

1. The teacher holds up a flashcard with the word written on it and says the word while underlining it with a finger or pointer.
2. The students repeat the word several times as the teacher underlines.

Spell Reading

1. Looking at the flashcard, the teacher or the students say the word, spell the letters, and then say the word again.
2. The teacher starts, and then the students complete the same task a few times while also looking at the flashcard.

Arm Tapping

1. Looking at the flashcard, the teacher or the students say the word, spelling out each letter while tapping two fingers on one arm, gradually progressing down the arm from shoulder to wrist.
2. The teacher or students then repeat the word again, sweeping the two fingers along the left arm.
3. Students then repeat this process while also looking at the flashcard.

Writing

1. Looking at the flashcard, the student writes the word on paper or their whiteboard.
2. The student repeats this process without looking at the flashcard.

These procedures can be adapted for individuals, small groups of students, or the whole class. Students need to be introduced to sight words with a consistent routine. Here's a sample from Georgina Alvarez's first-grade class:

Our first word is *where*. Take a look. Where [underlining with finger]. Where. Where. Your turn: Where. Where. Where.

Ready for spell reading? [Students: yes!] Where. W-h-e-r-e. Where. Where. W-h-e-r-e. Where. Your turn. [Students: Where. W-h-e-r-e. Where. Where. W-h-e-r-e. Where.]

Students need to be introduced to sight words with a consistent routine.

I'm hearing such good language from you [takes three sticks from the jar to call on students]. Karely, ready: [Where. W-h-e-r-e. Where.] Crystal, ready: [Where. W-h-e-r-e. Where.] Robert, ready: [Where. W-h-e-r-e. Where.]

Super! Time for arm tapping. My turn. Where. W-h-e-r-e. Where. Where. W-h-e-r-e. Where. Your turn. [Students: Where. W-h-e-r-e. Where. Where. W-h-e-r-e. Where.] [takes three sticks from the jar.] Ella, ready? [Where. W-h-e-r-e. Where.] Khalid, ready: [Where. W-h-e-r-e. Where.] Lucille, ready: [Where. W-h-e-r-e. Where.]

Amazing. Great practice everyone! We are ready for writing. Do you have your boards ready? [Where. Where. Where] Look at the card and let's see it! I see great letters forming! [takes three sticks from the jar]. Destiny, ready? [says *where* while the board is held up.] Sofia, ready? [says *where*.] Pablo, ready? [says *where*.]

And now on our own. I'll walk around and watch you. Let's write it a few times each so that I can see lots of you writing. Well done, Aneli. Luis, I see those letters forming. Danielle, I see you taking your time to show each letter.

Following the focus on the word *where*, Ms. Alvarez introduces several additional words. If students struggle, Ms. Alvarez immediately moves into corrections, saying, "That word is _____. What word is it?" And they practice a few more times.

In addition to the instruction of new words and practicing previously learned words, Ms. Alvarez has her students engage in a number of games at their learning stations, such as sight word bingo, sight word fly swat, sight word go first, sight word memory, and sight word dominoes, to name a few.

TAKE ACTION

In Appendices C–G, you'll find several Dolch sight word lists. These are grade-level estimates, and the lists include a sample of words that students at each grade should know. The ability to read these words on sight indicates that the student is developing as a reader rather than completing a specific list to drill. Administer one of the lists to your students, and identify words that students do not know.

1. What patterns do you notice? ______________________________

   ____

2. Which words need to be taught to the whole class? Remember, you can identify additional words with similar spelling patterns. ______________________________

   ____

3. Which words need to be taught to specific students during small-group instruction? ______________________________

   ____

HEART WORDS

As children begin to read, some of the words they encounter will have irregular spelling patterns, such as *today*, *other*, or *won*. Some have argued that these words are not decodable and need to be memorized, but Kilpatrick (2015) tells us that "the vast majority of irregular words have only a single irregular letter-sound relationship" (p. 105). Take the word *do* as an example. The /d/ can be decoded but the *o* is irregularly spelled for the sound that it makes in this word.

In the past, teachers identified these words and focused on rote memorization in an attempt to force these words into students' sight word vocabulary. They focused on the whole word, practicing the word many times until it stuck. More recently, the focus has been on word study. As Kilpatrick (2016) notes, "To be good orthographic mappers, children need to develop three skills: (1) automatic letter-sound associations, (2) highly proficient phoneme awareness, and (3) word study" (p. 41). Heart words invite students to study words and identify parts that need to be remembered because they are irregular versus parts of the word that are regularly spelled (Farrell et al., 2019). The process involves students studying words and literally writing hearts above the parts that are irregular. The students practice the sound that is made, while still using their knowledge of grapheme-phoneme correspondences in other parts of the word.

Figure 5.2 contains a list of words with unusual spelling patterns. Note that there are several high-frequency words that rely on these patterns. The place in the word that is irregular requires additional word study so that students learn these words. Figure 5.3 contains a list of high-frequency words that do not fit into spelling patterns.

WHAT'S YOUR ADVICE?

A colleague comes to you, suggesting that the team focus on teaching students 100 new high-frequency words during the year, and saying that students need to memorize these words because they are not decodable. Given what you know about the value of sight words and the fact that words that are traditionally considered not decodable typically have parts that rely on consistent patterns, what do you recommend?

____

____

____

Tommy Sukeo focuses on heart words with his students. They have index cards with holes in the corner so that new words can be added to a metal ring. Students write the target word and put a heart over the irregular spellings. Mr. Sukeo's students practice their heart words with peers and families, focusing on the parts that are decoded and the parts that they have to remember. A sample heart word card can be found in Figure 5.4. A set of video illustrations of example heart word cards can be found at www.reallygreatreading.com/heart-word-magic (Really Great Reading, n.d.).

Figure 5.2 Words With Unusual Spelling Patterns

59 Words Grouped by Similar Spelling Patterns

45 Words From the Dolch List and 14 Not on the Dolch List

(Numbers in parentheses are the Dolch frequency ranking.)

(A diamond [♦] indicates a word that is not on the Dolch list but fits the spelling pattern.)

Unusual Spelling Pattern	High-Frequency Words
1. **s** at the end of the word spells /z/	his (13), is (27), as (32), has (166)
2. **v** is followed by **e,** because no English word ends in **v**	have (34), give (144), live (206)
3. **o-e** spells short u /ŭ/	some (30), come (64), done (180)
4. **o** spells /Œ/ (as in *boot*)	to (2), do (41), into (77)
5. rhyming words spelled with the same last four letters	there (29), where (95)
6. **s** spells /z/ in a VCE word	those (179), these (212)
7. **all** spells /ŏl/ or /awl/ (depending on dialect)	all (25), call (167), fall (193), small (195), tall♦, ball♦
8. **oul** spells /œ/ (as in *cook*)	could (43), would (57), should♦
9. **e** added at end (*wer* and *ar* would be correct phonetic spellings)	were (50), are (63)
10. VCC and CVCC words with **o** spelling long o /ō/	old (102), cold (136), hold (173), both (190)
11. CVCC words with **i** spelling long i /ī/	find (167), kind (189), mind♦
12. words similar in meaning and spelling	one (54), once (160)
13. **a** after **w** sometimes spells short o /ŏ/	want (86), wash (201), watch♦
14. **ue** spells /Œ/ (as in boot)	blue (79), glue♦, clue♦, true♦
15. **u** spells /œ/ (as in *cook*)	put (91), full (178), pull (187), push♦
16. rhyming words—the letters **al** spell /ŏ/ or /aw/ (depending on dialect)	walk (121), talk♦
17. rhyming words—the letter **a** spells short i /ĭ/ or short e /ĕ/ (depending on dialect)	any (83), many (218)
18. **oo** at the end of a word spells /Œ/ (as in *boot*)	too (92), boo♦, moo♦
19. **or** spells /er/	work (145), word♦, world♦
20. **uy** spells long i /ī/	buy (174), guy♦

Source: Farrell et al. (2019).

Figure 5.3 Words That Do Not Fit Spelling Patterns

Heart Words

37 Words That Do Not Fit Into Spelling Patterns

(Numbers in parentheses are the Dolch frequency ranking.)

the (1)	very (71)	here (105)	does (154)	use (181)
a (5)	yours (74)	two (122)	goes (156)	carry (194)
of (9)	from (81)	again (126)	write (157)	because (204)
you (7)	don't (87)	who (128)	always (158)	together (214)
was (11)	know (89)	been (129)	only (168)	please (215)
said (12)	pretty (97)	eight (135)	our (171)	shall (219)
they (18)	four (100)	today (137)	warm (176)	laugh (220)
what (46)	their (104)			

Source: Farrell et al. (2019).

FIND THE MISTAKES

A student created the following heart word cards. Take a look at these cards, and see if you agree that the hearts are in the correct places. If the letter or letters follow a conventional spelling pattern, a block would be drawn under the letter(s), whereas a heart would be drawn for letter(s) that are unusual.

Figure 5.4 Sample Heart Word Card

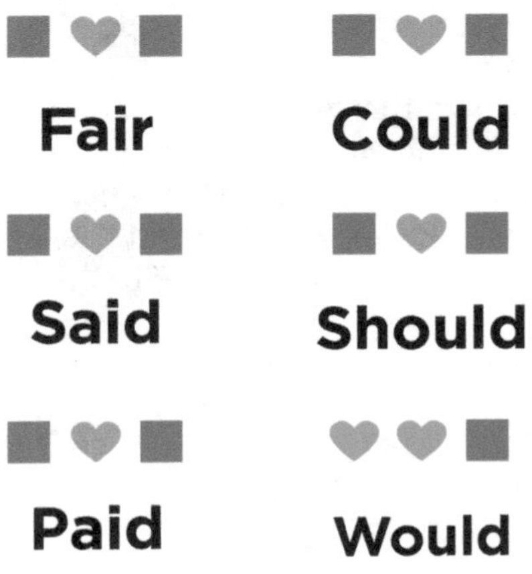

PRACTICING SIGHT WORDS

To build automaticity, students will need to practice the words. And they need to practice often. Despite how dated this may seem, flashcards are a useful way to encourage practice (Wissman et al., 2012). Putting individual words on flashcards and engaging students in practice builds their automaticity with these words. Importantly, students also need to encounter these words in print, which is inevitable with high-frequency words but may require some intentional planning with other sight words. There are number of digital formats for flashcards, such as Quizlet and Brainscape.

A specific way to ensure students practice high-frequency words until they become sight words that are recognized instantly is known as a *reading racetrack* (Rinalidi et al., 1997; Sullivan et al., 2013). The Iowa Reading Research Center modified the procedure so that the practice could be conducted with pairs of students or in small groups. They outline the following steps:

1. Identify 28 high-frequency words a student is unable to read with automaticity but that previously have been introduced.
2. Write each word on a notecard.
3. Prepare five copies of the reading racetrack form (see Figure 5.5).
4. Assign seven high-frequency words to each of four racetracks. The fifth racetrack is a review racetrack.
5. On one racetrack, write the first set of seven words in the seven cells. The selected seven words will appear four times in random order to fill the 28 cells of the racetrack. Repeat this with three other racetracks, using seven different words from the list of 28 total words on each racetrack, until all words have been used.
6. On the fifth or review racetrack, write all 28 words, one in each of the 28 cells of the racetrack in random order. Each word should appear one time. (Iowa Reading Research Center, 2018)

Jacqueline Santos devotes between 10 and 15 minutes per day to students' practicing high-frequency words until they become words that are instantly recognized by sight. She engages the whole class, but students work as partners at their tables. By third grade, her students know a lot of words by sight, and Ms. Santos knows that they still have more to learn. She begins the day's lesson reviewing each of the words with students. She shows students the flashcards one at a time and says, "This word is ____. Can you read this word?" The students respond in unison. Ms. Santos then calls on three students at random, in a rapid fashion, to read the word. If a student is incorrect, she says, "This word is ____. Try reading it again. What is this word?"

Figure 5.5 Reading Racetrack

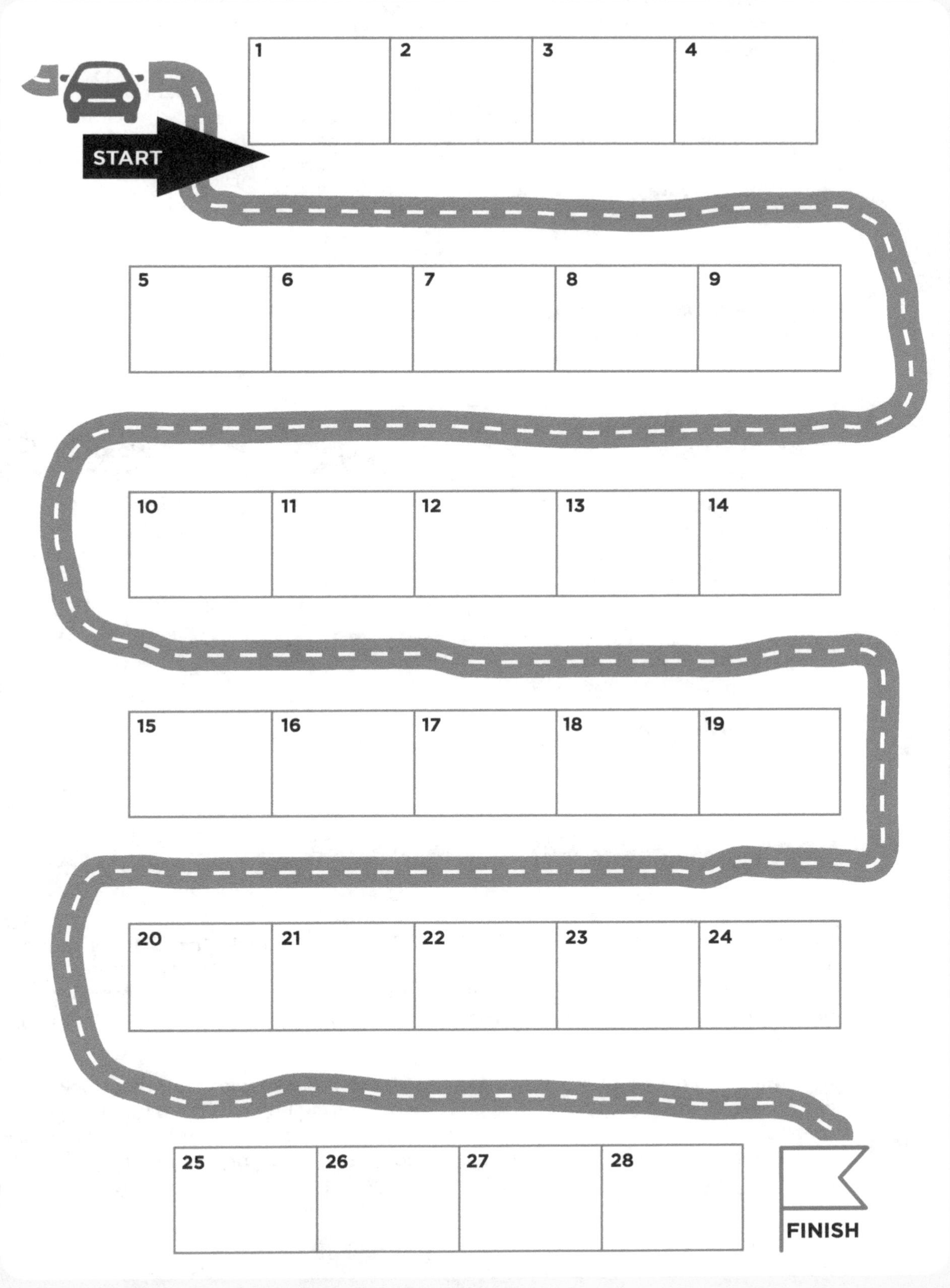

Source: Iowa Reading Research Center (2018). Reading Racetrack Sight Word Activity. https://iowareadingresearch.org/sites/iowareadingresearch.org/files/reading_racetrack_sight

She repeats the process until each of the words has been reviewed. Then she invites students to turn their attention to the racetracks. Students don't write on these, as she uses them again and again, rotating different words each day. Each set of partners has five racetracks, with the review racetrack copied on colored paper, and two score sheets.

"Keep the racetracks upside down," Ms. Santos says. "Partner A, select one of the racetracks. Ready?" Ms. Santos starts her timer, and Partner A reads the words. Partner B is there to encourage Partner A to keep reading if they get stuck on a word and to count the number of words Partner A reads correctly. When the one minute is up, the partners update the score sheet (see Figure 5.6).

Figure 5.6 Reading Racetrack Score Sheet

Name: Date:

			**Words to Practice**
My first turn			
My second turn			
Review			

The partners then change roles, selecting a different racetrack. This process continues through the review racetrack, and both students have an opportunity to use that one. Ms. Santos collects the score sheets, which are copied on ¼ size paper (four per page) and uses them for small-group instruction during which time she meets with students who have similar error patterns.

The students in Ms. Santos's class often request to practice with their racetracks during center time or when they have finished their other assignments. Ms. Santos makes the racetracks available for families who practice the game at home with their children. Each student in Ms. Santos's class has a personal journal in which on five different days they keep track of words that they recognize by sight. It's a source of pride with her students, and they like to share their lists with visitors to the class.

TEXT-TO-SELF CONNECTION

What are the key reasons for practicing sight words in my classroom?

____

____

____

Using the traffic light scale, with red being not confident, yellow being somewhat confident, and green indicating very confident, how confident am I in my ability to

- Identify the difference between high-frequency words and sight words?

- Select sight words and devote instructional time to students' learning?

- Teach students using the heart word approach?

Takeaways

- Phonemic awareness, letter-sound knowledge, and phonological long-term memory are used together to store words.
- High-frequency words can become sight words through instruction and practice.
- Sight word vocabularies expand as students use the visual outline of a word, recognize the letters that make the word, and then use the word without having to sound it out. This process is known as orthographic mapping.
- Words that are often considered not decodable typically have parts that follow conventional spelling patterns.

PS: Answers to the anticipation guide are F, T, F, T.

online resources

Visit the companion website at
resources.corwin.com/teachingreading
for this module's downloadable resources.

MODULE

6

Reading Fluency

In this module, we will

- Define reading fluency and describe the aspects that compose the term.
- Come to understand that developing reading fluency requires instruction and practice.
- Recognize that fluency is the bridge between phonics and comprehension as well as a critical aspect of reading.
- Identify when reading fluency rates suggest the need for targeted instruction and intervention.

Photo by Andrew Ebrahim on Unsplash

The students in the photo look really engaged with the text, don't they? They are reading and rereading together. Fluency—to be fluent—has many connotations in education. One focuses on the skills in learning to speak a language, as in describing a fluent speaker. Another focuses on learning additional languages, as in "she is newly fluent in Spanish." However, the meaning we will focus on in this module is the ability to read text accurately, smoothly, and with expression. Fluent readers recognize words automatically, without struggling over decoding issues.

Rasinski (2003) suggested that fluency is the bridge between decoding and comprehension. As students increasingly automate their decoding, they in turn become increasingly fluent readers.

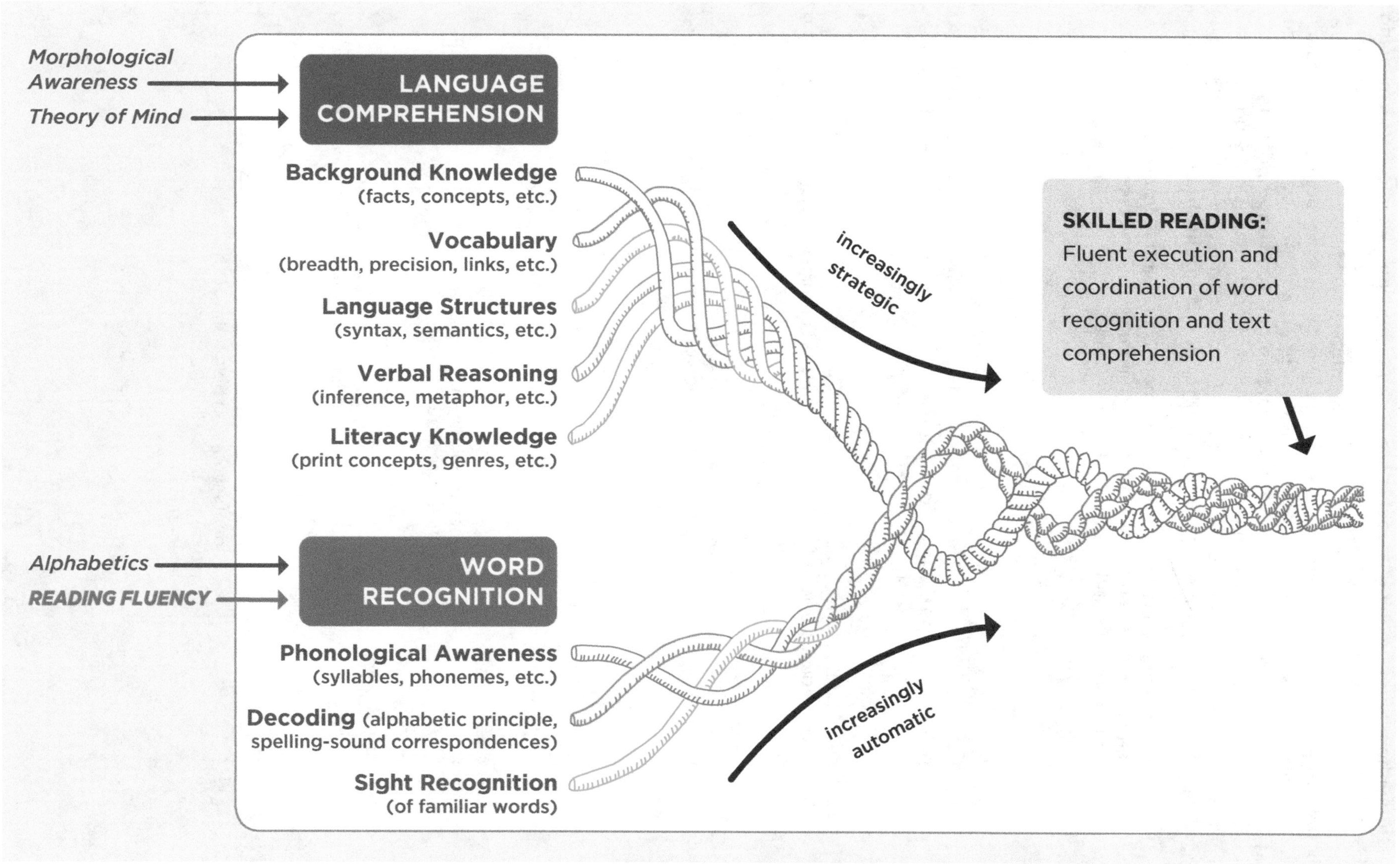

Source: Adapted from Scarborough, H. S. (2001). Connecting early language and literacy to later reading (dis)abilities: Evidence, theory, and practice. In S. Neuman & D. Dickinson (Eds.), *Handbook for research in early literacy* (pp. 97–110). Guilford Press.

But without word meaning, students are at risk of become "word callers," meaning that they can say the words but have limited knowledge of what they mean (Stanovich, 1986). One systematic investigation showed that 10% of fifth-grade students demonstrated normal reading fluency but below average comprehension skills (Meisinger et al., 2009). In other words, these students could say the words correctly at an appropriate rate but did not perform well on measures of comprehension. Students need to ascribe meaning to the words they are seeing while simultaneously activating vocabulary and background knowledge as they engage in the process of reading.

Fluency is the bridge between decoding and comprehension.

Read each statement and mark **T** if the statement is true and **F** if the statement is false. As you read through the module, you might change your responses. Be prepared to explain your responses and use the text for evidence.

<table>
<tr><th>Before Reading</th><th colspan="2">Statements</th><th>After Reading</th></tr>
<tr><td>T F</td><td colspan="2">1. Rate or speed is the most important factor in reading fluency.</td><td>T F</td></tr>
<tr><td colspan="2">Why did you indicate true or false?</td><td colspan="2">Has your thinking changed after reading?</td></tr>
<tr><td>T F</td><td colspan="2">2. Prosody is a dimension of fluency.</td><td>T F</td></tr>
<tr><td colspan="2">Why did you indicate true or false?</td><td colspan="2">Has your thinking changed after reading?</td></tr>
<tr><td>T F</td><td colspan="2">3. Fluency develops with repeated practice or repeated reading.</td><td>T F</td></tr>
<tr><td colspan="2">Why did you indicate true or false?</td><td colspan="2">Has your thinking changed after reading?</td></tr>
<tr><td>T F</td><td colspan="2">4. Students who read below the 50th percentile in reading fluency need intervention.</td><td>T F</td></tr>
<tr><td colspan="2"></td><td colspan="2"></td></tr>
</table>

What Is Reading Fluency?

Fluent readers should be able to read aloud and silently with speed, accuracy, and appropriate expression (National Institute of Child Health and Human Development, 2000). The National Reading Panel report cautions, "If text is read in a laborious and inefficient manner, it will be difficult for the child to remember what has been read and to relate the ideas expressed in the text to his or her background knowledge" (NICHHD, 2000, n.p.). It is far more likely that a comprehending reader is also a fluent one. We'll draw back on the previously discussed concept of automaticity in reading. Automatic word reading frees up a reader's cognitive resources, allowing the reader to dedicate more attention to understanding what is read.

Importantly, reading fast is not the true goal of fluency instruction. Readers must understand what they are reading. Students who read with expressiveness during their oral reading provide an important window into their comprehension. Comparing fluency with music, Worthy and Broaddus (2001/2002) note that fluency "consists not only of rate, accuracy, and automaticity, but also of phrasing, smoothness, and expressiveness. Fluency gives language its musical quality, its rhythm and flow, and makes reading sound effortless" (p. 334).

Reading fast is not the true goal of fluency instruction. Readers must understand what they are reading.

Let's define some of those terms that were just used.

- **Accuracy** refers to the ability to read the words correctly. Imagine reading this sentence—*The green house was haunted*—as *The greek horse was hunted*. Minor changes in three words drastically changed the meaning of the sentence.
- **Rate** is the speed at which the student reads. If the reader's rate is too slow (less than 50 words per minute at the beginning of second grade, for example), it will interfere with comprehension, because the reading becomes choppy and disconnected from other ideas in the sentences and paragraphs. If it is too fast, especially in oral reading, it may also interfere with comprehension, as the reader rushes too quickly past the details that make the passage meaningful.
- **Automaticity** is the ability to recognize words with a minimum of attention, allowing the reader to direct most of his or her attention to matters of comprehension (LaBerge & Samuels, 1974). Not surprisingly, automaticity is closely associated with decoding and spelling (encoding).

A major goal of reading is that students are able to do so independently for both enjoyment and information, and with understanding of what it is that they are reading. Again, they must read fast enough to make sense of the information and accurately enough to gain information. The majority of reading that students do is silent, especially after the first years of schooling. In addition to fluent *oral* reading, students must also be fluent in *silent* reading. In order to ascertain whether a student is reading fluently during silent reading, we rely on oral reading fluency (ORF) as one measure to monitor progress.

From a Surface Level of Reading Fluency to a Deep Level

The role of fluency in reading instruction continues to be shaped through research conducted since Scarborough first proposed the reading rope in the 1990s. Chief among those changes has been a shift away from a surface view of fluency that "leads to practices such as simply urging students to read faster" (Pikulski & Chard, 2005, p. 511). The purpose of surface-level fluency instruction sees oral reading performance as the end game. A deep view of fluency, on the other hand, understands fluency "far more broadly as part of a developmental process of building decoding skills that will form a bridge to reading comprehension." In this view, they continue, "efficient decoding is consistently related to comprehension" (p. 511). This deep view of fluency informs instructional practices that consider a child's understanding of the text as the endgame. In reconceiving the reading rope in light of contemporary practices, we propose that fluency is both a developmental process and a specific instructional target.

As Rasinski (2020) notes, slow, inefficient, and disfluent reading should be taken seriously. These readers will likely have reading difficulties for their entire school experience if nothing is done. Therefore, it is useful to attend to both silent and oral fluency rates throughout the academic year to monitor progress. Reading fluency is improved through repetition, including repeated readings of familiar text and instructional experiences that further develop automaticity and expressiveness (prosody).

NOTICE AND WONDER

Reading researcher Maryanne Wolf wrote, "Fluency is the developmental process that connects decoding with everything we know about words to make the meaning of the text come to life. Fluency is a wonderful bridge to comprehension and to a lifelong love of reading" (2009, p. 4).

Reading fluency is increasingly understood as a bridge between word recognition and language comprehension. Use the space below to create a visual or graphic representation of how you see this relationship. If you're not feeling particularly artistic, write a metaphor or simile about this relationship. How would you explain this relationship to a new educator who is coming to you for advice about reading fluency?

Oral Reading Fluency (ORF)

A widely accepted procedure for assessing a student's reading fluency is the curriculum-based measurement (CBM). A CBM is a simple assessment to measure the progress of a student using classroom tools. However, a CBM is not just a teacher-created assessment. In involves agreed-upon procedures to standardize its administration.

An easy-to-use CBM of oral reading accuracy and rate involves a one-minute timed reading of an unpracticed passage (Hasbrouck & Tindal, 2006). This is an individual assessment during which students are observed as they read from an unpracticed passage for exactly one minute. To determine the words correct per minute (WCPM), the teacher subtracts the total number of errors from the total number of words read in one minute. Errors include words that are mispronounced, substituted for another word, or left out. If a student transposes two words, it counts as two errors. If the student mispronounces the same word incorrectly later in the passage, the error is counted again. Words read correctly that are repeated more than once, self-corrected errors, extra words inserted by the student that are not in the text, and words mispronounced due to dialect or speech impairments are not counted as errors.

In some cases, it's useful to select several passages from the text and repeat the process two or three times to ensure that aspects of the text itself (such as information provided before the selected passage or concepts explained earlier) do not artificially lower the students' fluency scores. The students' reading rates (WCPM) are then compared with norms for the grade level and time of year. The fluency norms were last updated in 2017, as noted in Figure 6.1.

Figure 6.1 2017 Oral Fluency Reading Norms by Grade Level

Grade	Percentile	Fall WCPM*	Winter WCPM*	Spring WCPM*
1	90		97	116
	75		59	91
	50		29	60
	25		16	34
	10		9	18
2	90	111	131	148
	75	84	109	124
	50	50	84	100
	25	36	59	72
	10	23	35	43

(Continued)

(Continued)

Grade	Percentile	Fall WCPM*	Winter WCPM*	Spring WCPM*
3	90	134	161	166
	75	104	137	139
	50	83	97	112
	25	59	79	91
	10	40	62	63
4	90	153	168	184
	75	125	143	160
	50	94	120	133
	25	75	95	105
	10	60	71	83
5	90	179	183	195
	75	153	160	169
	50	121	133	146
	25	87	109	119
	10	64	84	102
6	90	185	195	204
	75	159	166	173
	50	132	145	146
	25	112	116	122
	10	89	91	91

*WCPM = words correct per minute

Source: Hasbrouck and Tindal (2017).

A question that often arises surrounds text selection. Hasbrouck and Tindal (2006), who have developed and updated the ORF norms for three decades, remind us that in order to maintain the validity and reliability of this CBM, students should read "an unpracticed, *grade-level* passage" (p. 640). This is in contrast to instruction of oral reading fluency, which has a different purpose than assessment does. As we will discuss in more detail later, fluency instruction involves a gradient of texts matched to the reader and includes modeling and discussion of the content before students begin reading aloud (e.g., Stahl & Heubach, 2005).

The goal is that the student is at the 50th percentile or above. For students who are at the 50th, routine classroom fluency lessons should be sufficient to maintain growth over the year. For students who are below the 50th percentile, supplemental or intensive instruction and intervention may be indicated, but Hasbrouck and Tindal (2006) caution that this CBM on its own should not be the sole indicator of the type of intervention. They draw an analogy to the way a physician uses body temperature to assess a patient. It is one indicator, and an important one, but it alone doesn't reveal some conditions, such as a torn ligament. Having said that, a high body temperature alerts the doctor to investigate further what might be happening. Likewise, a student who is scoring below the 50th percentile on a measure of oral reading fluency warrants further investigation.

With that caveat in mind, Endo (2021) notes that there are three profiles of learners to consider when viewing the results of an ORF CBM:

- **Low Accuracy, Low Fluency:** Students who are not reading at grade-level fluency standards and are instead reading word by word with low accuracy may need support with decoding and foundational literacy skills.
- **High Accuracy, Low Fluency:** Students who exhibit high accuracy on word reading but lower fluency scores will benefit from opportunities for ample fluency practice.
- **High Accuracy, High Fluency:** Students with high accuracy on word reading and high fluency scores will benefit from instruction that helps develop their prosody when reading (https://www.hmhco.com/blog/oral-reading-fluency-assessment).

A table of recommendations based on these three profiles can be found Figure 6.2.

Figure 6.2 Using Oral Reading Fluency Data to Inform Instruction

	Low Accuracy, Low Fluency	High Accuracy, Low Fluency	High Accuracy, High Fluency
Phonics Instruction	Targeted explicit systematic phonics instruction	Grade-level phonics instruction	Grade-level phonics instruction (if applicable)
Fluency Instruction	Explicit fluency instruction • Guided oral reading • Repeated reading of decodable or controlled text • Audio-assisted text	Fluency practice • Guided oral reading • Repeated reading of decodable or controlled text • Audio-assisted text	Focus on prosody • Develop prosody (reading with proper phrasing, expression, and intonation) • Independent silent reading
Comprehension Instruction	Explicit instruction on comprehension using text at the instructional level or challenging texts with teacher support	Grade-level comprehension instruction with teacher support	Grade-level comprehension instruction

Source: Endo (2021).

Prosody and Oral Reading Fluency

Prosody is the ability to adjust tone, pitch, stress, rhythm, and rate to read with expression appropriate to the meaning of the words. It is the "musical quality" Worthy and Broaddus referred to. After all, a reader can only properly use expression when the meaning of the message is understood. Prosody is one indicator that the reader understands some of the nuances in the text, and students with strong prosody in oral reading tend to have higher comprehension scores from silent reading as well (Zimmerman et al., 2019).

Prosody also includes the use of phrase boundaries. These are the meaningful chunks of words in a sentence that go together. As an example, read aloud the sentence, "I took a taste of the soup, but it was too hot." Chances are good that you chunked phrases such as *of the soup* and *it was too hot* using minute pauses and variances in your intonation. You might have stretched out *too* just a bit, and you signaled the end of the sentence by lowering the pitch of your voice. When we say to a reader, "Make it sound like talking," we are encouraging them to attend to the prosody of their oral reading.

Prosody as a function of oral reading fluency has received increased attention in the last two decades. The National Assessment of Educational Progress (NAEP) conducted an oral fluency study in 2018 to better understand oral reading fluency and foundational skills of students who score below basic on the comprehensive reading assessment. A nationally representative sample of 1,800 fourth-grade students who had previously scored at the below-basic levels read passages aloud. These recordings were analyzed using an automated speech analysis system to determine accuracy, rate, and the number of words correct per minute (WCPM). Trained human scorers then listened to the recordings and scored them according to a rubric of oral reading expression (see Figure 6.3). As a part of this same study, participants also read a list of words and a list of pronounceable pseudowords (e.g., *flam*, *nabble*) to gauge phonological decoding and word recognition.

Figure 6.3 NAEP Oral Reading Fluency Passage Reading Expression Scoring Rubric

Score	Level	Description
0	Insufficient Sample	• Insufficient sample for rating (fewer than 12 words read aloud correctly).
1	Word by Word	• Less than ¼ of the words read aloud with appropriate expression. • Reading focuses on individual words (not phrases, sentences, or the passage). • Reading is all or mostly monotone.
2	Local Grouping	• More than ¼ and less than ½ of the words read aloud with appropriate expression. • Reading focuses on local word groups (with little to no focus on phrases, sentences, or the passage). • Reading may be mostly arrhythmic or monotone.

Score	Level	Description
3	Phrase and Clause	• More than ½ of the words read aloud with appropriate expression. • Reading expresses the structure or meaning of words, phrases, clauses, and a few sentences (with little or no focus on the passage). • Intonation may sometimes reinforce rhythmic grouping, or reading may be monotone.
4	Sentence Prosody	• More than ¾ of the words read aloud with appropriate expression • Reading correctly expresses text and sentence structure and meaning (which may include non-local text connections). • Reading can be occasionally inconsistent, but not monotone. • Reading rate is at least 55 words per minute (at least 80 text-words-read to merit this level or above).
5	Passage Expression	• Passage read as if for a listener—of the passage portion read aloud, all or nearly all (at least 90 percent) is read with appropriate expression. The reading consistently expresses the structure and meaning of sentences, paragraphs, and the passage as a whole (which may include non-local text connections). • Reading may include a few word stumbles or misreading, but it is expressive throughout. • Reading rate is at least 80 words per minute (at least 120 text-words-read to merit this level).
8	Silent Reader	• Recording has audio signal, but no near-field speech from the student. • Audible background sounds, breathing, or microphone touching may suggest the reader did not speak throughout the recording period.
9	Anomaly	• Not 0, 1, 2, 3, 4, 5, or 8. Not a silent reader, nor any near-field reading aloud. • Possibly with off-task or irrelevant speech, evidence of confusion, or anything else unexpected, including electronic crackle or dead flat-line signal.

Note: Passage expression ratings of 8 and 9 were treated as missing as these students' expression level could not be determined because of the quality/content of the audio file.

Source: National Assessment of Educational Progress (NAEP) (2021b).

WHAT'S YOUR ADVICE?

Listen to two fourth graders as they read the same passage. One student scored at the below-basic level of the overall NAEP reading assessment; the other student scored at the proficient level. These illustrative audios are provided on the NAEP assessment website at https://nces.ed.gov/nationsreportcard/studies/orf/illustrative_audio.aspx.

As you listen to these, follow along with the passage they are reading, also posted on the same website.

Imagine that these two students are in the same fourth-grade classroom, and you have analyzed these samples with their teacher. What do you suggest their classroom teacher should emphasize to support each student? Consider what it is that you know about ORF norms as well as prosody. Draw on Endo's suggestions for using reading fluency data to make instructional decisions. In particular, how would you advise the teacher to fold in foundational skills with fluency development?

Advice Regarding Supports for the Disfluent Student	Advice Regarding Supports for the Fluent Student

Instruction in Reading Fluency

Effective oral reading fluency instruction rests on the goal that students engage in multiple readings of the same text in order to build automaticity, thereby increasing the cognitive resources for focusing additional attention on meaning. Two such practices are whole-class choral reading and fluency-oriented reading instruction (FORI).

WHOLE-CLASS CHORAL READING

Choral reading is a time-honored tradition in many elementary classrooms (e.g., Samuels, 1979). In choral reading, the students in the class read aloud simultaneously. This should not be confused with round robin reading, the particularly ineffective practice of single children taking turns reading aloud (Optiz & Rasinski, 2008). The emphasis in choral reading is on the performance and expression used to accurately convey the meaning of the text. The teacher is the first to read the text aloud, so students can focus first on meaning. Only then are children invited to join in the choral reading.

One of the advantages of choral reading is the sense of community created through the practice.

One of the advantages of choral reading is the sense of community created through the practice. The use of texts with community meaning, such as favorite songs and poems, dialogue, and other spirited texts, are particularly useful for choral readings. Rasinski et al. (2009) argue that the choice of text is an important one, noting that many texts, especially informational ones, "are meant to be read silently and are usually written in a third-person disembodied voice, one that does not lend itself to reading with expression" and therefore "do not lend themselves easily to reading fluency development" (p. 198).

In teaching choral reading, consider these points:

- Choose texts that are lively and engaging to read. Poems, predictable books, and song lyrics are ideal.
- Make sure the text is accessible to all, both in terms of difficulty and in visual display. Students may have their own copy, or the text can be projected digitally or written on a language chart.
- Be sure to model what the passage should sound like before students try it. Discuss why you are using particular expression, tone, pitch, or volume in order to model how you are inferring the meaning.
- Choose texts for choral readings that can be revisited over the course of the week. Remember that with fluency, repetition is the key.

Whole-class choral reading (WCCR; Paige, 2011) is one organizational model for doing so. In WCCR, a lively text of about 200 words is selected by the teacher, with modeling and discussion of the content preceding student readings. Although not specifically noted in the model, other research on repeated reading of texts notes that three to four repetitions seem to yield good results. (We will discuss the research on repeated reading more fully a bit later in this module.) A suggested procedure for WCCR can be found in Figure 6.4.

Figure 6.4 Procedure for Classroom Implementation of Whole-Class Choral Reading Using Repeated Reading of Text

Before Reading

1. Distribute or display reading text to students that represents an average reading level for the class.
2. Ensure that all students are attending to the passage; provide background knowledge about the passage to aid in comprehension.
3. On Monday, model aloud a fluent reading of the entire passage while students read along silently.
4. Review passage by reading aloud target words and phrases that may not be familiar to students.
5. Remind students to observe prosodic elements of oral reading such as commas, periods, and question marks.

During Reading

6. Count down "3, 2, 1" to help students begin reading on cue.
7. Read passage aloud along with students; everyone reads with one voice.
8. Listen for reading miscues and difficulties with text while modeling fluent reading and walking about the classroom.

After Reading

9. Review, through modeling aloud, pronunciation of words and phrases that were difficult for students.
10. Provide positive encouragement to the class, highlighting what was done well and what might be improved.

On Monday and Tuesday, you may have the whole class reread part or all of the passage as necessary to reinforce appropriate oral reading.

Source: Paige (2011, p. 436).

Hailey Lazo engages her second-grade students in whole-class choral reading almost daily. But she is using a little twist on this time-tested instructional routine in preparation for an upcoming performance her students will be doing for a school performance. She reads the text aloud as it is projected on her smartboard, modeling the rate, expressiveness, and rhythm of the first stanza of the poem, "Bed In Summer " by Robert Louis Stevenson (see Figure 6.5). She uses a digital pointer to follow along with the words as she reads, and then she discusses the meaning and humor of the poem. Then students are invited to read it chorally with her several times. On subsequent readings, she deletes words from the projected text, and the students rely on language skills and memory to chorally respond again, adding in the words that have disappeared from the text. If there are quiet spots, she reveals the words, and then her students practice the choral reading again.

Their practice continued daily for a week. Her students read it with her following her reading aloud to them. Their collective voices included a great deal of intonation and emphasis. The first set of deletions included *night* in the first line, *candle-light* in the second line, *way* in the third line, *day* in the fourth line, *you* from the ninth line, and *day* from the last line. Her students did not miss a beat. The choral reading sounded amazing, and all of the words were included. For the next round, she deleted six different words, and her students still experienced success. As Ms. Lazo notes, "It's fun, for the students and me. But more important, when I delete words, it gets them to read, and thus practice, again, which is great for their fluency development."

Figure 6.5 Excerpt from "Bed in Summer" by Robert Louis Stevenson

In winter I get up at night
And dress by yellow candle-light.
In summer, quite the other way,
I have to go to bed by day.

I have to go to bed and see
The birds still hopping on the tree,
Or hear the grown-up people's feet
Still going past me in the street.

And does it not seem hard to you,
When all the sky is clear and blue,
And I should like so much to play,
To have to go to bed by day?

Source: Stevenson (1885).

NOTES

Fluency-Oriented Reading Instruction

Fluency instruction, like many other elements of reading, should follow a developmental trajectory. Children in kindergarten who are reading at expected levels are not yet developmentally at the point where whole-group fluency instruction makes much sense. As well, students in fifth grade who are performing at expected levels aren't as likely to benefit from an investment in whole-group instruction. For older students who are disfluent, interventions such as repeated reading (discussed later) are warranted. Having said that, students in grades 2 and 3 are especially receptive to whole-group fluency instruction. A proven approach for whole-group fluency instruction at these grade levels is fluency-oriented reading instruction (FORI; Stahl & Heubach, 2005) and a variation, called Wide FORI (Kuhn et al., 2006). Both emphasize the use of shared reading of text over the course of five days. FORI uses a single text for the five days, while Wide FORI uses several texts that are conceptually related (Kuhn, 2020; see Figure 6.6 for a comparison of the two approaches).

Figure 6.6 FORI and Wide FORI Lesson Plans

FORI Lesson Plan				
Monday (40 minutes)	**Tuesday** (30 minutes)	**Wednesday** (20 minutes)	**Thursday** (30 minutes)	**Friday** (30–40 minutes)
The teacher uses prereading activities to introduce the selection to the class. The teacher then reads the selection to the class; students should follow along on their own copies. The teacher and students discuss the selection, thereby keeping the focus on comprehension.	The teacher and students echo read the selection. The teacher should integrate comprehension and vocabulary strategies throughout the reading. The teacher and students discuss the selection further.	The teacher and students chorally read the selection.	The students partner and read the selection to each other while the teacher monitors and supports their reading.	The students complete extension activities designed to broaden their understanding of the text.

Wide FORI Lesson Plan				
Monday (40 minutes)	**Tuesday** (30 minutes)	**Wednesday** (30–40 minutes)	**Thursday** (30 minutes)	**Friday** (30 minutes)
Text #1 The teacher uses prereading activities to introduce the selection to the class. The teacher then reads the selection to the class; students should follow along on their own copies. The teacher and students discuss the selection, thereby keeping the focus on comprehension.	Text #1 The teacher and students echo read the selection. The teacher should integrate comprehension and vocabulary strategies throughout the reading. The teacher and students discuss the selection further.	Text #1 The students complete extension activities designed to deepen their understanding of the text.	Text #2 The teacher and students echo read a second selection for the week. The teacher should integrate comprehension and vocabulary strategies throughout the reading. The teacher and students discuss the selection.	Text #3 The teacher and students echo read a third selection for the week. The teacher should integrate comprehension and vocabulary strategies throughout the reading. The teacher and students discuss the selection.

Source: Kuhn (2020).

The developers of both models caution that the texts selected should be of a length appropriate for a sustained reading of about 20 minutes, rather than a series of short reading passages. In addition, the text chosen should be challenging enough for students to stretch their decoding and comprehension skills but not so difficult that they need extensive scaffolded supports. Each of these draws on instructional principles of learning:

- **Modeling fluent reading** as students follow along with the text. Point out to students how you are using phrase boundaries and expressiveness to model rate and prosody, not just accuracy.
- **A focus on vocabulary and comprehension** such that the purpose of reading—understanding—is not lost.
- **Repetition** to build automaticity in word recognition and confidence in their oral reading.
- **Echo reading** to release responsibility to students. Echo reading is the process of reading a short portion of the text aloud to students and then having them repeat it back to you at the same rate and expressiveness. Remind students that this isn't a memorization task. Their eyes should be on their own texts as they read it back to you. As students become accustomed to the routine, increase the amount of text they are reading during each portion of the echo reading, going from line by line to a paragraph or more at a time.

- **Choral reading** is a further extension of echo reading. As students' familiarity with the text grows due to repetitions, they read aloud simultaneously with the teacher.
- **Partner reading** as students work in mixed ability pairs to read together, alternating by page or by paragraph. Kuhn (2020) cautions that the difference in skill level should not be so wide that the partners have difficulty supporting each other. One way to create effective pairs is to use an alternate ranking system using a relevant skill level (in this case fluency) from the top-performing student to the lowest-performing student. Privately, the teacher then cuts the list at the midpoint and forms pairs by selecting students from each side of the list. For example, a teacher listed 32 students in order of skill (see Figure 6.7). The list was cut in half after Student 16. The second list comprised the names of Students 17 through 32. The lists were placed side by side, and the first name from the first list was paired with the first name on List 2. Therefore Students 1 and 17 were a pair, while students 2 and 18 were paired, et cetera. In this way, every pair maintained heterogeneity, but the membership is not so different from one another that they cannot produce. Maintaining a balance of abilities within each pairing is important, so that the more able students do not take over the task altogether and limit the participation (and learning) of their partners.

Figure 6.7 Alternative Ranking System for Partner Reading

1. Keisha	17. Rudolfo
2. Arturo	18. Sara
3.	19.
4.	20.
5.	21.
6.	22.
15. Leighanne	31. Felicia
16. John	32. Sam

Source: Frey et al. (2018).

The Wide FORI approach is used by all the second- and third-grade classes in the school where Julia Cruz teaches. The teachers at her school often choose texts for the fluency instruction that parallel what the students are learning in science and social studies. It's the first quarter of the school year, and since her students are currently learning about magnetism, she has selected three texts to use in this week's fluency lessons:

- *Magnetism* (Dunne, 2017): 510L
- *Magnets* (Gaertner, 2019): 470L
- *The Science of Magnets* (Vogel, 2018): 500L

The teacher explains her rationale for the text selections. "They're accustomed to the routine, as nearly all of them were in this school last year. But I'm still getting to know their strengths and interests. I chose these texts because there's some challenge to them, but it's not over the top." She has also finished with administering her fluency assessment, so she has a better idea of how to rank them. "The first few weeks until I got it done, I really just relied on observation to figure out pairs. Now I've got some more data to guide me," says Ms. Cruz.

TAKE ACTION

Administer a curriculum-based measure of oral reading fluency to your class, and compare the results to the national norms to identify students at, above, or below grade level in ORF. Use an alternate ranking system of your students, and draft pairs of students to work together on fluency practice. (Adjust as necessary based on your knowledge of their history of productive work, behavior, and personality). Provide time for daily FORI approach for two weeks, and then reflect.

What early gains are you noticing? ______________________________

____

Are there unexpected difficulties? If so, how do you address them? ______________

What people do you need to consult with, and resources do you need, to strengthen your oral reading fluency practice? ______________________________

____

NOTES

Repeated Reading for Disfluent Students

For students not yet making expected progress in their oral reading fluency and prosody, more intensive intervention may be warranted. Repeated reading is a highly effective intervention approach for students who need more practice with building automaticity. In repeated reading, the student reads the same passage aloud multiple times. While earlier repeated reading interventions focused on rate and accuracy, the practice has evolved to include prosody and reading comprehension. A 2020 systematic review of 39 repeated reading studies of students in grades 2 to 5 reported that this approach made solid contributions to students' more fluent reading and their comprehension (Hudson et al., 2020). A different set of researchers used another statistical tool, called a meta-analysis, to examine practices and conditions that yielded good results with repeated reading for those with a reading disability (Lee & Yoon, 2017). Those practices include previewing vocabulary and a teacher modeling of the reading, four repetitions by the student, and reading comprehension activities.

Repeated reading is a highly effective intervention approach for students who need more practice with building automaticity.

Preview vocabulary and model the passage. Provide the student with the opportunity to practice isolated vocabulary words that will appear in the passage and discuss the meaning. Then read the passage aloud to the student as they follow along with their own printed version, pointing out how you use expression to understand the text.

Student repeats the reading aloud. The researchers found that results were significantly higher with each repetition, up to four repeats. More than four repeats did not yield further gains.

Make sure the student comprehends the text. Include reading comprehension activities to promote summarization, generation of questions, and retelling. Keep in mind that improved fluent reading creates a cognitive space for students to attend to the meaning of the text. Make sure you are filling that space (Hudson et al., 2020).

What did these studies show not to be meaningful variables in repeated readings? Both studies noted that small-group repeated readings were not as effective as individual instruction. One-to-one arrangements make repeated reading instruction more time intensive. Therefore, make use of CBM and other data to identify and monitor student progress.

Fifth-grade teacher Sarita Youngblood and special education teacher Marcus Harris collaborated to analyze the data following Ms. Youngblood's winter administration of the oral reading fluency assessment. There were several students who scored below the 25% level on grade-level texts. For the smaller group of students, several of whom receive special education supports in Ms. Youngblood's classroom, Mr. Harris administered and recorded an additional fluency assessment, and he used the NAEP prosody rubric to further analyze the results. The data they collected about five of their students appears in Figure 6.8.

Figure 6.8 Ms. Youngblood's Students for Fluency Intervention

Aniya		Ben		Ceci		James		Jeremy	
ORF	Prosody	ORF	Prosody	ORF	Prosody	ORF	Prosody	ORF	Prosody
71	1	88	2	101	2	67	1	107	3

Together, the two educators made plans for how to implement repeated reading as an intervention for these students. In addition to conducting repeated reading practice several times a week for these students, Ms. Youngblood, the fifth-grade teacher, paired each of these students with a peer in the class who could partner read with them. Mr. Harris, the special educator, planned to conduct choral readings with the five students during some of the times he was in the classroom. "I want to be sure to tie this to the word recognition work that I'm doing with Aniya and James," he said, "as well as the reading comprehension work I'm doing with Ben, Ceci, and Jeremy." In order to do so, he reviewed his materials to locate opportunities to embed more reading fluency activities into the word recognition and comprehension materials. "It's all about braiding these skills together," he said.

FIND THE MISTAKES

Oral reading fluency instruction, intervention, and assessment is rife with misinformation. Here are some common mistakes.

1. **Telling students that rate is the only thing that really matters**. Telling a child to "read as fast as you can" often results in mechanical and monotone reading. Pay attention to expressiveness, too.
2. **Failing to teach prosody**. Help students identify phrase and clause boundaries, and model and discuss the connections between expressiveness and a reader's understanding of the text.
3. **Asking students to read aloud "cold" texts.** Despite evidence that it is ineffective, round robin reading is rampant in classrooms (Ash et al., 2009). Don't ask students to take turns reading texts aloud they have not yet had time to read to themselves silently, or that have not first been read aloud by the teacher.
4. **Teaching fluency without bridging it to word recognition and language comprehension.** Oral reading fluency is both an indicator of and a link to the word recognition and language comprehension skills of your students. Leverage these strands to consolidate their developing reading.
5. **Failing to understand the difference between assessing and instructing in fluency.** When oral reading fluency is *assessed*, a grade-level text is used to ensure validity and reliability when using the ORF norms (Bolaños et al., 2013). When fluency is part of *instruction*, the text selection is closer to what the student can reasonably read on their own or with some assistance. In the words of Paige (2011), it should be "appropriate and sensible" so that the student can access it (p. 436).

From this list of mistakes, inventory your classroom practice and talk with your colleagues. Are there mistakes that you could correct to increase students' oral reading fluency?

TEXT-TO-SELF CONNECTION

What are the key reasons for focusing on oral reading fluency in your grade level?

____

____

____

Is oral reading fluency in your grade level primarily for instructional purposes, primarily for intervention purposes, or for a combination of both reasons?

Using the traffic light scale, with red being not confident, yellow being somewhat confident, and green indicating very confident, how confident are you in your ability to

- Teach oral reading fluency?
- Teach prosody?
- Integrate oral reading fluency with foundational skills?
- Integrate oral reading fluency with reading comprehension skills?

Takeaways

- Oral reading fluency is a crucial bridge between word recognition and language comprehension and assists in further consolidating the strands of the reading rope.
- Measurement of oral reading fluency and prosody allow teachers to monitor development.
- Readers benefit from routine reading fluency instruction. Examples of fluency routines are fluency-oriented reading instruction (FORI) and Wide FORI, as well as whole-class choral reading.
- Repeated reading is a proven activity at the heart of fluency instruction and intervention.
- Assessment practices for oral reading fluency are different from instructional practices. The assessment protocol for determining ORF norms requires the use of unpracticed, grade-level passages. This is in contrast to instructional practice, which allows for a wider gradient of texts that are grounded in teacher modeling and discussion of the content.

PS: Answers to the anticipation guide are F, T, T, T.

PART

II

Language Comprehension

Reading is more than decoding the squiggly black lines on a page. As Thorndike (1917) noted more than one hundred years ago, comprehension requires the cooperation of many forces. This "cooperation of forces" requires complex coordination of skills and concepts that together represent true reading. Chief among these forces is the ability to comprehend language. Language comprehension is the ability to make meaning from spoken and written language (Silverman et al., 2020). It requires that students correctly process the meanings of words and phrases. Of course, they also need to decode those words and phrases, which was the focus of Part I. In this section, we attend to dimensions of language comprehension that contribute to meaning making.

One dimension of language comprehension focuses on how a reader integrates new information with what they already know. Every reader in your class possesses background knowledge that can be leveraged to advance reading. They also come to school with prior experiences, including those that may be unfamiliar to us, or not conventionally fortified in the classroom. Our ability to effectively activate their background knowledge is crucial. When teachers are strength spotters rather than deficit detectors, they recognize the academic and cultural background knowledge that their students already possess. Further, they use that knowledge to expand students' understanding of the world and the texts with which they engage.

In addition to **background knowledge**, students all have reading-specific background knowledge that contributes to their language comprehension. Of course, there is unfinished learning, which is why students are in school. The modules on **vocabulary** and **morphological awareness** draw further attention to how students learn and use academic words and phrases. Importantly, instruction on these strands of the reading rope impacts students' spelling and writing.

Semantic knowledge must be paired with an understanding of the grammar and syntax of the language. The module on **language structures** highlights learning about the mechanics and conventions needed to understand sentences.

We also recognize the impact that **verbal reasoning** has on students' comprehension. Verbal reasoning is used by readers to attain higher-level language skills and includes making inferences using logical steps to reach logical conclusions not stated explicitly in the text. Notably, students who are poor comprehenders have difficulty in making inferences, especially those that require more effort and elaboration (Bowyer-Crane & Snowling, 2005).

Literacy knowledge of how texts work plays an important role in comprehension. We start with what young students need to know in terms of concepts about print, drawing in newer research about how primary teachers use print referencing to teach these skills. We then continue with discussion of genres, text features, and expository and narrative text structure to expand their knowledge in an ever-widening circle so that they can use it to understand increasingly complex texts.

Finally, newer research on language comprehension has demonstrated that children must develop a **theory of mind (ToM).** This is likely to be newer to you, at least in terms of reading comprehension, and our choice to feature it as part of the expanded reading rope will be new too. Theory of mind involves the ability to think about mental states, your own and those of others. These mental states include emotions, desires, beliefs, values, and knowledge. It requires that readers understand the thoughts and feelings of others, or really what might be going on in another person's head. Importantly, our students are not in the heads and minds of others, so they must develop theories about what is happening with characters, peers, adults, officials, and so on. We develop our theories of mind as we observe what people say, how they act, what motivates them, and what we know about their personalities. This allows us to infer their intentions and understand their motivations. Dore et al. (2018) propose a possible link between theory of mind and reading comprehension. In their words, "Increased ToM leads to increased representation of and inferencing about characters' thoughts, motives, goals, and emotions, which then lead to increased reading comprehension" (p. 1084).

Language comprehension and word recognition need to be taught with intention from the first day of school. Diminishing language comprehension instruction in a misguided effort to boost word recognition is not effective. As Scarborough (2001) has noted, it weakens the entire rope. If we are to teach reading to every child, we must ensure that we attend to both.

MODULE

7

Background Knowledge

Photo by Andy Kelly on Unsplash

In this module, we will

- Explore the role and impact of background knowledge on students' reading ability.
- Identify techniques for building background knowledge through instruction and text selection.
- Consider the ways in which prior knowledge can be activated.
- Discuss ways background knowledge can be assessed.

How much do you know about robotics? For example, did you know that the term *robot* comes from the Czech word *Robota,* which means "drudgery" or "hard work" and "forced labor"? Imagine you are reading up on the VEX Robotics Competition and encounter the following text:

> There are seventy-two (72) **Rings** and seven (7) **Mobile Goals** on a VRC Tipping Point Field. Each Alliance has two (2) **Alliance Mobile Goals**, with the remaining three (3) Goals being neutral. Each **Alliance** also has a **Platform** located in their **Home Zone**. (https://www.vexrobotics.com/v5/competition/vrc-current-game)

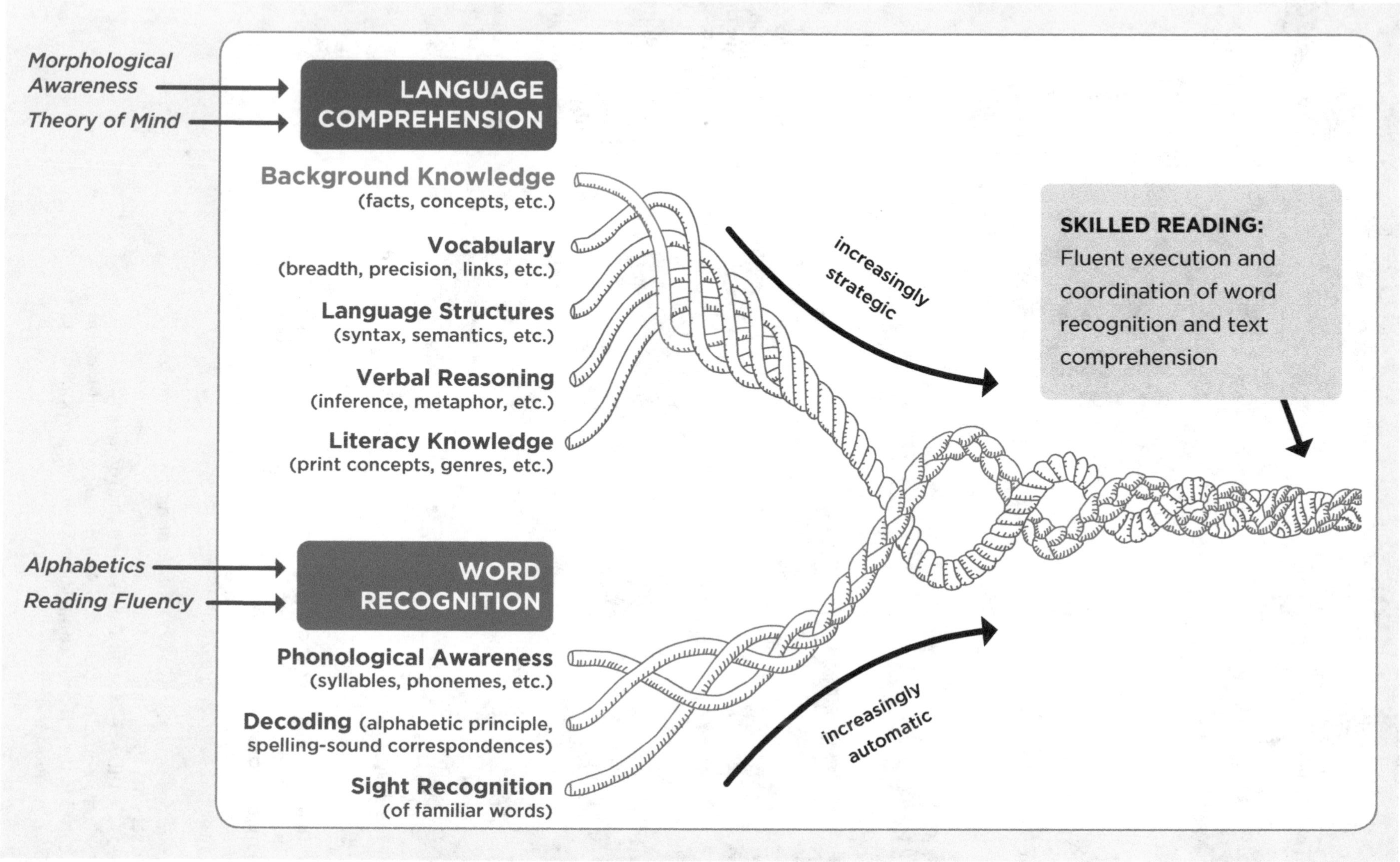

Source: Adapted from Scarborough, H. S. (2001). Connecting early language and literacy to later reading (dis)abilities: Evidence, theory, and practice. In S. Neuman & D. Dickinson (Eds.), *Handbook for research in early literacy* (pp. 97–110). Guilford Press.

Your ability to understand the text is impacted by the knowledge you already have. While many of the words are familiar in their general meaning, your lack of knowledge about robotics impacts your ability to use the information. It's easier to go from the "known" to the "new" rather than just encounter unanchored new information, which is why background knowledge of information is so important in reading.

Now imagine you're reading Asimov's (1950) three laws of robotics:

> First Law: A robot may not injure a human being, or, through inaction, allow a human being to come to harm. Second Law: A robot must obey orders given it by human beings, except where such orders would conflict with the First Law. Third Law: A robot must protect its own existence as long as such protection does not conflict with the First or Second Law. (p. 40)

It's easier to go from the "known" to the "new" rather than just encounter unanchored new information.

What knowledge would you need to understand this information? It's not the technical information about robotics that would be important, but rather you would need to understand logic, the value of human life, the language being used to share the information, and the ways in which robots are perceived. Again, your background knowledge helped you interpret this, although in this case the knowledge you were using likely drew on your ethical and cultural experiences. Here's the breathtaking part: You drew on your factual knowledge, as well as your experiences, to make sense of the texts and to notice what you did not understand. And you accomplished this is a split second.

The National Research Council's report entitled *How People Learn: Brain, Mind, Experience, and School* (2000) describes a framework for understanding how background knowledge supports new learning:

> The new science of learning does not question that facts are important for thinking and problem solving. . . . However, the research also clearly shows that "usable knowledge" is not the same as a mere list of disconnected facts. Experts' knowledge is connected and **organized** around important concepts (e.g., Newton's second law of motion); it is "**conditionalized**" to specify the contexts in which it is applicable; it supports understanding and **transfer** (to other contexts) rather than only the ability to remember. (National Research Council, 2000, p. 11)

Let's take a closer look at those three ideas: that the knowledge must be organized, conditionalized, and transferrable:

- **Organized:** This is your schema, which is to say how you link facts and concepts together. Here's a visual way of thinking about schema. Throw a handful of paper clips on the table. They scatter into a random mess, much like the bits of knowledge in some students' heads. But, when a large magnet is used, the individual pieces gather together and connect to something bigger. And that is schema. Your usable background knowledge is retrievable, because it is organized and connected to other facts.
- **Conditionalized:** That means you know when and where to apply your background knowledge. Once you've retrieved that schema, you have to sort through what is useful in this condition, and what isn't. Wolfe and Goldman (2005) studied the relationship between background knowledge, reasoning, and explanation of sixth-grade students who read two conflicting accounts about the fall of the Roman Empire. The researchers noted the types of associations and reasoning the students used to understand the documents, including irrelevant associations ("My family visited Rome last year") (p. 481). Interestingly, nearly 50% of the background knowledge associations drawn by these students did not contribute to text understanding. But more to our point, students who appropriately utilized their background knowledge scored higher on measures of reasoning for the task.

Knowing what was relevant and what wasn't for a particular condition influenced their comprehension.

- **Transferrable:** Transfer—the *application* of new learning—is the ultimate goal of our teaching, right? But the evidence is that novices have difficulty transferring background knowledge to novel situations, because they attempt to memorize a sequence rather than pay attention to the conceptual aspects of the task (Atkinson et al., 2003). When the steps are grouped into conceptually similar chunks, transfer in reading improves (Fisher & Frey, 2016).

Read each statement and mark **T** if the statement is true and **F** if the statement is false. As you read through the module, you might change your responses. Be prepared to explain your responses and use the text for evidence.

<table>
<tr><th colspan="2">Before Reading</th><th colspan="2">Statements</th><th colspan="2">After Reading</th></tr>
<tr><td>T</td><td>F</td><td colspan="2">1. Students who have successfully completed the previous grade level have similar levels of background knowledge.</td><td>T</td><td>F</td></tr>
<tr><td colspan="3">Why did you indicate true or false?</td><td colspan="3">Has your thinking changed after reading?</td></tr>
<tr><td>T</td><td>F</td><td colspan="2">2. Background knowledge can be gained through direct experiences such as visiting a museum.</td><td>T</td><td>F</td></tr>
<tr><td colspan="3">Why did you indicate true or false?</td><td colspan="3">Has your thinking changed after reading?</td></tr>
<tr><td>T</td><td>F</td><td colspan="2">3. Background knowledge is a factor in whether a student can learn from a text.</td><td>T</td><td>F</td></tr>
<tr><td colspan="3">Why did you indicate true or false?</td><td colspan="3">Has your thinking changed after reading?</td></tr>
<tr><td>T</td><td>F</td><td colspan="2">4. It is difficult to assess background knowledge of students.</td><td>T</td><td>F</td></tr>
<tr><td colspan="3">Why did you indicate true or false?</td><td colspan="3">Has your thinking changed after reading?</td></tr>
</table>

What Is Background Knowledge and Why Is It important?

Background knowledge is the network of information we draw upon as we read and listen to make meaning. It is a complex stew of topical knowledge about a subject, the prior experiences we have had, and what we know about the structure of the language that is used. The background knowledge we possess makes it possible to draw inferences, form conclusions, and engage in critical analysis *with* the text ("what knowledge am I gaining?") as well as *against* the text ("what information is causing me to question?").

Background knowledge makes it possible to draw inferences, form conclusions, and engage in critical analysis.

Background knowledge factors into our understanding of words with multiple meanings. Importantly, for instance, it isn't simply a list of facts. The word *stable* in a story about horses is different than *stable* in the context of a science experiment on working machines. The word *bug* has 17 different meanings. A child with sufficient background knowledge can immediately discard the 16 other meanings that distract their reading comprehension and home in on the one they need when reading about spying devices.

READING LEVELS AND BACKGROUND KNOWLEDGE

While we often consider reader profiles in terms of measures of accuracy and comprehension generated through assessments (e.g., informal reading inventories, Lexile levels), a less considered but intriguing method of assessment is listening to how (or whether) a reader uses background knowledge while reading. Researchers in the Netherlands devised an ingenious method to understand how and when children ages 9 to 11 used their background knowledge (Karlsson et al., 2018). They read narrative and informational passages, with each sentence printed on a separate sheet of paper. After each sentence, they asked, "What are you thinking now?" to encourage the child to think aloud about how they were understanding the developing story. They analyzed each think-aloud to determine whether it was a literal repetition of what was in the text, a paraphrase, or a response that indicated the child was using their background knowledge to make inferences. What emerged were three distinct profiles of readers:

- **Literal readers** who adhered tightly to the text and made few inferences
- **Paraphrasing readers** who extracted meaning from the text and made some connections and inferences
- **Elaborating readers** who regularly made inferences, used their background knowledge, and thought ahead about what might happen next through predictions.

Not surprisingly, elaborating readers scored at higher levels on measures of word decoding skills, vocabulary knowledge, reading comprehension, and reasoning ability. Once more, we are reminded of Scarborough's 2001 observation reported in the first module about the reciprocal relationship between the word recognition and language comprehension bundles.

TOPICAL KNOWLEDGE

These are concepts and information needed to understand the subject of the reading. Importantly, topical knowledge is more than a list of facts; it is what Neuman et al. (2014) call "knowledge networks" (p. 147). Think again of the visual of the magnet picking up all those paper clips—it's an organized schema that can be readily retrieved. More extensive knowledge of the topic makes it possible for the reader to accumulate and recall more information as they build their schema, while those with less topical knowledge "are less able to select and recall premises required to make inferences about a text and are also less able to suppress irrelevant information" (Smith et al., 2021). In other words, the text is less useful to them, even if they can accurately decode it. They further note that the studies they reviewed confirmed that students with low background knowledge must devote more of their cognitive resources to maintaining meaning, and therefore are less able to attend to storage of the information for learning. Consider the implications of that last statement. Students with more background knowledge are better able to acquire new information during the reading, while those with little background knowledge struggle to build schema. It is analogous to the seed on poor soil, which is less likely to take root than the seed on fertile ground.

PRIOR EXPERIENCES

When children know more about a topic, they are able to read and understand more complex texts about that topic because of their background knowledge of the topic and of the language used to convey the information. However, this will not be true for all. Some texts place demands on a reader that extend far beyond one's experiences and language and provide little in the way of explanation, whereas other texts contain content that closely match the reader's life experiences. The baseball study is illustrative. Recht and Leslie (1988) had students read about a baseball game. They divided readers into four groups:

- Group 1: Good readers who were high in baseball knowledge
- Group 2: Good readers who were low in baseball knowledge
- Group 3: Poor readers who were high in baseball knowledge
- Group 4: Poor readers who were low in baseball knowledge

The assumption at the time was that comprehension scores would be strongest among students in Group 1, who were good readers with strong baseball knowledge. That was supported in this study. But the surprise was that the performance of the students in Group 3—poor readers with strong background knowledge in baseball—did pretty well, almost as well as those in Group 1. Of course, this is only one study, but it does highlight the ways in which prior content knowledge impacts reading.

The good news is that we can create some of these prior experiences in the classroom. Dempsey (2020) worked with three- and four-year-olds. The children who had short (5–10 minute) play-based experiences linked to a topic they would be learning about in a subsequent interactive read-aloud were better able to attend to the information in the text and replicate the sequence of information learned. As an example, prior to a read-aloud about how pizza is made, they had an adult-directed play experience using props and pictures to learn about the process. The adult narrated their thinking (e.g., "First I roll the dough. Find the picture of the girl rolling dough") and then allowed the child to similarly repeat the four steps for making a pizza. Other children had access to the same props and pictures but did not have adult guidance. Later, after hearing a story about making pizza, those who had had the adult-guided play-based experience made more inferences and answered comprehension questions with higher accuracy than those in the free-play condition (Dempsey, 2020). Having an experience that is intentionally aligned to the subsequent reading mattered.

As classroom educators, we similarly create experiences that build students' background knowledge through experiences. Field trips are great, of course, but prohibitively expensive and time-consuming if that's all we ever did. But consider all the hands-on opportunities you create for students. A demonstration of a scientific phenomenon, a multimedia experience of a historical event, conducting virtual field trips of museums, building sensory experiences—all of these techniques can augment the prior experiences students bring to their reading.

NOTICE AND WONDER

We've written that "background knowledge is the missing piece of the comprehension puzzle" (Fisher & Frey, 2009, p. 1). Some researchers have called on educators to devote more time to building background knowledge while somewhat reducing the amount of instructional time on generic comprehension strategies (e.g., Dole et al., 2009; Elleman, 2017; Smith et al., 2021). How do you build background knowledge with your students? Inventory your practice and make note of examples of building topical knowledge and prior experience.

Ways I Build Topical Knowledge	Ways I Build Prior Experiences

Instruction to Build Background Knowledge

Build students' background knowledge at the word level and at the concept level. Consider some of the ways you can incorporate practices like these into your teaching.

CONCEPT WORD SORTS

Concept sorts are a variation of the open and closed sorts we discussed in Module 4 on phonics. However, rather than focusing on the orthographic characteristics, students are sorting words in phrases to align to categories. This is a tactile version of what is happening in their brains, which is to say that they are building schema. The purpose is for students to develop relationships held in common by a set of terms. Although this is often described as a vocabulary instructional strategy, it serves the dual purpose of organizing knowledge. As with phonics sorts, these can either be open sorts (the student determines the category) or closed sorts (the categories are given).

List-Group-Label is an open-concept sort that students collaboratively develop (Taba, 1967). Fourth-grade teacher Kendra Jenkins uses this technique to build the background knowledge of her students during their study of the Klondike Gold Rush. She begins by projecting photographs taken in Washington State during the time, explaining that "Seattle was a gateway to the gold fields" of the Yukon. As she slowly previews the photographs, she asks her students to think about words they would expect to see in their readings about this time in history. She then displays photographs from *Yukon Gold: The Story of the Klondike Gold Rush* (Jones, 1999), a book she'll be reading to them. After showing the pictures, she invites the class to suggest words, which she writes on the smartboard. It should come as no surprise that terms like *Gold Rush, railroads, miners*, and *rich* are immediately suggested.

Having an experience that is intentionally aligned to the subsequent reading has a positive impact.

After this presentation to the whole class, she says, "Let's go back to your tables so you can work together." She explains that they will generate predictions (List), then sort them into clusters of concepts that seem to "hang together" (Group), and then name the categories (Label). Her students have done this before, so they are familiar with the routine. However, Ms. Jenkins initially did List-Group-Label as a whole-class activity several times during the first month of school to guide the process.

Her students return to their desks, where they find several pads of stickie notes and markers. They start by writing one word or phrase from the list on the smartboard on each stickie note. Once they have done so, they negotiate how the terms are linked. During the process, they speculate, discard, and refine possible category labels. One group's List-Group-Label product can be found in Figure 7.1.

"What I appreciate about it is all the oral language development that's happening, and how the students are really building each other's background knowledge," said the teacher. After each group is done, they conduct a gallery walk around the classroom, leading to further class discussion. "They'll be totally ready for this reading tomorrow," remarked Ms. Jenkins. "And it gives me a great window into what it is they already know and where I need to fill in the gaps."

Figure 7.1 List-Group-Label for Yukon Gold Rush

NOTES

Build Background Knowledge With Text Sets

Kindergarten teacher Mayra De León is preparing for an upcoming unit on weather. The teacher knows that her young students have had experience with weather in their daily lives, but they do not necessarily possess a scientific understanding of weather patterns. It's early in the school year, but Ms. De León has already been preparing her students in advance of this unit of instruction. "Since the first day of school, I've included a weather report during calendar time," she explains. "Each day a child is selected to put on the 'weather glasses' [oversized plastic eyeglass frames] to look outside and report on the current weather conditions." The daily weather is logged on the calendar "so that the kids can begin to see local and seasonal weather patterns."

Because they will be exploring the science of weather more deeply, Ms. De León knows that she needs to further build their content knowledge and language skills. In addition to their daily experiences observing and discussing the weather, and science instruction aligned to the content standards, she will be using text sets. **Text sets** are widely used to build content knowledge throughout the grades and are typically organized according to a theme, topic, or essential question. These related titles build knowledge of the concepts being taught by providing students with cognitive resources to draw upon.

However, text set development is more than consulting a list of thematically linked titles, which may or may not contribute to language comprehension. This hit-or-miss approach may in fact exacerbate linguistic and knowledge gaps. "I used to just gather up books that said they had a particular theme," said Ms. De León. She explained that she realized over the years that this method did not always lead to adequate gains in knowledge resources for them to draw upon. She now uses an approach called a "quad text selection" to ensure that her students are exposed "to a variety of texts that provide different challenges and varying modes and purposes" (Lupo et al., 2020, p. 515). The **quad text selection** framework leverages what is known to be essential in reading development: multimodal texts, informational texts, motivational texts, and texts that are more complex:

Text set development is more than consulting a list of thematically linked titles.

- **Multimodal texts** to build knowledge visually
- Easier **informational texts** to build knowledge
- A **hook text** to build interest and activate motivation
- A **challenging target text** to apply their growing content knowledge

Using the quad text selection framework, Ms. De León selected the texts in the table that follows to augment her weather science unit. In addition, she identified how these would be utilized instructionally.

Text Type	Selected Text	Instructional Mode
Multimodal/visual text	National Science Teacher Association's "Introduction to Weather" https://www.generationgenius.com/videolessons/introduction-to-weather-video-for-kids/	Whole-class viewing and discussion to build a language chart of what we learned.

Text Type	Selected Text	Instructional Mode
Informational text	*National Geographic Little Kids First Big Book of Weather* (Seve, 2017)	Interactive read-alouds aligned to students' questions
Motivational texts	*Come On, Rain!* (Hesse, 1999) *On a Magical Do-Nothing Day* (Alemagna, 2017)	Interactive read-alouds
Challenge text	*Tap, Boom Boom* (Bluemle, 2017)	Shared readings

In this case, the teacher's use of daily calendar experiences has contributed to the students' general language development about noticing, observing, and discussing weather phenomena. By using quad text selection, she is ensuring that her students are being exposed to the "complex language and ideas [needed] to independently read complex texts" (Lupo et al., 2020, p. 513).

NOTES

Concept-Oriented Reading Instruction

One of the many wonderful things about elementary children is their curiosity about the natural world around them. Researchers have noted the potential for using science as a lens for literacy instruction, especially in the parallels between inquiry in science and inquiry as active reading (Pearson et al., 2010). When we talk about "reading like a scientist," we're capitalizing on overlapping cognitive tools used in both fields: applying reasoning, drawing inferences, posing questions, and making evidence-based claims.

Concept-oriented reading instruction (CORI) is a method for teaching reading through science concepts (Guthrie et al., 2004). Originally developed for use in grades 3 to 5, CORI has been utilized for older students as well. The central tenet of CORI is that a child's curiosity about a scientific concept fuels a motivation to read and engage. In the process of reading more, they develop and refine word recognition and language comprehension skills. An inquiry might begin with a focus on an ecological concept, such as how the tree cover benefits the community. Students engage in hands-on activities and observations, such as examining Google images of tree canopies in their neighborhood, reading a range of informational books about trees, and choosing subtopics of their own to investigate (e.g., what birds in my neighborhood are threatened by tree loss?). Additional instructional supports include teacher-directed small-group reading of texts, developing concept maps of their books, and writing about what they are learning.

Our attention to CORI for the purposes of this module is on the activation and building of background knowledge. The questioning that launches a unit of instruction is intended to activate their existing background knowledge, while the ongoing unit further builds background knowledge, organizes their schema, and promotes transfer of learning through their growing literacy and investigation skills. More recent innovations of CORI have included other disciplines, such as social studies, to build content knowledge. It should also be noted that practices like CORI are not intended to be a substitute for coherent science and social studies instruction, but rather are intended to complement the learning accomplished in these subjects using a literacy lens.

WHAT'S YOUR ADVICE?

It's not uncommon for teachers to assemble a text set or inquiry without deeply considering how background knowledge will be built. Imagine that a teacher who is new to your grade level comes to you for advice about building a thoughtful text set and inquiry for an upcoming unit. What advice do you have? What mistakes should the teacher avoid? What sources do you find useful for building text sets?

Advice About Text Sets	Mistakes to Avoid	Sources to Consult

Activating Background Knowledge

K-W-L AND ITS MANY VARIATIONS

The **K-W-L** instructional routine is well known among teachers as an effective way to activate background knowledge and cause students to link it to new information. In its classic form (Ogle, 1986), the teacher leads a discussion and summarizes it on a three-column chart with the column headings:

- What I know
- What I want to know
- What I learned

K-W-L was conceived as a way to engage students in active reading by causing them to focus on what is known and not yet known. This hearty routine works well in so many subjects in part because it mirrors aspects of the scientific process. To our thinking, the K phase allows us to rapidly assess background knowledge; the W phase focuses student attention on what can be learned based on the specific text when students plan for reading, reevaluate their questions, and activate helpful background knowledge; and the L phase provides an opportunity for consolidating understanding in light of the text and the purpose for reading in the first place.

Educators and researchers have adapted the original K-W-L format to further refine it. Their adaptations include the following:

- K-W-L-H (Ogle, 1986)—How can I learn more?
- K-W-L Plus (Carr & Ogle, 1987)—Adds mapping or writing to the process
- K-W-L-H-S (Reid et al., 1989)—How will I learn it? How will I share it?
- K-W-L-S (Moore et al., 2000)—What do I still need to learn?

The selection of a particular variant of K-W-L is guided by your teaching purpose. When you want your students to concentrate on their background knowledge, you might insert a column of your own. K-**H**-W-L invites students not only to list what they know, but *how* they know it. This is quite challenging for students, who are not accustomed to naming their sources.

The second graders in Paul Rincon's class are learning about life cycles. Mr. Rincon uses the K-H-W-L process to help students organize information for learning. This strategy uses brainstorming and listing to promote student interest and sustain learning before, during, and after the information is taught. In addition to activating background knowledge, K-H-W-L provides students an opportunity to expand their language.

Mr. Rincon arranges the questions into four columns and prompts a discussion to activate students' prior knowledge. This organizer mirrors the process of scientific inquiry inherent in any investigation and can be created by individual students, small groups, or the whole class, with the teacher acting as recorder for the last.

What do we KNOW?	HOW do we know it?	What do WANT to know?	What did we LEARN?

To get started, students talked with a partner about what they knew or thought they knew about the topic. Angie and her partner Ben discussed size and shape differences in things that grow, whereas Leah and Karina talked about babies and their changes as they grow. Mr. Rincon recorded students' facts or ideas on chart paper (which could be done digitally on Google Slides). All student ideas were charted, because the content of the lessons allows students to correct their misunderstandings and misconceptions. Contested ideas can be marked with a question mark.

The second phase—HOW do you know?— proved to be more challenging. The teacher was patient in letting his students process this reflective question, and in time they developed some ideas:

- We see our brothers and sisters grow up.
- Some of us have chickens and have seen them lay eggs and hatch.
- Some of us have planted a garden and seen the seeds change into plants.

Working in groups of three or four, students then looked at the information written under the *K* and *H* columns to generate questions about the topic. After reconvening as a whole group, the questions were entered in the *W* column. For example, the students asked

- Is the life cycle always the same?
- Does everything have a life cycle?
- What can change the life cycle?

The K-W-L chart was displayed, and the class returned to it throughout the lesson so that they could check off questions as they were answered. At the conclusion of the unit a week later, the *L* column was added as students identified what was learned. In the *Plus* or writing phase, the information appearing in the *What Is Learned* column was organized into categories or topics. Students then used these categories to generate a summary.

Martin's summary read as follows:

> I learned about the life cycle. It is for things that are alive. All alive things have a life cycle. Like the frog starts in the egg like a chicken. That is when they are babies. But then they grow. They change when they grow. And then they have babies.

In this case, the teacher activated students' background knowledge and then facilitated students' interest in the lesson through the use of student-generated questions. In doing so, students relied on language comprehension to leverage their reading and learning.

FIND THE MISTAKES

Background knowledge is a crucial component for making meaning during reading. Both students' ability to build background knowledge and teachers' ability to assess it has been interrupted by the disruptions in schooling caused by an extended pandemic (e.g., Zierer, 2021). However, there are some mistakes to avoid when it comes to building and activating background knowledge.

- **Failing to identify what background knowledge is necessary for students to access in upcoming units of instruction.** Planning processes should identify what content knowledge and skills are needed such that students are able to benefit from new learning.
- **Adopting a remediation approach to building necessary background knowledge.** A study of two million math students in grades 3 to 5 found that classrooms that used an acceleration approach to build necessary background knowledge completed 27% more grade-level work (TNTP, 2021). How was this accomplished? Teachers identified the background knowledge students would need for a unit of study, taught specific lessons from the previous grade level to build background knowledge, and then pivoted to grade-level appropriate instruction. Doing this requires a revised scope and sequence that allows for a few days of background knowledge instruction on what students need to know (not what's neat to know) such that you can rapidly move back into grade-level instruction.
- **Making assumptions about what students don't know.** This is especially treacherous territory that puts multilingual learners, BIPOC students, and students with disabilities at risk. These students come with assets, cultural knowledge, and experiences that may be unfamiliar to you. Take the time to engage with students to learn about what they know, and be open to understanding your content in new ways.

What steps do you want to take to avoid these mistakes?

Mistakes to Avoid	What I Can Do to Avoid Them
Overlooking what background knowledge students need to access grade-level content	
Remediating rather than accelerating	
Making assumptions about what students know and do not know	

Anticipation Guides

Each of the modules in this book begins with an anticipation guide, and for good reason—an anticipation guide is an effective way to address misconceptions students may have. In addition, using an anticipation guide with students can give you insight about what they already know (Tierney et al., 1995). From the standpoint of activation of background knowledge, anticipation guides can "prime the pump" by introducing questions in the minds of learners. There is mounting evidence that "errorful learning" matched with an "analysis of the reasoning leading up to the mistake" improves memory and retrieval of new knowledge (Metcalfe, 2017, p. 465).

From the standpoint of activation of background knowledge, anticipation guides can "prime the pump" by introducing questions in the minds of learners.

Use an anticipation guide near the beginning of a lesson or unit of instruction. It gives you formative evaluation data to plan your instruction, and it draws the learners' attention to assumptions they hold.

To create and use an **Anticipation Guide**,

- Devise five or so statements constructed for true/false responses.
- Deliver the questions verbally, or present them as a written handout.
    - Variation: Pose statements verbally to younger students, and ask them to give you a thumbs up/thumbs down hand signal (held close to their chest so it's only you that sees).
    - Variation: Use digital polling to get a sense of what it is students know or believe they know.
- Don't grade them: Use anticipation guides as a barometer of class understandings and as prompts for an initial discussion of the topic at hand.
- Follow up: Often, it's useful to pose the same statements again near the end of the lesson or unit, when students can provide justification for true statements and reasons for why false statements are incorrect. This provides you with excellent pre/post quantitative data, as well as qualitative information about the extent to which the learner understands key concepts.

Jon Cato prepared an anticipation guide for his sixth-grade students, who would be reading informational and narrative passages about ancient Egypt (see Figure 7.2). "I want to whet their appetite, but I also want an early heads-up about what they know or think they know. As I meet with the groups, I ask them about the content, of course. But I also want them to source their information," said Mr. Cato. "It ties together the claims, evidence, and reasoning work that we're doing as part of their argumentative reading and writing."

Figure 7.2 Ancient Egypt Anticipation Guide

<table>
<tr><th colspan="2">Before Reading</th><th colspan="2">Statements</th><th colspan="2">After Reading</th></tr>
<tr><td>T</td><td>F</td><td colspan="2">1. Egyptian hieroglyphics are a secret code.</td><td>T</td><td>F</td></tr>
<tr><td colspan="3">Why did you indicate true or false?</td><td colspan="3">Has your thinking changed after reading?</td></tr>
<tr><td>T</td><td>F</td><td colspan="2">2. Education was valued for both boys and girls.</td><td>T</td><td>F</td></tr>
<tr><td colspan="3">Why did you indicate true or false?</td><td colspan="3">Has your thinking changed after reading?</td></tr>
<tr><td>T</td><td>F</td><td colspan="2">3. Ancient Egyptians worshipped cats.</td><td>T</td><td>F</td></tr>
<tr><td colspan="3">Why did you indicate true or false?</td><td colspan="3">Has your thinking changed after reading?</td></tr>
<tr><td>T</td><td>F</td><td colspan="2">4. Upper Egypt is in the northern part of the country, and Lower Egypt is in the south.</td><td>T</td><td>F</td></tr>
<tr><td colspan="3">Why did you indicate true or false?</td><td colspan="3">Has your thinking changed after reading?</td></tr>
<tr><td>T</td><td>F</td><td colspan="2">5. Ancient Egyptians were thankful for the annual flooding of the Nile.</td><td>T</td><td>F</td></tr>
<tr><td colspan="3">Why did you indicate true or false?</td><td colspan="3">Has your thinking changed after reading?</td></tr>
</table>

PS: Answers to the sixth-grade anticipation guide are F, T, F, F, T.

TAKE ACTION

Plan an anticipation guide for an upcoming unit of instruction. Consider misconceptions your students typically have about the topic. Intersperse false statements with true ones. What percentage of your students do you predict will answer incorrectly in advance of instruction?

Item	True/False?	Percentage Predicted to Answer Incorrectly Before Instruction
1.		
2.		
3.		
4.		
5.		

TEXT-TO-SELF CONNECTION

What key background knowledge (skills and concepts) do students in your grade level need in order to access grade-level content?

____

____

____

Do you and your planning team identify background knowledge needed for students to access grade-level units of instruction?

____

____

____

Using the traffic light scale, with red being not confident, yellow being somewhat confident, and green indicating very confident, how confident are you in your ability to

- Build and activate background knowledge?

- Integrate background knowledge with other reading comprehension skills?

Takeaways

- Background knowledge isn't just a list of facts. Our instruction can help children organize and retrieve background knowledge to use as they read and learn.
- More skilled readers are able to use their background knowledge to make inferences, generate questions, and elaborate on what they are learning.
- Students who don't have sufficient background knowledge devote more attention to trying to make meaning of the text, leaving them with fewer cognitive resources to store information.

PS: Answers to the anticipation guide are F, T, T, F.

online resources

Visit the companion website at
resources.corwin.com/teachingreading
for this module's downloadable resources.

MODULE

8

Vocabulary Knowledge

In this module, we will

- Link vocabulary development to language comprehension and word recognition.
- Explain differences in types of vocabulary to support selection.
- Discuss a decision-making frame for selecting vocabulary to teach.
- Demonstrate practices for fostering explicit and incidental vocabulary acquisition.
- Consider vocabulary assessments that inform our instructional practices.

Photo by CDC on Unsplash

It's after lunch in Mario's third-grade class and time for social studies. Mario is previewing a worksheet that features 10 vocabulary terms related to geography, including *cardinal directions, poles, equator, geography, latitude, longitude, map key, legend, hemisphere,* and *compass rose*. His task is to alphabetize the list, write definitions for each word, and then use each in a sentence. Like many of his classmates, Mario spends 15 minutes diligently looking up the words online and in the textbook's glossary before cobbling together the definitions. He adapts the first meaning presented in the dictionary for the word *legend*: "A story from the past."

He then wrote a sentence containing the word *legend*:

The legend of the coyote was told by Indigenous people.

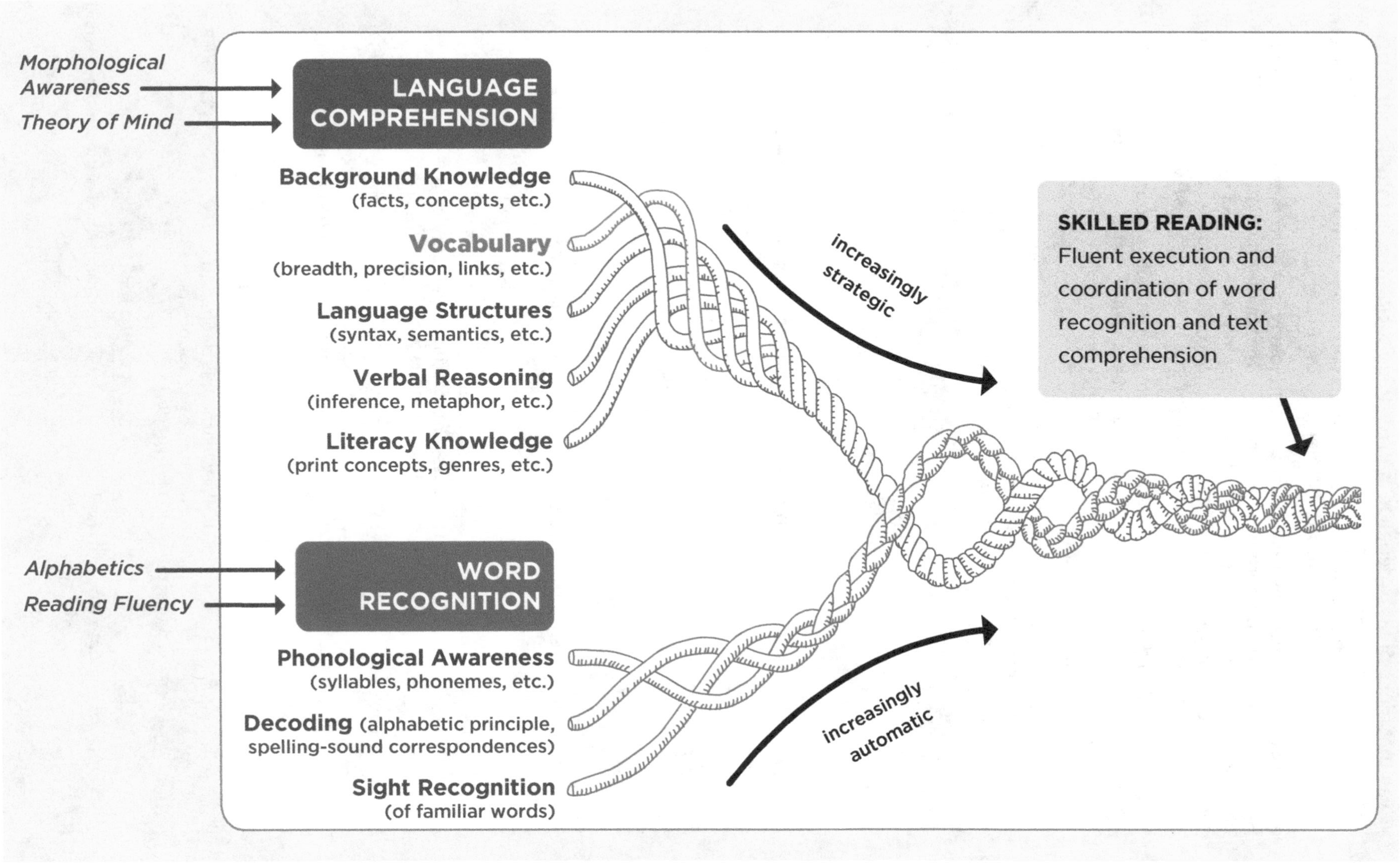

Source: Adapted from Scarborough, H. S. (2001). Connecting early language and literacy to later reading (dis)abilities: Evidence, theory, and practice. In S. Neuman & D. Dickinson (Eds.), *Handbook for research in early literacy* (pp. 97–110). Guilford Press.

Given that much of his experience in third-grade social studies thus far has focused on native peoples in his state, the definition and sentence are reasonable guesses. Mario slogs through the rest of the task, completing definitions and sentences for the other nine words designed to introduce students to the unit.

It's not surprising that the task did not get Mario any closer to mastering the content standards focused on geography. Nor did this vocabulary task prepare him for the reading he was expected to complete, the mapping skills he was expected to develop, or his participation in the classroom discussions. The vocabulary work took class time but did not scaffold his understanding of content in any significant way.

Quite frankly, we don't have this time to waste on ineffective approaches. Vocabulary knowledge is critical, and students need an intentional vocabulary effort that is part of the overall classroom experience, rather than a series of random activities to episodically engage them in word learning.

Read each statement and mark **T** if the statement is true and **F** if the statement is false. As you read through the module, you might change your responses. Be prepared to explain your responses and use the text for evidence.

<table>
<tr><th colspan="2">Before Reading</th><th colspan="2">Statements</th><th colspan="2">After Reading</th></tr>
<tr><td>T</td><td>F</td><td colspan="2">1. Vocabulary knowledge is strongly associated with comprehension.</td><td>T</td><td>F</td></tr>
<tr><td colspan="3">Why did you indicate true or false?</td><td colspan="3">Has your thinking changed after reading?</td></tr>
<tr><td>T</td><td>F</td><td colspan="2">2. Vocabulary is best taught through direct instruction.</td><td>T</td><td>F</td></tr>
<tr><td colspan="3">Why did you indicate true or false?</td><td colspan="3">Has your thinking changed after reading?</td></tr>
<tr><td>T</td><td>F</td><td colspan="2">3. The process for selecting vocabulary is idiosyncratic to the teacher.</td><td>T</td><td>F</td></tr>
<tr><td colspan="3">Why did you indicate true or false?</td><td colspan="3">Has your thinking changed after reading?</td></tr>
<tr><td>T</td><td>F</td><td colspan="2">4. Vocabulary learning is deepened when students have opportunities to produce language.</td><td>T</td><td>F</td></tr>
<tr><td colspan="3">Why did you indicate true or false?</td><td colspan="3">Has your thinking changed after reading?</td></tr>
</table>

What Is Vocabulary Knowledge?

Vocabulary knowledge is a crucial bridging process that joins language comprehension and word recognition. To "know a word" means that a person develops a representation using the phonological skills to recognize the word, and a semantic representation to know what it means. It's not one or the other, however. Learning a word requires the joint development of word recognition and language comprehension.

Learning a word requires the joint development of word recognition and language comprehension.

Let's take on language comprehension first. Vocabulary is among the strongest predictors of reading comprehension (Baumann et al., 2003). Vocabulary knowledge is especially important when it comes to understanding informational texts and appears to have an interesting relationship with reading motivation (Liebfreund, 2021). There's a reason vocabulary knowledge is so influential when it comes to reading: words and phrases serve as labels for the concepts we understand. A reader who knows the concepts represented by the academic vocabulary in a text is likely to be more intrinsically motivated to read the passage.

Vocabulary knowledge also influences and is influenced by the reader's word recognition knowledge. These include the ability to discern the sounds of language and bolt them onto the letters of the language (phonics). Learning a new word or phrase is more efficient when both the meaning and the form are presented (Adlof & Patten, 2017).

NOTES

What Does It Mean to Know a Word?

Vocabulary knowledge is discussed it two ways: breadth and depth (see Figure 8.1). It goes hand-in-hand with schema, which we explored in the previous module. How many words does the learner know, and how well does the learner know the words? Beck et al. (2002) make an important distinction between shallow and deeper word knowledge. Shallow word knowledge refers to memorizing definitions of words without understanding them at a deeper conceptual level. If students have deep word knowledge, they understand the concept(s) the word represents, and they can use the word flexibly in a variety of contexts. They can acquire this depth of understanding if they are actively engaged in the repeated, gradual learning of vocabulary in rich instructional contexts (Blachowicz & Fisher, 2000).

Figure 8.1 Breadth and Depth in Vocabulary

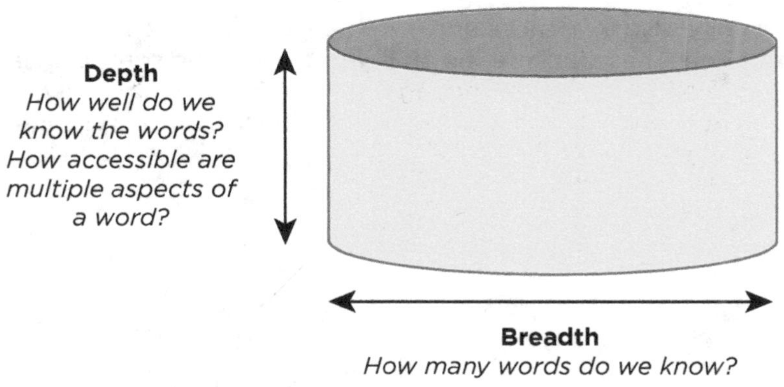

Source: Stahl et al. (2008).

NOTES

Types of Vocabulary

Over the past two decades, a great deal of agreement has been reached about vocabulary instruction. In general, experts agree that there are three types of words that students need to know. Beck et al. (2002) identify these as Tier 1, Tier 2, and Tier 3 words. Others, such as Vacca and Vacca (2007), identify these words as general, specialized, and technical, respectively. If Mario's teacher had used this classification system, the words she selected might appear in these categories.

General (Tier 1) Words	Specialized (Tier 2) Words	Technical (Tier 3) Words
(none for the words chosen for instruction but many in the readings themselves)	legend	cardinal direction
	poles	hemisphere
		compass rose
		equator
		geography
		latitude
		longitude
		map key

GENERAL VOCABULARY

The general vocabulary or Tier 1 words that are basic for reading. These words are typically in the spoken vocabulary of most students and are typically acquired through interactions with other people and texts. Unfortunately, in many classrooms, too much instructional time is devoted to instruction for words students can learn in other ways. These words develop as students read and are read to. General vocabulary words are not conceptually difficult but may require explicit instruction for very young children as well as emergent multilingual learners.

In many classrooms, too much instructional time is devoted to instruction for words students can learn in other ways.

SPECIALIZED VOCABULARY

Tier 2 or specialized words are those high-utility terms that often change meaning in different contexts. They can confuse readers and are significantly undertaught in most classrooms. This category also includes words for which students know some part of the meaning but do not have mastery of the complexity of the word's meaning. Importantly, these words are critical for understanding. Imagine the student who is working with the word *expression* as it relates to a character's expression in a piece of fiction. Later that day, the student might be expected to write an *expression* during math. Mario's teacher acknowledged that these words were critical for understanding the content but failed to recognize the role that multiple meanings and contexts play on words such as *legend*.

TECHNICAL VOCABULARY

Tier 3 or technical words are bound to a specific discipline. These are the "sexy" content words that teachers love to focus on: *photosynthesis*, *pointillism*, *hieroglyphic*, *metaphor*, *parallelogram,* and so on. Sometimes these words need to be directly taught, but they are best learned when coupled with lots of opportunities to use them in reading, discussion, and writing. The decision to teach the word versus explain the word should be based on the future utility of the word and its relative importance in facilitating or blocking understanding.

Again, conceptual difficulty plays a role in what gets taught, and how. The term *parallelogram* represents an intricate knowledge set in mathematics and defies simple definitional instruction, especially due to its contrastive concepts, *quadrilateral* and *rhombus*. By contrast, it is possible to teach *pointillism* through definition—it is a painting method that uses very small colored dots to create a larger image. There are additional concepts that represent a deepening schema to pointillism: It uses primary colors to fool the eye into believing there are secondary colors, and George Seurat is a major artist associated with the technique. However, goals of recall, recognition, application, and precision influence the extent to which an art teacher spends on instruction. Most obviously, the important words to teach are those that are critical for understanding the text or the content.

NOTICE AND WONDER

Reflect on your context and practices as they relate to tiers of vocabulary. Tier 2 words are often undertaught relative to Tier 3 words. What types of words are highlighted in your curricular materials? How might you increase the number of Tier 2 words you teach?

NOTES

Choosing Words

The oft-quoted statistics about vocabulary knowledge are daunting. Nagy and Anderson (1984) estimated that by the time students enter high school, they need to know 88,500 word families. The researchers arrived at this figure by analyzing printed school materials, and they developed a six-point scale that ranged from semantically transparent to semantically opaque words. For example, *teacup* is quite semantically transparent, meaning that the word parts—*tea* and *cup*—are quite literal. In contrast, *honeymoon* is semantically opaque, as simply taking apart the term isn't going to reveal what the actual meaning is. *Blueberry* is semantically transparent, while *strawberry* is not. Semantically transparent words are readily understandable (a *cup* that holds *tea*) and are easier to decode. Semantically opaque words (what do *honey* and *moon* have to do with a post-wedding trip?) are also more challenging to decode, let alone understand (Kim et al., 2019).

By the time students enter high school, they need to know 88,500 word families.

Many word families transcend more than one category. Therefore, knowing the Latin root *port* can be easily transformed into knowing *portable* and *airport*, but *import, portly,* and *transport* might prove to be a bit more challenging. The majority of word families (about 54,000) contain semantically opaque words, many of which are encountered primarily in reading but not in everyday speech. Semantically opaque words and phrases can be especially confounding for English learners. Doug recalls a meeting about an upcoming overnight school trip in which a student was advised to wear shower sandals to prevent athlete's foot. "But I would like to have the foot of an athlete," responded this budding soccer player.

It is impossible to directly teach each and every word to students. There isn't enough time, and besides, doing so would not allow learners to develop word-solving skills. But choosing the "hard" words in a text and teaching those is also ineffective. Instead, use a decision-making framework (Frey & Fisher, 2009). The bullet list that follows represents such a framework; it is drawn from the work of Graves and Slater (1996). (See Figure 8.2 for a visual portrait of this decision-making model.)

1. **Representative: It is essential to understand the text?** It's hard to imagine understanding a science textbook passage about the *solar system* without understanding what that phrase means.
2. **Repeatability: Will this word be used again in the text or lesson?** If the answer is yes, it might be worth teaching directly. But hold off until you consider the questions about contextual and structural analysis.
3. **Transportable: Can this be used in other subjects?** Tier 2 words are sometimes neglected because no single discipline owns them. Yet words like *verify, label,* and *examine* have a high degree of usefulness across subjects.
4. **Contextual analysis: Can students arrive at the meaning through context?** If the answer is yes, this might be a great word-solving opportunity that need not be wasted on direct instruction.
5. **Structural analysis: Can students arrive at meaning through structure?** For semantically transparent words, word derivations and morphological analysis (units of meaning) can be used to break a word apart. *Teacup* and *transportation,* for instance, might be developmentally appropriate words for your students to take apart. We'll dive further into teaching for morphological analysis in the next module.

How many words are reasonable to teach directly? Once you have arrived at a selection of words and phrases to teach directly, consider the cognitive load. It is a judgment call, to be sure. However, two to five words is probably sufficient for a short reading in one lesson.

Figure 8.2 A Decision-Making Model for Selected Targeted Vocabulary Words and Phrases

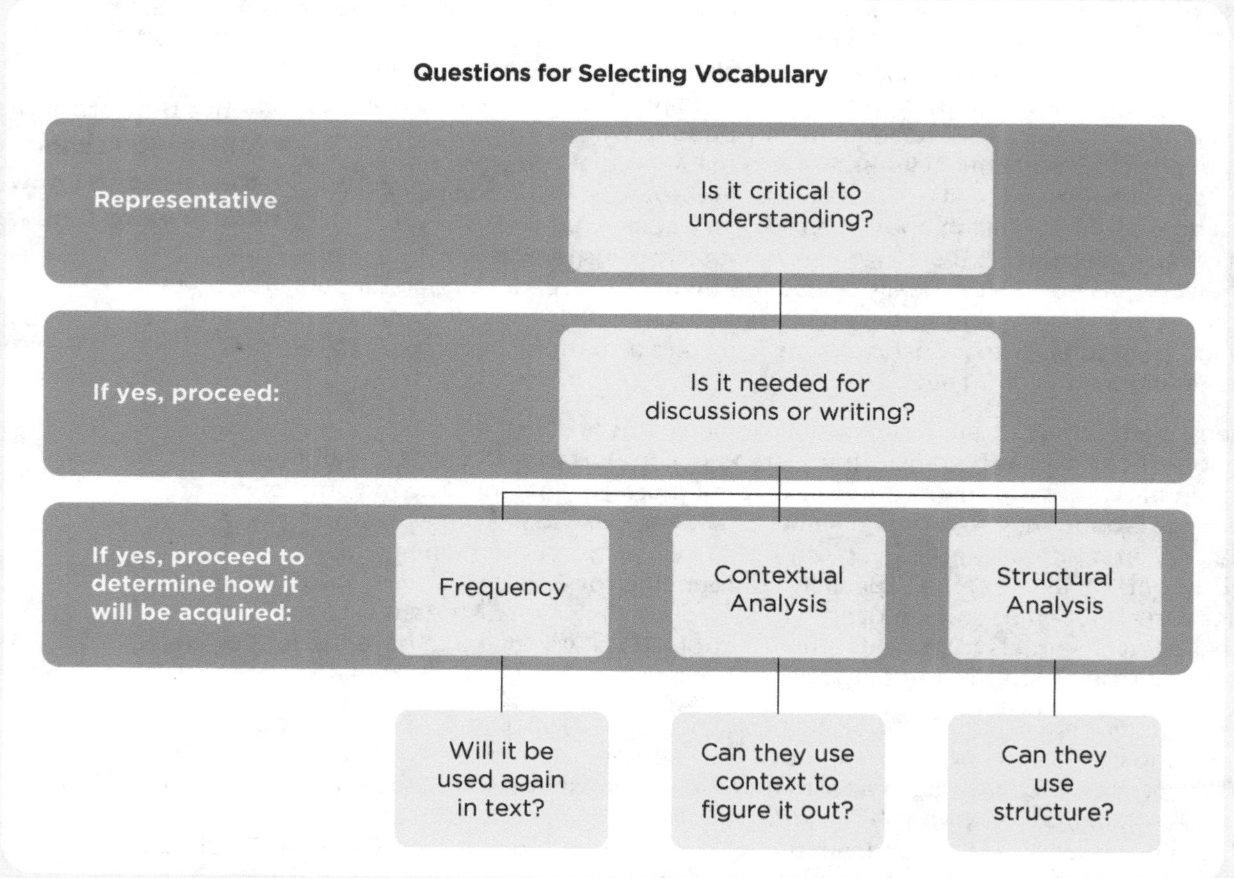

Source: Fisher et al. (2021).

FIND THE MISTAKES

Despite volumes of research on vocabulary development and instruction, misconceptions exist. Here are five common mistakes to avoid.

1. **Assigning words for students to look up in the dictionary.** These resources are useful when you know something about the word but are often too complex for a person completely new to the term.

2. **Believing that using a word in a sentence is sufficient.** This is only one dimension of vocabulary learning. Most students can pull off a superficial sentence using a term. But can they use it in authentic writing?

3. **Mistaking recognition for understanding.** Matching and multiple-choice tasks tell you that students have a superficial knowledge of the word, which is a good start. But the true measure is when they produce it in their spoken and written language.

4. **Failing to cycle back to previously taught words.** Keep vocabulary alive by periodically returning to words learned in past weeks or months. Use these opportunities to link to other vocabulary they are learning or experiences they have had.
5. **Failing to teach for word nuances**. Relatively few words have true synonyms and antonyms. Make sure that students are learning about the shades of meaning of a set of words. For example, *rage, anger,* and *annoyance* represent a range of emotions, but are not the same.

What other errors have you encountered in vocabulary instruction, either as a student or a teacher? Are there ineffective practices you used in the past but have now abandoned? Why?

NOTES

Explicit Versus Incidental Vocabulary Teaching and Learning

Vocabulary knowledge is acquired both directly and indirectly. There are many words and phrases that students learn due to the explicit instruction afforded by their teachers. Methods for doing so typically include any number of routines that promote understanding of word meanings and their parts, pronunciations, and usage in oral and written language. In the section that follows, we will discuss several routines that promote word learning. Having said that, effective vocabulary routines possess these characteristics:

- They are multimodal and support students' visual and auditory skills to internalize the words and phrases selected.
- They provide students with opportunities to produce language through speaking and/or writing.
- They allow for multiple exposures to the words and phrases to encourage application and transfer of learning.
- The routines are just that: routines, not novelties. Students develop a familiarity with the routines chosen such that less time is needed for instructions while more time can be dedicated to instruction.

Importantly, students also learn vocabulary through incidental exposures. Many words and phrases are rarely spoken but occur more commonly in texts. Children making expected progress typically grow their vocabulary by about 3,000 words per year, and as Adams (1990) notes, "This order of growth cannot be ascribed to their classroom instruction, nor could it be attained through any feasible program of classroom instruction" (p. 172). Students who read more often are exposed to more words, and many of these words slip into their vocabulary. A fifth grader who reads for 15 minutes a day outside of school is exposed to an additional 600,000 words per year; a classmate who reads for only one minute a day gains exposure to only 8,000 additional words (Anderson et al., 1988). Little wonder that a large-scale study of first- and fourth-grade classrooms reported that the most effective classrooms ensured that students had eyes on text for a cumulative 90 minutes a day (Allington & Johnston, 2002; Pressley et al., 2001). The opportunity to read throughout the day—during shared readings, small-group instruction, and collaborative tasks; from textbooks; and during independent reading—results in gains in vocabulary knowledge. Figure 8.3 summarizes these methods.

Figure 8.3 Indirect and Direct Word Learning

Indirect Word Learning	Incidental vocabulary learning	New words are learned through the context of the students' environment, including listening and reading tasks.	• Notice and discuss unfamiliar words during daily interactions with students. • Use new words in songs, chants, or rhymes and in interactions with others. • Ask students to read books that introduce new words.
Direct Word Learning	Explicit vocabulary teaching and learning	Words are learned as teachers clearly demonstrate or explain what a word means and show students how to solve for unknown words.	• Provide direct instruction in pronunciation, word meanings, parts of speech, etc. • Use videos, discussions, pictures, and examples to expose students to the new word. • Demonstrate how readers actively solve the meanings of unknown words. • Engage in activities that require students to use the new word.

Source: Adapted from Iris Center (n.d.).

NOTES

Instruction in Vocabulary Knowledge

DIRECT INSTRUCTION OF VOCABULARY

You've read the text that you have chosen for your upcoming lesson. You've selected the vocabulary terms that students need to know and determined that some of the words are going to require some direct instruction and modeling by you. But where to begin? It should come as no surprise that having a structure for instruction and modeling is going to increase the effectiveness of your instruction. Tennyson and Cocchiarella (1986) outlined a five-step structure for teachers to use to systematically introduce students to words using direct instruction. We'll use the word *analyze* to illustrate the process (Fisher et al., 2020).

1. **Label and define.** Students first need to be able to attach a short meaning and a label to an unfamiliar word. The teacher might pause to say, "*Analyze* means to look at something carefully so you can solve a problem."
2. **Contextualize.** After defining, ground the word or phrase within the author's use. "I'm going to reread that sentence now. 'The police detective analyzed the crime scene for clues.' Since *analyze* means to look closely to solve a problem, I know she's trying to figure out what happened."
3. **Give a best example.** Link the word to something they might already know. "Some of you have told me about your use of Fortnite analysis videos on YouTube to improve your online gaming skills. You're not just watching. You're solving problems to get better at the game."
4. **Elaborate on attributes.** Contrastive examples help students understand what it is *not*. "When someone is analyzing something, they're breaking it apart into smaller pieces, so they can look more closely to understand. A police detective that wasn't looking carefully wouldn't be able to analyze the scene."
5. **Provide strategy information.** Tell students a strategy you used to figure out the word. "I've heard this word used before on other TV crime shows. So, I thought about how it was used and then made a connection to the story we're reading now."

Leticia DeLeón uses the same approach with her second-grade learners. "They're soaking up lots of new vocabulary. But I want to make sure I follow a familiar pathway for them to be able to make the most of my instruction." Ms. DeLeón identified the term *mysterious*, as a target word in the book, *Hey, Water!* (Portis, 2019). It appeared in the sentence, "Ocean—you cover most of the earth—salty, surging, and mysterious." After reading the sentence, she says, "Mysterious means something that is unknown and hidden" [label and define].

She writes it on the board, then rereads the sentence, commenting, "I think that the author is using that word because she wants me to understand that I can only see the surface of the water, but not what is below" [contextualize].

Ms. DeLeón then anchors the new word to something they already know. "We read a mystery about Cam Jansen trying to figure out who stole the diamond jewelry. That type of story is called a mystery, because the reader doesn't know the answer until the end of the book. Let me write that word on the board so you can see how similar they are" [best example]. "When something is not mysterious, it is known to the person. An ocean probably would not be mysterious to a creature who lived in it" [elaborates on attributes].

She finishes her direct instruction by saying, "I figured out that word by thinking about a similar word I already knew. Since I knew *mystery*, it helped me figure out *mysterious*" [strategy information].

Word Solving: Developing Habits for Analyzing and Understanding Words

In addition to the direct instruction of target vocabulary words, readers use specific actions to figure out the meaning of unknown words. Teachers model word solving so that it becomes a habit for students to look inside words and look outside words to determine what those words mean. Reading is an active process that requires monitoring understanding and deploying strategies, as needed, to make sense of the text. We have organized teacher modeling of word-solving strategies into three components: context clues, morphology and word parts, and resources. To demonstrate each of these, we'll look inside Amanda Hart's third-grade classroom.

TEACHER MODELING OF WORD-SOLVING STRATEGIES

Context Clues

One of the ways that readers figure out unknown words is with context clues. This is an example of an outside-the-word strategy. The goal of modeling context clues is to provide students with enough examples so that they can use this approach independently. Of course, context clues don't work 100% of the time, and students need examples of when this approach fails and what else they can do. Before we consider when to use context clues, let's note when they don't work. **Misdirective** context clues are those in which the reader would assume an incorrect definition from the words surrounding the target or unknown word. A **nondirective** context clue is of little or no assistance to the reader. These clues fail to help the reader make meaning. **General** context clues provide readers with some information, but not a level of detail that would allow them to identify specific nuances or connotations of the words. Thankfully, there is a type of context clue that really helps the reader: a **directive** one. These clues provide readers with information that they can use to determine the word's meaning, and even the nuances of the word, from reading around the word. Modeling the five ways in which authors provide context clues helps students develop their skill in using context to discover words and their meanings. We'll use text written at an adult level so you can see how context clues help us understand less familiar words.

The goal of modeling context clues is to provide students with enough examples so that they can use this approach independently.

1. **Definition/Explanation Clues.** The most obvious clue occurs when the author explains the word immediately after its use. For example,

   Access to clean water would ameliorate, and improve upon, living conditions within the village.

2. **Restatement/Synonym Clues.** Using this clue, authors provide a restatement or synonym of a harder word. For example,

   Access to clean water would ameliorate living conditions within the village such that life would be tolerable for the people who live there.

3. **Contrast/Antonym Clues.** These clues provide a contrast for the target word such that readers infer the word's meaning while reading. For example,

   Access to clean water would ameliorate living conditions within the village. However, a continued reliance on a polluted river will exacerbate a bad situation.

4. **Inference/General Context Clues.** Sometimes a word or phrase is not immediately clarified within the sentence. Relationships that are not directly

apparent are inferred or implied. The reader must look for clues before or after the sentence in which the word is used. For example.

Access to clean water would ameliorate living conditions within the village. Clean water would make life tolerable, as residents could focus on other pressing needs such as finding food and shelter.

5. **Punctuation Clues.** Readers can also use punctuation and font style to infer word meanings. Quotation marks (showing the word has a special meaning), dashes, parentheses, or brackets (enclosing a definition), and italics (showing the word will be defined) all help readers determine what the word means in the given context.

   Access to clean water would ameliorate—make tolerable—living conditions within the village.

For example, Ms. Hart read aloud to her third-grade students and modeled context clues after reading the following passage from *The Incredible Journey* (Burnford, 2018/1961):

> It would have been impossible to find three more contented animals that night. They lay curled closely together in a hollow filled with sweet-scented needles, under an aged, spreading balsam tree, near the banks of the stream. The old dog had his beloved cat, warm and purring between his paws again, and he snored in deep contentment. The young dog, their gently worried leader, had found his charge again. He could continue with a lighter heart. (p. 101)

Pausing, the teacher commented, "I appreciate how the author reminded me about the word *contented*. 'It would have been impossible to find three more contented animals that night.' I know from the sentences that follow it that she's using the word to mean that the animals are satisfied with the way things are right now. They're not quite happy, but they're also not scared. I have this image in my mind that they're all safe again and that they'll continue the journey after they have a little rest."

Structural: Morphology and Word Parts

In addition to looking outside words for clues about their meanings, students need models of looking inside words to determine meaning. We can ensure that students apply this strategy on their own by providing examples of how to use morphology and word parts. We're using morphology here in the linguistic sense, to mean the smallest meaningful units of language. For example, adding an -s to the end of many words adds meaning (more than one), as in *dog* becoming *dogs*. But morphology is more complex than that. In addition to prefixes and suffixes, morphology also includes knowledge of word derivations. English is a language system that draws from many other languages, so Latin and Greek root words play a significant part in determining the meaning of a word. Teaching students to look inside words for their morphology and word parts requires a sophisticated knowledge of the language. Because of its vital role in reading, we'll place more detailed attention on building students' morphological awareness in the next module. Having said that, we use knowledge of word parts as a way of getting to unknown words.

Third-grade teacher Ms. Hart used an inside-the-word strategy while modeling during a science lesson. This is a form of structural analysis to allow readers to break a word down into its meaningful parts. In this case, she used a cognate, which is a word from another language that has a similar meaning and spelling. Many of her students come from Spanish-speaking homes, so she uses cognates when appropriate. For example, when she came across the word *carnivore* while reading, she said, "I remember that *carne* is a Spanish word for meat, as in *carne asada*. I also know that *-vore* means that it is about eating. So, I can easily figure out that a *carnivore* is a meat eater. That's different from *herbivore*, which I remember because herb is a plant. It's also different from *omnivore*. *Omni-* means everything or all, so an omnivore eats both plants and meat."

Resources

When the first two approaches fail—context and word parts—teachers model the use of resources. These take readers even further outside the word to determine meaning. Commonly, teachers use peer resources, dictionaries, and the internet in their modeled quests for figuring out word meanings. For example, Ms. Hart modeled using a peer when she called the teacher next door to ask about word *cirrostratus* as it was presented in the sentence "Soon, the blue sky begins to fill up with milky veils of cirrostratus clouds, formed lower down on the front" (Farndon, 2007, p. 36). The teacher next door replied on speaker phone and described a very interesting type of cloud, one that is "almost transparent with a whitish veil of fibrous, almost hair-like, appearance. These clouds usually cover the whole sky and often produce a halo phenomenon. These clouds are made of ice crystals and are thin. These clouds are in high altitudes, usually between 20,000 and 40,000 feet." Thanking her colleague, Ms. Hart added, "I'm never embarrassed to ask a friend about a word. Now I know the word and can help another person. I want to find this kind of cloud and see what else it offers."

WHAT'S YOUR ADVICE?

You are the supervising teacher to a student teacher from the local university. Their reading instructor has been teaching them about vocabulary instruction, but the student teacher is still clinging to the way they were taught in elementary school years ago: a weekly list of words to look up, define, and use in a sentence, followed by a test. What do you want to model for them so that they can apply research-based practices?

NOTES

Routines That Allow Students to Practice and Use Vocabulary

To consolidate their word knowledge, students must use the target vocabulary in their interactions with others as well as in their writing. There are any number of routines and techniques that allow students to do this. What we have learned is that students grow bored when the same vocabulary instructional strategies are used too often. Thus, teachers need a lot of ideas for encouraging students to use the words they are learning.

First-grade teacher Angel Zavala provides her students with sentence frames that allow them to use their growing vocabulary in increasingly complex sentences. As she notes, "It's about apprenticing. They try on the frames using their new vocabulary and it starts to stick." For example, during their discussions about comparing two stories on the same topic, Ms. Zavala provides her students with the following sentence frames. As they discuss the stories, she listens to their vocabulary and notes terms they use and those that they do not use.

- __________ and __________ are the same/different because __________.
- The evidence I use to support __________ is __________.
- I agree __________ because __________.
- I disagree __________ because __________.

Consider the opportunities reciprocal teaching provides students to practice, use, and apply their vocabulary knowledge. Ruth Padilla's second-grade students were studying insects. A group of four students read an informational website for children about insect metamorphosis. During the reading and the reciprocal teaching discussion that followed, the students in this group experimented with several new ideas and new words. Some of the words they wrestled with were specialized terms. For example, *creature* is used generically on this informational website, whereas students think of creatures like scary monsters. The text also uses the term *order* in a scientific way, as in groupings.

In addition to using the specialized words, the students in this group used several technical, content-specific words, including *thorax*, *abdomen*, and *exoskeleton*. As evidence that they used these words in their discussions, consider the following excerpts from their conversation about the reading:

Bradley: But I thought a spider was an insect, 'cause my mom always says, "Kill that bug."

Micha: But they can't be insects. They're a different creature because they don't have the same 'xact parts, like it says here [points to text]. It's not the same order.

Janae: Yeah, insects gotta only have six legs, and spiders have eight.

Bradley: And they don't have the three body parts, only two. They don't have the thorax or abdomen. Do spiders have an exoskeleton?

Ms. Padilla had taught these words, but the reciprocal teaching routine provided students an opportunity to actually use the words.

As noted in Figure 8.4, there are specific vocabulary tasks that provide students opportunities to practice and learn new words. Some of these techniques have been discussed in previous modules.

Figure 8.4 Routines for Using Vocabulary and Academic Language

Technique	Definition	Example
Barrier Games	One partner has a picture or information that the other partner does not have. Students sit back-to-back or have a visual obstruction to block their view (barrier). Using oral language only, students communicate to complete the task.	Tasks may require partners to draw a picture, place objects in specific positions, or find the difference in two pictures. For example, students might describe positions on a map using directional vocabulary.
Concept Sort	Students sort words, phrases, or sentences into categories that relate to the concept they are studying. Sorting may be by category, sequence, characteristics, or something else.	Students sort descriptions of the major characters in a book based on whether they have positive, neutral, or negative connotations and meaning.
Frayer Model Cards	Using an index card divided into four quadrants, students (1) name the target word; (2) provide a definition in their own words; (3) identify a word that has the opposite meaning or is a nonexample of the target word; and (4) draw a picture to illustrate it. These are used as personal flashcards.	After developing their own Frayer cards, students practice using target words identified for a chapter book they are reading.
List-Group-Label	This is a prereading strategy similar to concept sorts, but categories (labels) are developed by the students rather than predetermined. Students brainstorm words they expect to encounter in a reading (list), and then group them based on similarities (group). Finally, they develop categories (labels) for the groups.	In advance of a reading about polar bears, students list words they expect to read, then sort them based on similar features, and then title the emerging categories.
Graphic Organizers and Word Maps	Students create visual displays of relationships between and among concepts and words. The purpose is to build schema and deepen knowledge.	Students build a graphic organizer that reflects the expository text structure of an article they are reading about birds of prey.

GRAPHIC ORGANIZERS

Graphic organizers are an opportunity for students to think, in words, about the content. They provide students a way of organizing information, again in words and sometimes images, in a way that helps them understand and remember. Looking through the lens of academic vocabulary development, we see that the power of graphic organizers lies in their ability to facilitate conversations among students. Students need to be taught several types of graphic organizers and then be encouraged to use an appropriate graphic organizer to visually represent information (again, almost always words).

To appreciate graphic organizers in action, let's turn to a discussion a group of second graders had about plant and animal life cycles. The group had selected a vocabulary word map, which is especially effective for helping students engage with and think about new terms or concepts in specific ways. (Other small groups used a timeline and a compare/contrast chart.) The key is the conversation that occurs as students complete the task, for it's here that academic vocabulary gets bandied about and refined by peers.

The group used a vocabulary Venn diagram graphic organizer highlighting the term *offspring*. Their task was to build a graphic organizer comparing and contrasting the offspring of birds and mammals, noting their similarities and differences. Here are a few of the comments made by group members as they constructed their Venn diagram:

Jeremy: Ms. Brown said that the babies look like their parents, but the baby chickens don't look like their mom.

Brian: But they do when they grow up. They have to get bigger first. The offspring grow up to look like the adults.

Natalie: Just like the puppies and kitties have to grow up to look like their mommy. Well not exactly like them. But kinda like them, like a mix of the mom and the dad.

Hunter: When my dog had babies, some looked more like her, but some looked like the dad.

Brian: But they all looked like dogs, right? They didn't look like cats because dogs can't have baby cats. That's the wrong offspring.

Natalie: But that's funny. What if a chicken had a baby cat!

Brian: That's crazy! It can't happen that way.

Natalie: I know, but it's funny to me.

In this brief excerpt, it's striking to see how this group of students used general, specialized, and technical vocabulary, isn't it? Notice how they incorporated words they'd encountered in texts and from their teacher into their own conversation. They clarified ideas and made connections with one another as they negotiated the task of creating the vocabulary graphic organizer. Again, the power is in the conversation, not the paper. Students need multiple opportunities such as this to build their academic vocabulary with their peers.

TAKE ACTION

Graphic organizers are an intermediate step to writing or discussion; they aren't the final destination. Examine the table below, and reflect on your uses of typical graphic organizers. Do you use them to support writing? To support discussion? If you don't currently use graphic organizers in your practice, how could you use them to support academic vocabulary development?

Type	Do you use it to support discussion?	Do you use it to support writing?	Ideas for Future Applications
Venn Diagram			
Compare-Contrast			
Cause and Effect			
T-Chart			
Sequence Chart			
Problem-Solution			

WORD MAPS

Deepen students' vocabulary knowledge by using word maps that challenge them to consider the nuances of words and phrases. A word map is a visual organizer that frames the various aspects of the word or phrase through definition and analogies. While graphic organizers typically foreground the concepts the terms represent, a word map draws students' attention to related categories, such as analogies that highlight the similarities between the word and an example. *Between* is the operative word—a word map assists students on the between-space of the ideas. In other words, the point with analogies is the comparison itself, as a form of verbal reasoning. (We will explore verbal reasoning in Module 12.)

Sixth-grade teacher Noel Lemieux uses word maps regularly to teach and formatively evaluate her students' vocabulary knowledge. She introduces the process during the first week of school, folding it in to her instruction on classroom procedures. "My classroom uses lots of collaborative learning, so we actually start off with defining what it means to work collaboratively," she said.

In her lesson on working collaboratively, she introduced a word map on a language chart (see Figure 8.5). Over the course of 30 minutes, the class co-constructed the map through discussion of the definition (*what is it?*) before moving to the more challenging task, which was developing analogies (*what is it like?*).

"That's where it gets interesting, because they have to dig deeper," said the teacher. This part of the discussion yielded three analogies:

- "It's like the pieces of a puzzle that fit together to make a picture."
- "It's like when everyone in a boat is rowing in the same direction."
- "It's like a school of fish that are all swimming together to keep each other safe from a predator."

They finalized their word map with classroom promises they could agree upon (*what are examples?*). "I hang up the word map for each period so that I can refer to the language we used to determine what it meant. Each class period is a little different, and I like to use their words," said Ms. Lemieux. "When I use the same kind of word map for content instruction, they already know how to develop them as a table or individually. It gives me a sense of how their knowledge is deepening in the terms we use."

Figure 8.5 Word Map

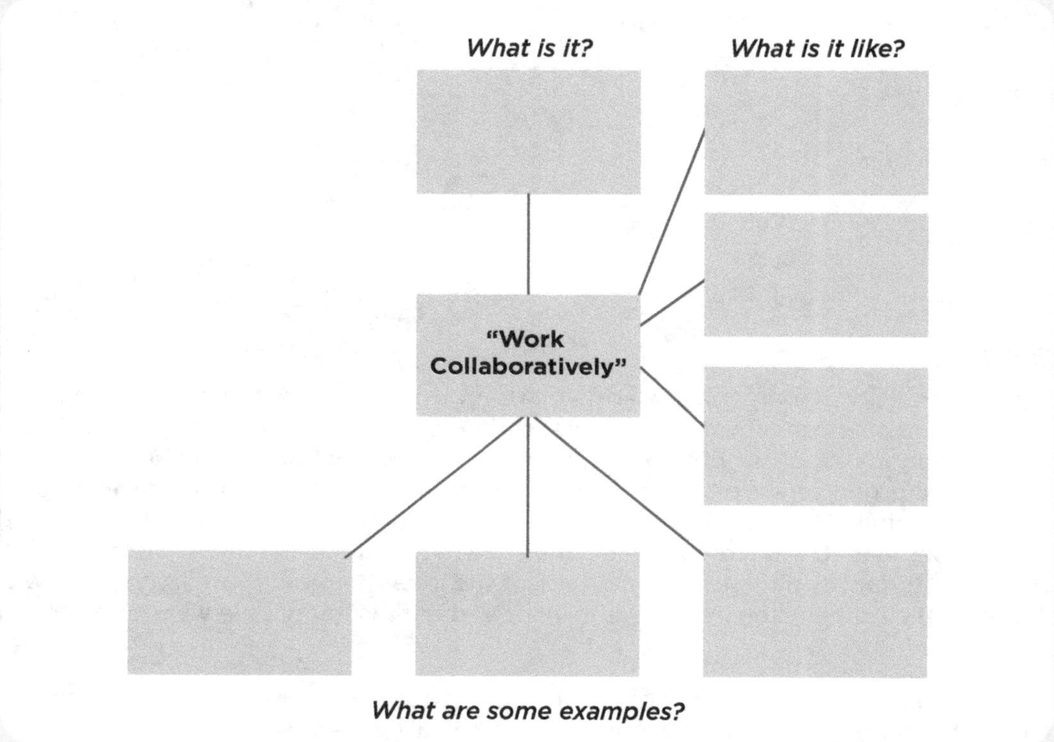

SEMANTIC FEATURE ANALYSIS

Semantic feature analysis (SFA) requires readers to consider the attributes of a set of related terms and to determine how they are similar to and different from one another (Bos & Anders, 1990). We like to think of this as a two-way sort, going both down the columns and across the rows. The process encourages students to think about the relationships between concepts and to determine whether particular attributes are a feature of the term. This approach is particularly useful with nouns.

The students in Gustavo Perez's fifth-grade class are studying natural disasters. They have read a lot, and some of their experiences were with specific types of disasters. The teacher used the semantic feature analysis as an ongoing notetaking device for his students to use throughout the science unit.

"I want them to be able to identify the characteristics of various natural disasters, but it can be confusing when we're studying so many of them," he said. "I have them use the SFA so that they can organize their schema around the meaning of each of these terms. It's really not useful information to them if they only learn definitions," the teacher continued. "I want them to be able to compare the features in terms of similarities and differences."

Yarely, one of his students, completed a version that can be found in Figure 8.6.

Figure 8.6 Yarely's Semantic Feature Analysis

Vocabulary Word/ Feature	Occurs in or Near Oceans	Occurs in Mountains	Occurs on Plains	Advance Warning System
Hurricane	+	–	–	+
Tsunami	+	–	–	+
Mudslide	+	+	–	–
Tornado	+	–	+	+
Earthquake	+	+	+	+
Wildfire	+	+	+	–
Flood	+	+	–	+
Drought	–	+	+	+

FIND THE MISTAKES

Yarely has made several meaning errors. What does this tell you about the vocabulary knowledge and attending schema this student has, and what might be the next steps to advance their learning?

Strengths: ____

____

Areas for Instructional Focus: ______________________________

____

TEXT-TO-SELF CONNECTION

This is a summary strategy called 3-2-1. What are three confirmations you had regarding vocabulary knowledge?

Confirmation 1: ___________________________________

Confirmation 2: ___________________________________

Confirmation 3: ___________________________________

What are two surprises about vocabulary knowledge you learned in this module?

Surprise 1: ___________________________________

Surprise 2: ___________________________________

What is one action you will take regarding vocabulary knowledge in your classroom?

Action 1: ___________________________________

Using the traffic light scale, with red being not confident, yellow being somewhat confident, and green indicating very confident, how confident are you in your ability to

- Build vocabulary knowledge?

- Teach students about using an inside-the-word/outside-the-word approach with unfamiliar vocabulary?

Takeaways

- Vocabulary knowledge is predictive of reading comprehension. Students with deep and broad vocabulary knowledge are likely to have a better understanding of the texts they read.
- Vocabulary acquisition comes through two channels: direct and indirect learning. Students acquire some vocabulary through reading and discussion. This is augmented with direct instruction of some words that are carefully selected.
- Vocabulary selection must include a balance of Tier 2 and Tier 3 words. Selection criteria include the extent to which a word represents important concepts, its repeatability, and its potential to be used for structural and contextual problem solving.
- Production is key to vocabulary knowledge. Words and phrases should be paired with ample opportunities to use them in discussion and in their writing.

PS: Answers to the anticipation guide are T, F, F, T.

online resources

Visit the companion website at
resources.corwin.com/teachingreading
for this module's downloadable resources.

MODULE

9

Morphological Awareness

Photo by Amy Humphries on Unsplash

In this module, we will

- Examine the research on and practical application of morphological awareness for readers.
- Utilize knowledge of affixes and Latin and Greek roots to build students' ability to resolve unknown or unfamiliar words.
- Explore suggested instructional sequences for teaching for morphological awareness.

Do you remember Mario, the third-grade student in the opening scenario of the previous module on vocabulary, who had difficulty with some of the map-related terms in his social studies reading? His teacher, Thomas Richland, observed many of his students making similar errors that school year. As a teacher who sees himself as a lifelong learner, he decided he needed to know more about vocabulary development. A major insight for him was in adding more explicit morphological awareness instruction in his classroom. When it came time to teach the same unit again the following year, Mr. Richland chose some different terms that would

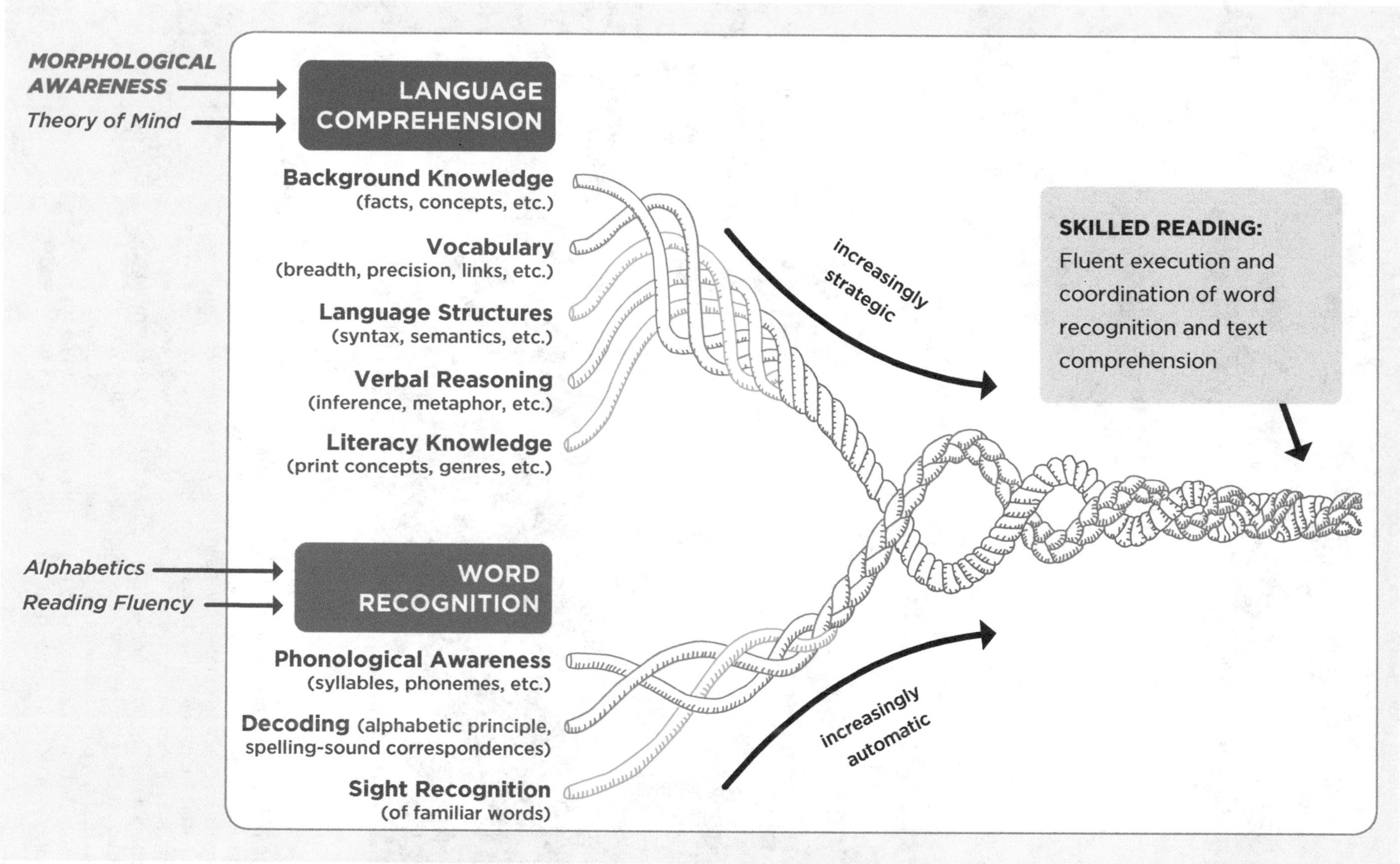

Source: Adapted from Scarborough, H. S. (2001). Connecting early language and literacy to later reading (dis)abilities: Evidence, theory, and practice. In S. Neuman & D. Dickinson (Eds.), *Handbook for research in early literacy* (pp. 97–110). Guilford Press.

be useful for fostering morphological awareness with his students. (Morphemes are the smallest units of meaning in words and include affixes as well as word parts that can unlock the meaning of a longer word.) The teacher spotlighted these words to use in his morphological instruction (see Figure 9.1).

Figure 9.1 Mr. Richland's Word Categories

Specialized (Tier 2) Words	Technical (Tier 3) Words
elevation	equator
position	geography
	hemisphere

"I selected these words because they give me the chance to reinforce and extend the vocabulary work we're doing during other parts of the day," he explained. "The *-ion* words are a great way to profile this suffix as a way to describe a process or action. I want to use *hemisphere* and *equator* to connect these to what they know from math about spheres and things being equal. And *geography* presents a nice opportunity for me to teach *geo-* as a referring to the Earth, and I could present *-graph* as something that is written. They already know *biography*, for instance."

Ellie, a student not yet making expected progress in her reading, is one example of students experiencing accelerated growth this year. "She's making some important gains this year, and the attention to morphological awareness is helping her with decoding new multisyllabic words while also figuring out their meaning."

Mr. Richland is seeking to foster an increasing ability in his students to draw on what they know about a word not only through word recognition but also by using their growing ability to analyze morphemes within the word to make meaning. This requires rapid shifts in thinking to draw on multiple thinking resources. We'll use a fancier term—*graphophonological-semantic cognitive flexibility* (Cartwright, 2007). Can you use your vocabulary knowledge and morphological awareness to formulate the meaning of that term? You know that the sounds of a language (phonemes) bolt on the written letters of the language (graphs). So *graphophonological* refers to the ability of readers to decode. *Semantic* refers, in this case, to the meaning of the words. *Graphophonological-semantic* is the further twining of the reading rope such that a reader can rapidly decode the word and draw on knowledge of the meaning of said word. *Cognitive flexibility* is a term used to describe what a reader does in a given moment, which is the rapid "processing of, and links between, these features of print" (p. 175).

Much like what we did with the new fluency and alphabetics strands, we have called out morphological awareness as an essential process. In Scarborough's original description, concepts related to morphological awareness, such as semantics and links to vocabulary, existed. However, morphological awareness has drawn considerable research and instructional attention in the decades since then.

Read each statement and mark **T** if you think the statement is true and **F** if you think the statement is false. As you read through the module, you might change your responses. Be prepared to explain your responses and use the text for evidence.

Before Reading	Statements	After Reading
T **F**	1. Morphology should be taught separately from other elements of instruction.	**T** **F**
Why did you indicate true or false?		Has your thinking changed after reading?
T **F**	2. Most students can acquire knowledge about prefixes and suffixes through wide reading.	**T** **F**
Why did you indicate true or false?		Has your thinking changed after reading?
T **F**	3. Morphological awareness extends into other aspects of literacy development, such as spelling.	**T** **F**
Why did you indicate true or false?		Has your thinking changed after reading?
T **F**	4. Effective morphology instruction relies on memorization and repetition.	**T** **F**
Why did you indicate true or false?		Has your thinking changed after reading?

NOTES

What Is Morphological Awareness?

Morphological awareness is a critical tool used by readers to analyze unknown or unfamiliar words. In fact, we'll do a little morphology on the term *morphological awareness* (MA). If you know that a morpheme is the smallest unit of meaning, then you'll understand that MA is being aware of the bite-sized chunks present in many words that can help to unlock their meanings. More formally, MA refers to "children's conscious awareness of the morphemic structure of words and their ability to reflect on and manipulate that structure" (Carlisle & Feldman, 1995, p. 194).

Morphological awareness is a critical tool used by readers to analyze unknown or unfamiliar words.

Morphology is an important dimension of vocabulary knowledge, as discussed in the previous module. You recall that we profiled a three-part model of how to teach problem solving for unknown words:

- Looking inside the word for structural clues.
- Looking outside the word for contextual clues.
- Looking outside the word to consult resources.

Morphological awareness is crucial for examining structural clues. The morphemes and attendant word parts can unlock the meaning of a word.

It is useful to have a shared understanding of the vocabulary of morphology, so, here's a glossary of terms we'll use throughout this module. The chart in Figure 9.2 offers quick definitions of morphology terms. We note that some linguists have somewhat different definitions of these terms, but we wanted to share the definitional meanings of terms we will use in this module. Investing in our own vocabulary about morphological awareness makes it possible for us to teach it with intention, so our students can use this inside-the-word approach to determining meanings.

Young children are introduced to morphology through the most common suffixes, such as *-s, -es, -ed, and -ing.* Of course, these also parallel the oral language experiences they have beginning as toddlers learning to speak. A two-year-old who says, "Truck go" while pointing to several large vehicles might be encouraged by her caregiver to say, "The trucks are going," thereby adding two basic morphemes *(-s* and *-ing*) to her developing language.

Morphological awareness provides a gateway to a broader expanse of word families, rather than individual words. As we noted in the previous module, the 88,500 word families Nagy and Anderson (1984) estimated students need to know by the end of eighth grade is daunting, and there isn't anywhere enough time to teach all of them directly. (It actually wouldn't be very effective either. Readers need to develop the cognitive flexibility, which is to say the ability to rapidly shift attention during a task, to apply knowledge of known words to go after the unknown ones.) A third grader who has acquired a reasonable number of morphemes in their vocabulary bank can use the base word *act* along with several affixes to get to *react*, *actor*, and *enact*. But here's further evidence for a strong MA component in your reading instruction. The same researchers estimated that about 60% of the words encountered by third graders in their reading contain derivational morphemes (affixes, roots, and base words) and that there are on average three other words in printed school English that have a meaning similar to the root (Nagy & Anderson, 1984).

To be sure, there is a strong relationship between a student's vocabulary knowledge and their morphological awareness. But a well-designed study analyzed the relationship of vocabulary knowledge and morphological awareness to reading outcomes and spelling performance of second and third graders. In a series of tasks, researchers

Figure 9.2 Morphology Terms Used in This Module

Morphemes fall into two broad categories: **free morphemes** and **bound morphemes**.

Free morphemes can stand alone as a word (e.g., *duck, do, farm*) and many can be altered by an affix (e.g., *duckling, redo, farmer*).

Bound morphemes cannot stand alone. Prefixes and suffixes are bound morphemes.

Affixes is a collective term used to describe both prefixes and suffixes.

Component	Definition	Example
Prefix	Prefixes are bound morphemes that appear at the beginning of a word and cannot stand alone (e.g., *un-, dis-, re-*). A prefix is added to the beginning of a base word to create a new meaning.	*Hypo-* means "under," as in *hypodermic* (under the skin).
Suffix	Suffixes are bound morphemes that appear at the ends of words and cannot stand alone (e.g., *-ed, -s, -es*). A suffix is added to the end of a root or base word to create a new meaning.	*-est* creates a superlative word, as in *tallest*.
Root	Often Latin or Greek in origin, these are bound morphemes that cannot stand alone as words. Prefixes and suffixes are also roots.	*Aqua-, mal-,* and *-spect* are examples of roots. They form words when affixes are added, such as *aquatic, malady,* and *inspect*.
Base Word	These are free morphemes that can stand alone as words. Base words can be added to other bases or affixes to make a new word.	*Act* meaning "to do" can be changed to *action*. Act can also stand by itself as a word.
Cognate	Two words having a shared ancestral language meaning.	*Rehabilitation* and *rehabilitación* both mean "to restore or improve."
Word Family	A group of words sharing a common morphemic element.	*Judge, judgment, adjudicate, adjudication*

Morphological awareness provides a gateway to a broader expanse of word families, rather than individual words.

asked students to write a word, for example, *friend*, and then finish the sentence, "The teacher is ________." Thus, students had to draw on their knowledge of derivational morphemes. Other tasks were designed to measure word-level reading, spelling, and reading comprehension. The researchers found that MA is a uniquely strong predictor of word reading and spelling (Apel et al., 2012).

NOTICE AND WONDER

Review Figure 9.2 on morphology terms. What are the emphases of your MA instruction in your grade level?

Are there dimensions of MA that you suspect might be useful additions to your lessons for the students you teach? Why?

Consider a student you have who may not be making expected progress in MA. What signs do you see in their reading, writing, speaking, or listening that might indicate difficulty with morphology?

NOTES

Instruction in Morphological Awareness

SYSTEMATIC INSTRUCTION OF AFFIXES

There is widespread agreement that there is a scope of morphemes that all students learn.

Like other elements of reading instruction, morphological awareness requires a systematic, rather than hit-or-miss, approach to instruction. While sequences vary somewhat in the research literature and in reading/language arts materials, there is widespread agreement that there is a scope of morphemes that all students learn. Affixes are essential for young readers to master, because they equip children with tools they can draw upon to resolve unfamiliar words. Primary students benefit greatly from learning these commonly used affixes. Figure 9.3 is a suggested list of high-utility prefixes and suffixes for primary grade students.

Figure 9.3 Affixes for Grades K–2

Basic Prefixes		Basic Suffixes	
un- (not)	unlock	s (plural)	cups, books
re- (again)	rewrite	-es (plural)	dishes, boxes
re- (back)	return	-ing (present part.)	jumping
		-ed (past part.)	jumped
		-er (person)	teacher
		-er (comparative)	larger
		-est (superlative)	largest
		-ful (full of)	careful
		-less (without)	nameless

Source: Van Cleave (2019, p. 3). © William Van Cleave, 2019, WVCED.com.

As students advance in schooling, the affixes they need broaden in scope and meaning. Manyak et al. (2018) developed a list of 41 affixes to be taught systematically in grades 3 to 5 (see Figure 9.4). Baumann, a member of the research team, did extensive analyses of published lists and mapped them onto curricular materials and textbooks used in these grade levels in order to develop a scope and sequence across the grades. Note that the list also is grouped according to the function of the affix, such as those that indicate a position (e.g., *pre-, mid-, fore-*) or a person (e.g., *-er, -ist, -ee*). Such clustering further strengthens students' ability to analyze for meaning.

Figure 9.4 Affixes for Instruction

Family	Grade 3	Grade 4	Grade 5	Meaning	Example Words
Not prefixes	*dis-*			not, opposite	*dislike, disobey, disagree*
	un-			not, opposite	*unhappy, unlock, unafraid*
	in-			not, opposite	*incorrect, invisible, inappropriate*
		im-		not, opposite	*impossible, impolite, impatient*
		non-		not, opposite	*nonfiction, nonstop, nonliving*
			il-	not, opposite	*illegal, illogical, illegible*
			il-	not, opposite	*irregular, irresponsible*
Position prefixes	*pre-*			before	*pretest, preheat, preschool*
		post-		after	*postgame, postwar, postseason*
		mid-		middle	*midnight, midday, midair*
			inter-	between	*intercity, interstate, interact*
			intra-	among	*intrastate, intracellular*
			fore-	before	*foresee, foretell, forewarn*
			trans-	across	*transatlantic, transnational, transplant*
Over/ under prefixes	*over-*			more than, too much	*overheat, overwork, overpriced*
		super-		over, high, big, extreme	*superheat, superstar, supermarket*
		under-		low, too little	*undersea, underachiever, undercook*
			sub-	under, below	*subset, subtitle, subcommittee*
Against prefixes			*anti-*	against	*antifreeze, antiwar, antidiscrimination*
			counter-	against, opposite	*counterclockwise, counterargument*
Bad prefixes	*mis-*			bad, wrong	*misspell, misunderstand, misbehave*
			mal-	bad, wrong	*malnutrition, maltreat, malformed*

(Continued)

(Continued)

Family	Grade 3	Grade 4	Grade 5	Meaning	Example Words
Number prefixes		*uni-*		one	*unicycle, unicolor, unicellular*
		mono-		one	*monorail, monotone, monoplane*
		bi-		two	*bicycle, biweekly, biplane*
		tri-		three	*tricycle, triangle, trimotor*
Other useful prefixes	*re-*			again, back	*rewrite, rebuild, rearrange*
		de-		take away, from	*deice, debug, defrost*
			co-	with, together	*coauthor, coequal*
More and most suffixes	*-er*			more of something	*taller, smarter, warmer*
	-est			more of something	*tallest, smartest, warmest*
Person who suffixes	*-er*			person who	*teacher, writer, banker*
	-or			person who	*sailor, actor, explorer*
			-ist	person who	*artist, guitarist, nutritionist*
			-ee	person who	*employee, trainee, attendee*
Other useful suffixes	*-ful*			full of	*useful, joyful, cheerful*
	-ness			state or quality of	*weakness, illness, careless*
	-ly			like, full of	*clearly, costly, carefully*
		-y		like, full of	*lengthy, chilly, wealthy*
		-less		without	*hopeless, worthless, careless*
		-able		can be, worthy	*doable, workable, knowledgeable*

Source: Manyak et al. (2018, pp. 292–293).

Like many other strands in the reading rope, morphological awareness instruction often touches upon other facets of reading. Given the connective nature of MA as a tie to both word recognition and language comprehension, instruction frequently integrates these other skills to foster consolidation. In other words, to foster graphophonological-semantic cognitive flexibility.

WHAT'S YOUR ADVICE?

The teachers at Iron Ore Elementary are meeting in grade bands to discuss vertical alignment. They have conducted these grade band meetings monthly to address different parts of their literacy curricula. Principal Sanjay Reddy explains, "Our state standards are arranged in grade bands, but it was only a few years ago that we realized we rarely had vertical alignment conversations. Honestly, people in one grade level really didn't have any idea what was happening at the grade level before and after theirs."

This month's grade band meetings are focused on morphological awareness. Select the grade band below that reflects your own current assignment. What principles should the teachers for this band keep in mind? What errors should they avoid? Keep these in mind as you complete the module, returning to this activity to add new ideas.

Grade Band	Grades K-1	Grades 2-3	Grades 4-5	Grades 6-8
Principles of MA				
Relevance to Literacy Learning				
Errors to Avoid				
Recommendations				

NOTES

Direct Instruction in Morphology

A primary way to build morphological awareness for your students is to provide them with direct instruction. The purpose is not only to build skills but to surface their ability to notice small changes in print. In doing so, children come to understand that these changes to print are not capricious but rather orderly, rule-bound, and meaningful. Having said that, since MA influences and is influenced by other strands in the reading rope, make these links explicit, too, such as connecting the changes to word recognition, comprehension, vocabulary, and spelling. When it comes to building MA, note that the structure of the direct instruction lesson follows a general pattern:

- **Meaning**—What does the word mean?
- **Built**—How is the word built?
- **Relatives**—Is the word related to other words?
- **Pronunciation**—How do we say the word?

Kindergarten teacher Elizabeth Jones often uses the free texts provided by textproject .org for her instruction. These texts can be used for many purposes across the day and can even be printed and sent home for students to use. Ms. Jones introduced the text "In the Chicken Coop" to her students, reading it aloud to them. Once she finished reading, she returned to the first page, circled the word *chickens,* and wrote the word off to the side of the text, spelling it out loud for her students. She chunked the letters as follows: *ch - i - ck - en - s.* And then said *chickens* again. She then asked her students, "What does this word mean?" She got answers that it was the kind of bird in the picture, and it was the bird that laid eggs.

She then wrote the word *chicken* and spelled by chunks. She asked her students, "What is this word? Let's say that word all the way through the end: *chicken*."

As she moved her finger from left to right under the letters, they responded *chicken*. She then asked, "What's the difference between these two?" They answered *-s*!

"What does the *-s* do to this word? Natalie?"

Natalie responded, "*-s* makes it more."

"Class. More what?"

"More chickens!" they responded.

"Yes, I see more than one chicken. So, the base word is *chicken,* and if I want to say more than one, I can add the *-s* as a suffix. Adding the *-s* changes the meaning from one bird to more than one bird. There's another word on this page that ends with *-s* and changes the meaning from one to more than one. Do you see it?"

"*Nests*!" the students respond.

"Yes. Nests. n - e - s - t - s. Nests. What does that mean?"

"It's the place where the chicken has the eggs."

"It's like the place that they sleep."

Ms. Jones continues, "Great. If *-s* means more than one, what is the base for *nests*?"

"Nest," they reply.

"Perfect. Let me write that, *nest,* n - e - s - t. So, *nest* is the base and adding the *-s* tells us that there is more than one. We can add that to the base."

The lesson continued with the words *seeds* and *eggs*. In their final repetition, she used echo reading to further promote their fluency, word recognition, and comprehension of the text.

NOTES

Building Words With Word Sums

A *word sum* is a visual representation of the structure of members of a morphological family. It includes a base as well as possible prefixes and suffixes. The third graders in Marisa Gomez's class use a word sum matrix to continue their learning about morphology.

At the start of the year, Ms. Gomez produces the word matrix for students and has them produce word sums. A word sum shows how a word is built by inserting a plus sign (+) at the points where the word joins with prefixes and suffixes.

For example, the word matrix for *help* is found in Figure 9.5. As one of their literacy tasks, students apply what they have learned from the direct instruction lessons to make words. Of course, the matrix can produce words that do not exist, and students must differentiate real words from pseudowords. For example, the *help* matrix could produce the following word sum:

> un + help + er = unhelper

The vertical lines in the word matrix correspond to the plus sign in the word sums.

***Figure 9.5 Word Matrix for* Help**

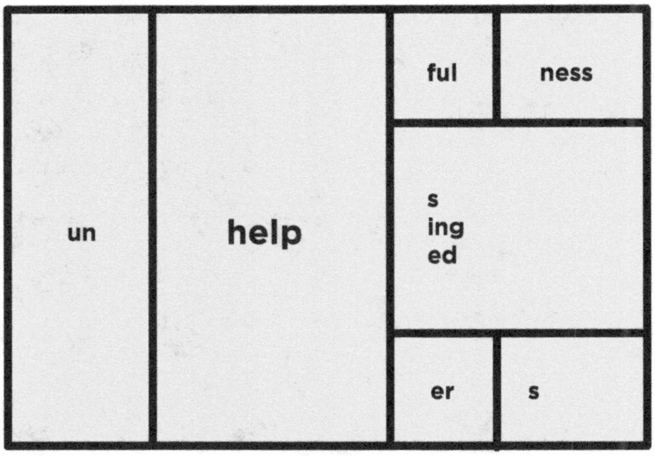

Carter asked Maricella if *unhelp* was a word. She responded that she thought so, but that she didn't think she had ever heard that word before. "But I have heard of *unhelpful,* so maybe *unhelp* is a word. I think we should add it, and if it is, then we learned a new word together."

At another table, Jai said, "I think I found a word that should have been added. I wrote help + ing + s = helpings. That's a word. My grandpa used that word at Thanksgiving when we were passing food around the table. But the matrix doesn't have that choice. I think Ms. Gomez has to make these harder for us."

Another important dimension to morphological awareness instruction is in assisting readers in recognizing that morphology impacts the spelling of the words. For example, on the matrix for *image*, students would learn

image + es = images

un + image + ine + able = unimaginable

image + ine + ate + tion = imagination

Once students have had considerable practice with the word matrices that have been provided by their teacher, Ms. Gomez invites students to create additional matrices. It becomes a collaborative and a bit of a competitive experience in her class, all in the spirit of strengthening their ability to read and spell.

Dinah Zike, the inventor of Foldables™, created an interactive tool that accomplishes the same thing as the word matrix. She calls it visual kinesthetic vocabulary, or VKV, but it's built on a foundation of morphology. As you can see in the picture below, it's a piece of paper with folds so that students can manipulate the matrix and see the words. This allows them to create their word sums more easily and to practice, adding and changing affixes to bases to see how words are made.

Understanding Affixes With Word Sorts

Use word sorts, as profiled in Module 4 on word building and in Module 7 on vocabulary concepts, to build students' MA. Word sorts with affixes look like this:

- They can use either an open system (categories are student-generated) or a closed system (categories are furnished by the teacher).
- Young children can sort words using prefixes and suffixes they are learning. For instance, students can sort using the comparative suffixes *-er* and *-est* (*kind/kinder/kindest, smart/smarter/smartest*).
- Add challenge to the sort by creating two more categories that require a more significant spelling change. Some comparative words change the *-y* to *-ier* or *-iest (empty/emptier/emptiest; murky/murkier/murkiest*). Sorts such as these are invaluable for assisting students in understanding the meaning and the spelling patterns needed (Bear et al., 2000).

Other affixes can seem arbitrary at first blush but are actually bound by rules of orthography (spelling) as well as morphology. To learn about *-ion* and *-ian* suffixes, students can sort the words *education, institution, magician, technician, election*, and *electrician* by endings. The end result of this visual display of sorted words (see Figure 9.6) can lead to a discussion about how the meaning of the root influences the choice of suffix: *-ion* is used for abstract nouns while *-ian* is used for people and animals (Bryant, 2006, cited in Goodwin et al., 2012).

Figure 9.6 ***-ion/-ian*** **Closed Sort**

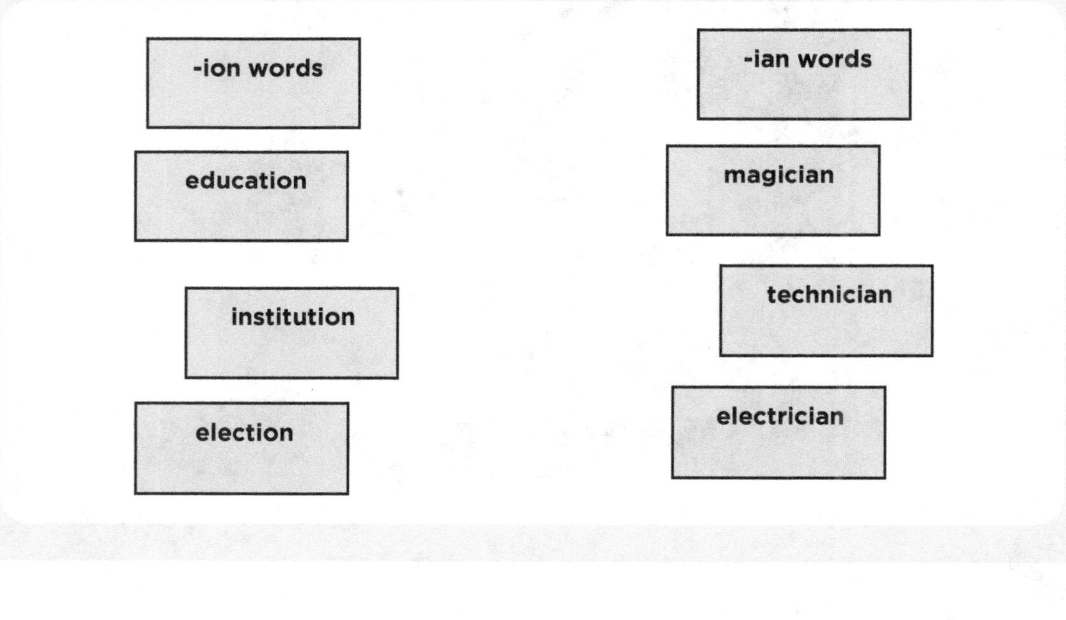

Affix Awareness

There are several ways to determine whether students are aware of the various affixes that convey meaning. One method is to teach about a particular prefix or suffix, and then give students tasks that require them to make a word choice using a pseudoword. By using a nonsense word instead of a real word, you require students to use what they know about the function of the affix, rather than draw on their content or vocabulary knowledge. Here is an example, which comes from the Morphological Awareness Test in Reading and Spelling (MATRS), currently in development (Apel et al., 2021):

> **Instructions:** This activity has lots of silly words you've never seen or heard before. You will hear and see a made-up word in a sentence and then circle a new made-up word that best fits the description in the sentence. Don't worry that you have not heard of the words before or are not sure what they mean; just choose the answer you think is best.
>
> 1. If *wame* means "horse," then which word means "without a horse"?
>   a) wameful
>   b) wameless
>   c) wamely
>   d) wamer

Another method is to have students identify which part of pseudowords is a real prefix or suffix.

> **Instructions**: Your job is to find these real add-ons (prefixes or suffixes) and circle them.
>
> 1. meckness
> 2. retage
> 3. gretting

You might also include items that challenge students to consider how target words are used as derivations, which further reinforces the cognitive flexibility they need to process words simultaneously at the semantic, syntactic, and phonological levels. Again, this example comes from the MATRS (Apel et al., 2021):

> Instructions: For this activity, you will see a word. Read the word, and then read the sentence that is missing a word. Use the word you read before the sentence to help you think of the missing word to fill in the blank line. Then write that word on the blank line.
>
> 1. **Achieve.** When she realized how much needed to be done, she realized the goal was not _______.
> 2. **Drivable**. I had to _______ my car to the market.

By embedding such items into your instruction, you can gain insight into your students' morphological awareness.

TAKE ACTION

Choose one of the approaches discussed, and formulate a plan to use it in your classroom. Why did you select it? When will you use it? What will you need to teach your students about the routine?

Routine I selected: ______________________________

____

Why I selected it: ______________________________

____

When I will use it: ______________________________

____

What do I need to teach about the routine? ______________________________

____

NOTES

Morphological Awareness Through Latin and Greek Roots

The English language derives words from languages all over the world—*luau* from Hawaiian, *bazaar* from Persian, *shampoo* from Hindi. Other words like *blog* enter our language because they represent a new concept. However, many of the words in the English language are derivatives of the Latin and Greek languages. Teaching some of the more common Latin and Greek root words gives students a transportable set of strategies to use as they spell new words. For example, when a student knows that *fac-* means "to make something," they can use that information to figure out both the spelling and meaning of *factory* and *manufacture*.

As students advance through the grade levels, they face an increasing number of academic words, which can test their comprehension abilities. As Rasinski et al. (2017) note, "The academic register is vast and complex but not haphazard: The majority of academic words are connected by morphemic (meaning-based) patterns" (p. 42). Most Latin and Greek roots are bound morphemes, meaning that they don't stand alone. While readers may acquire some indirect knowledge of Latin and Greek roots through reading academic texts, there is good evidence that a combination of explicit instruction paired with reading accelerates their word knowledge at elementary (Baumann, Edwards et al., 2003) and middle school levels (Crosson et al., 2019), especially for multilingual learners.

As with teaching affixes, we want students to be able to see the patterns of meaning in words that use morphemes derived from Latin and Greek. The general consensus is that formal instruction in this realm should begin in grade 4, paired now with the continued instruction of affixes (Manyak at al., 2018). Grade-level lists abound on the internet and in curricular materials, and they vary slightly from one another. We are appreciative of the work performed by Manyak and his colleagues to map the frequency of occurrences in curricular materials in grades 4 and 5 to other published lists. In addition, they considered those Latin and Greek roots that were consistent in meaning. Their recommendations can be found in Figure 9.7.

Word games are a great way to engage students in active learning, and Latin and Greek roots are no exception. Here is one method to try:

- Introduce students to a root for the week, with initial practice using five words that illustrate its meaning.
- Once the root is introduced, ask students to BOLO (be on the look out) for other words with this root to add to a class list of words. Students should include their names with their listing, and indicate the source where they found the new word (Padak et al., 2020).
- The friendly competition to locate similar words can keep students alert and more aware of what they are hearing and reading.

Fifth-grade teacher Stefani Torres uses word games like this with her students. One week, she identified the Latin root *-rupt*. She began by explaining that the root signals that something is broken or breaking. "I'll give an example. Let's watch a short video of a volcano erupting and then talk about why this root would make sense in the word." The teacher showed a 30-second video of an eruption, which sparked immediate discussion. After Liam first said that it was the Earth breaking, she nodded in agreement but said, "Liam, go deeper with that idea. Can you use what you've learned in science to be a bit more precise?"

He thought for a moment and said, "It's the Earth's mantle that's breaking, and the lava on the ground is erupting from the volcano."

Figure 9.7 Latin and Greek Roots for Instruction at Grades 4 and 5

Family	Root	Meaning	Example Words
Look and light roots	*scope*	to look at	*telescope, microscope, kaleidoscope*
	vis, vid	to see or watch	*vision, video, visibility*
	photo	light	*photograph, photocell, photon*
Communication roots	*dict*	to speak or say	*predict, dictator, dictaphone*
	script, scribe	write	*scribble, transcribe, manuscript*
	phon/phone	sound	*telephone, headphone, symphony*
	graph	to write or draw	*biography, autograph, paragraph*
	aud/audi	to hear	*audience, audible, auditorium*
Build or break roots	*rupt*	break	*eruption, interrupt, bankrupt*
	fract	break	*fracture, fraction, refract*
	struct	build	*construct, structure, destruct*
Movement roots	*tract*	drag, pull	*tractor, subtract, distract*
	mot, mov	move	*motion, remote, demote*
	port	carry	*export, import, portable*
Other useful roots	*bio*	life	*biology, biofuel, symbiotic*
	tele	far	*telescope, television, telegram*
	geo	earth	*geology, geography, geode*
	therm	heat	*thermometer, thermostat, hypothermia*
	micro	small, tiny	*microscope, microwave, microchip*
	astr	star	*astronomy, astronaut, astrobiologist*
	path(y)	feeling, suffering	*sympathy, empathy, telepathy*
	phobia	fear	*zoophobia, hydrophobia, acrophobia*

Source: Manyak et al. (2018, p. 295).

"I love that!" the teacher said, "Let's use that sentence on the chart to illustrate *erupt*." Over the next few minutes, she similarly expanded their word schema by introducing *disrupt* and *corrupt*.

Throughout the week, students added other words as well as derivations to the chart and initialed their entries. One student wrote, "I watched Pardon the Interruption on YouTube with my brother."

Another wrote, "I couldn't open the file because it was corrupted."

Others added sentences using the words *incorruptible, abruptly*, and *ruptured* to the list. On Friday, Ms. Torres issued a challenge for them to work together to develop word families using affixes to expand the words. The week's winning group produced this list:

Corrupt	Erupt	Disrupt	Interrupt	Abrupt	Rupture	Bankrupt
corrupted	eruption	disrupted	interrupts	abruptly	ruptures	bankrupted
corrupts	erupted	disruption	interruption	abruptness	ruptured	bankrupt
corruptly	erupts	disrupt	interrupted			bankruptcy
incorruptible		nondisruptive	interrupters			
corruptness		disruptively	interrupting			
anticorruption						

The fourth-grade teacher team at Hillside Elementary identified the Latin and Greek roots they would be teaching their students during the first semester of school. They developed a teacher-constructed assessment to be administered during the first month of school in order to learn about their new students' morphological knowledge of these Latin and Greek roots. Gabriella, a multilingual learner, wrote these answers (shown in italics) to the questions in their assessment:

1. What does the root -*scope* mean in these words? *For looking*
   telescope, microscope, periscope, horoscope

2. What does the root -*graph* mean in these words? *IDK*
   graphic, telegraph, photograph, biography

3. What does the root -*struct* mean in these words? *IDK*
   structure, instruction, construction, destructive

4. What does the root *port* mean in these words? *Fly*
   airport, transportation, portable, supporting

5. What does the root astr- mean in these words? *Man*
   astronaut, astronomy, astronomer, Astrodome

FIND THE MISTAKES

Gabriella made several errors that may indicate some gaps in her morphological awareness.

What does this tell you about the morphological awareness this student has, and what might be the next steps in moving her learning forward?

Strengths: ____

____

Areas of Focus: ____

____

What existing resources do you have for teaching Latin and Greek roots and for teaching affixes? Do a resource inventory. How often do you use them? What gaps have you identified in availability or usage?

Materials for Teaching Latin/Greek Roots	Used Frequently or Infrequently?	Materials for Teaching Affixes	Used Frequently or Infrequently?

Resource Gaps I Have Identified

Morphological Awareness Through Spelling Instruction

In an article about spelling instruction and morphology, Templeton (2012) quotes a teacher who says, "You learn one word, you learn ten!" (p. 103). The research on spelling instruction has moved far beyond the Friday tests the three of us recall from our childhoods, which emphasized seemingly random lists of words to be memorized over the week. Spelling is now recognized as a series of stages that reflect a child's growing literacy knowledge. Generally speaking, students in the intermediate grades are in spelling stages that increasingly draw on their knowledge of morphology to accurately spell multisyllabic words, and in particular those whose spelling changes depending on the part of speech (e.g., *curious* versus *curiosity*). These stages, referred to as *syllable juncture* and *derivational constancy*, can be successfully mastered with spelling instruction that includes morphology. We have constructed a description of these two stages (see Figure 9.8) based on the work of a number of spelling researchers (Bear et al., 2000; Ganske, 2000; Henderson, 1985; Sheets, 2013).

Figure 9.8 Two Stages of Spelling Development

Spelling Stage	Description of Stage
Syllable Juncture	• Frequent errors in spelling unstressed vowels (the schwa) in multisyllabic words and also in consonant doubling • Doubling and e-drop with inflectional endings (*-s, -es, -ed, -ing*) • Long vowel patterns (*ladle, complain*) and *r*-controlled vowels (*dreary, inspire*) in the stressed syllable • Consonant assimilation (*ir* + *relevant* = *irrelevant*) • Prefixes and suffixes (known as affixes) • Typical of students 9 to 11 years of age
Derivational Constancy	• Relationships between spelling and meaning (morphology) • Morphemes are preserved even when pronunciations change (*condemn-condemnation; discuss-discussion*) • Silent and sounded consonants (*haste, hasten*) • Consonant and vowel changes or alternations (*express-expression*; *compose-composition*) • Greek and Latin roots and affixes • Typical of students 11 years of age through adulthood

Generative word instruction can build the vocabulary of students while highlighting their morphological awareness. Each week, sixth-grade teacher Jawan Thomas introduces word families to his students, many of whom are multilingual learners who speak Spanish as a heritage language. "When I can, I make connections to cognates to show them how they appear in their home language," explained the teacher. Each week Mr. Thomas identifies a "word of the week" that has a common Latin or Greek root. In addition, he asks his students to teach him words in their native language that have similar cognates. "We build a word tree throughout the week, and I challenge them to use variations of the word in their speaking and writing."

During a week when his students were studying about the scientific process in their science class, Mr. Thomas introduced them to the word *significant*. He explained that the Latin root *sign* means a mark or a seal. After writing it on the trunk of a tree he drew on the board, he added variations, discussing the affixes he can use to generate related words:

Significant

Significance

Signify

Signifying

Signified

Signifies

Insignificant

Insignificantly

"My goal's always to try to get as close to 10 as I can," Mr. Thomas says, "but I've only got eight words so far. Can you help me out? Do these words remind you of ones in Spanish? I'm looking for cognates. Go ahead and talk to your table first."

After a quick check-in with their classmates, several students tell him that the words *significativa* and its masculine form *significativo* are cognates that mean something is very important or meaningful. Mr. Thomas adds those to the board.

"Thank you! That got us to 10 words! Now how can you use it? Let's see if we can't practice some of those variations together."

NOTES

Assessing for Morphological Awareness

As we noted in the previous module on vocabulary, we are cautious about subdividing assessments of morphological awareness (MA) too narrowly, at the risk of sacrificing a more holistic view of your students. Because MA is so intertwined with vocabulary, comprehension, and word attack skills, we advise that your unit-specific vocabulary assessments include, when appropriate, soliciting students' knowledge of MA in the context of academic learning.

INITIAL ASSESSMENT OF LATIN AND GREEK ROOTS

Initial assessments provide you with information in advance of instruction such that you can make the most of the time you have. Further, results can better equip you to provide needs-based instruction in small groups to students. One method for initial assessment is to identify grade-level morphemes you will be teaching, and then find out what your students already know about them.

TEXT-TO-SELF CONNECTION

Why should morphological awareness be included as part of a vocabulary instruction program? What are the risks of overlooking MA?

____

____

What new decisions have you formed based on your learning about morphological awareness?

____

____

Using the traffic light scale, with red being not confident, yellow being somewhat confident, and green indicating very confident, how confident are you in your ability to

- Teach morphological awareness?

- Integrate morphological awareness with vocabulary instruction?

Takeaways

- Newer research has highlighted the crucial role of morphological awareness in reading and writing development.
- Knowledge of morphemes, the smallest units of meaning, is utilized to recognize words, make orthographical (spelling) decisions, and determine the meaning of words.
- Morphological awareness instructional routines focus on active learning though approaches that allow children to build words.
- Instruction in word families that use similar morphemes can further expand oral and written language expression.

PS: Answers to the anticipation guide are F, F, T, F.

online resources

Visit the companion website at
resources.corwin.com/teachingreading
for this module's downloadable resources.

MODULE

10

Text and Language Structures

Photo by Santri Vendri on Unsplash

The student in the photo looks pretty committed to his writing. There's little doubt that he is consolidating what it is that he knows about language structure to get his ideas on paper. To do so, he needs to internalize the grammar of the language to get his message down. And given his apparent engagement, it's highly unlikely that he is filling out a boring grammar worksheet. Yet teaching grammar is something that causes many teachers to figuratively hold their noses. "Grammar," wrote Hausmann in 2003, "is the skunk at the language arts garden party" (quoted in Gartland & Smolkin, 2016, p. 391).

All languages have structures that allow for meaningful communication to take place. Different languages assemble

In this module, we will

- **Examine new thinking about grammar through a contrastive analysis lens.**
- **Discuss the teaching of language structures through integrative approaches.**
- **Highlight techniques for instruction on grammar and syntax.**

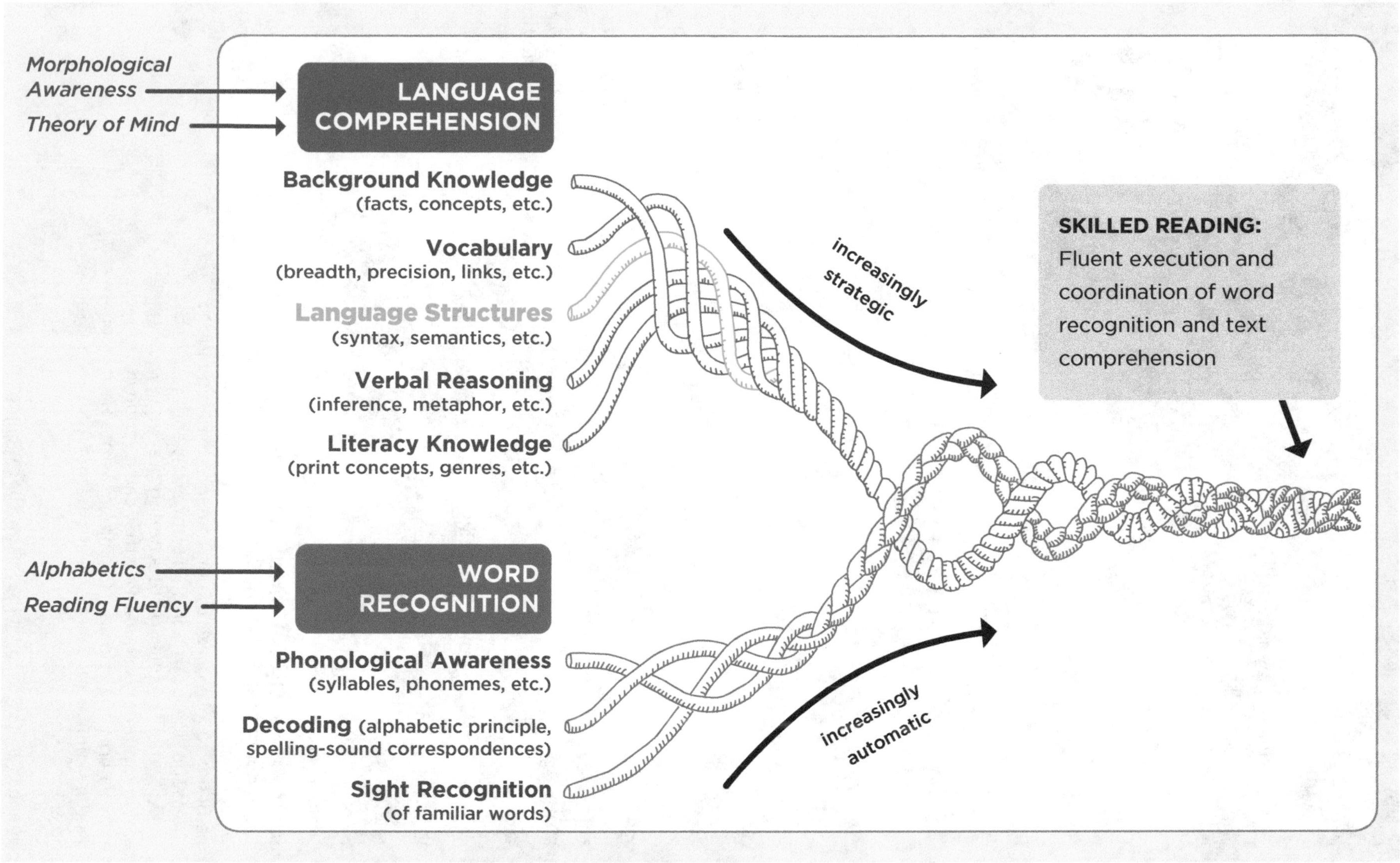

Source: Adapted from Scarborough, H. S. (2001). Connecting early language and literacy to later reading (dis)abilities: Evidence, theory, and practice. In S. Neuman & D. Dickinson (Eds.), *Handbook for research in early literacy* (pp. 97–110). Guilford Press.

elements of words together in different ways, lining them up in a comprehensible order. Each word carries a specific meaning, and understanding those words draws on one's vocabulary knowledge and morphological awareness. While vocabulary and morphological awareness support a child's comprehension of a word or phrase, knowledge of the language structure makes it possible for them to interpret the meaning of full sentences, whether spoken or written.

This lining up of words is referred to as *syntax.* Moving a single word out of order might change the meaning or render the whole message meaningless. A comprehensible sentence might be: *The garbage truck picks up the trash and recycling every Tuesday.* Change the order just a bit and it no longer makes sense: *Truck garbage the Tuesday every and trash picks recycling* is just gobbledygook. Syntax is informed by the grammar of the language, which also governs phrases. For instance, *garbage truck* is a meaningful phrase, as is *every Tuesday.* Gartland and Smolkin explain that "grammar is a set of rules that explain how a system operates, and in language, this system typically refers to syntax (the arrangement of words and phrases to create well-formed sentences in a language)" (2016, p. 391). Like other dimensions of reading, language structures inform speaking and writing. In the case of writing, knowledge of language structures is necessary for writing conventions, including punctuation and capitalization.

Knowledge of language structures is necessary for writing conventions, including punctuation and capitalization.

Read each statement and mark **T** if you think the statement is true and **F** if you think the statement is false. As you read through the module, you might change your responses. Be prepared to explain your responses and use the text for evidence.

<table>
<tr><th>Before Reading</th><th>Statements</th><th>After Reading</th></tr>
<tr><td>T F</td><td>1. Descriptive grammar instruction emphasizes the rules that govern the language.</td><td>T F</td></tr>
<tr><td colspan="2">Why did you indicate true or false?</td><td>Has your thinking changed after reading?</td></tr>
<tr><td>T F</td><td>2. All languages and dialects have rules that impact understanding, and these include the order of words in sentences.</td><td>T F</td></tr>
<tr><td colspan="2">Why did you indicate true or false?</td><td>Has your thinking changed after reading?</td></tr>
<tr><td>T F</td><td>3. Typically, developing readers don't need instruction on language structures after fourth grade.</td><td>T F</td></tr>
<tr><td colspan="2">Why did you indicate true or false?</td><td>Has your thinking changed after reading?</td></tr>
<tr><td>T F</td><td>4. Sentence-level analysis fosters understanding of language structures.</td><td>T F</td></tr>
<tr><td colspan="2">Why did you indicate true or false?</td><td>Has your thinking changed after reading?</td></tr>
</table>

Grammar Through a New Lens

If you are of a certain age, you may recall your own grammar instruction as being mostly about diagramming sentences. If you're younger, this may be completely unfamiliar, and instead you remember "daily oral language" as an exercise in noticing errors. It is true that interest in grammar instruction has waxed and waned over the decades. But grammar is a crucial dimension of language learning for all students.

The English language assigns parts of speech to describe the role of a word in a sentence. Figure 10.1 lists eight of them. This is by no means an exhaustive list, as some words can shift in terms of the part of speech they fulfill depending on their use in a sentence. The word *nest* is one of many examples.

- The bird's *nest* is full of eggs. (noun)
- The birds *nest* in the same tree every year. (verb)

Differences in grammar between languages may be puzzling to students who speak a language that differs from the language of instruction.

There has been renewed interest in language structures as educators seek ways to effectively support multilingual learners. Differences in grammar between languages may be puzzling to students who speak a language that differs from the language of instruction. As an example, Mandarin and Japanese do not use articles (a, the, an). As well, the function of a word or phrase may change depending on how it is used in a sentence, which can add to confusion for both monolingual and multilingual children.

Figure 10.1 Quick Guide to Eight Parts of Speech

Eight Parts of Speech	Role	Examples
Nouns	person, place, or thing	woman, Bennie, Yellowstone National Park, table
Pronouns	substitutions for nouns	he, she, they, it
Adjectives	describe nouns	red (plate), hilarious (book), beautiful (destination)
Verbs	actions	draw, argue, love, be
Adverbs	describe a verb, adjective, or another adverb	The boy ate his lunch *slowly.* Movies are *never* as good as the book.
Conjunctions	Linking words or phrases to make more complex sentences	and, but, as, because, not only, so, for

Eight Parts of Speech	Role	Examples
Articles	A word that precedes a noun to show whether it is specific (definite: *that* cat) or general (indefinite: *a* cat)	the, a, an, this, that
Prepositions	Describes the relationship between words in terms of direction, time, location, or space	under, inside, in front of, in back of, above, below, through, within, for, at

But grammar instruction is also fraught with concerns about the privileging of a standard for English versus variations used at home, in communities, and in settings outside of the classroom. When one version of English (referred to as standard English, or SE) is set up as the "correct" form, it perpetuates a wrongheaded message that other forms (Vernacular English, or VE) are "wrong" or "incorrect." This is a prescriptive form of grammar instruction that limits language use to standard English only.

Contrastive analysis is an approach that teaches children to look for patterns in dialects. Rather than looking for errors, students are asked to notice how language and its variations are all governed by rules (patterns). Rather than a prescriptive approach, contrastive analysis emphasizes a descriptive way of understanding the features of English and its dialects. In using this approach, we pivot away from correctness to codeswitching, focusing on appropriateness and suitability for the context and task. Wheeler and Swords (2006) discuss contrastive analysis by contrasting it (pun intended) with a more limited prescriptive approach to grammar instruction (see Figure 10.2).

Figure 10.2 New Ways of Discussing Language Structures

Instead of This	Try This
Thinking in terms of • proper or improper • good or bad	Seeing language as • appropriate or inappropriate • effective or ineffective in a specific setting
Talking about • right or wrong • correct or incorrect	Talking about • patterns • how language varies by setting

(Continued)

(Continued)

Instead of This	Try This
Thinking that students • make mistakes or errors • have problems with plurals, possessives, tenses, etc. • leave off *-s, 's, -ed*	Seeing your students as • following the grammar patterns of their home language
Saying students • "should have," "are supposed to," "need to," "should correct"	Inviting students to • code-switch (choose the language pattern to fit the setting)
Making red notes in the margin • correcting students' grammar	Leading students to • compare and contrast language • build on existing knowledge to add new knowledge—standard English • code-switch to fit the setting

Source: Wheeler and Swords (2006, p. xvii).

A contrastive analysis approach emphasizes detection and use of the patterns of dialects and languages. As one example, African American Vernacular English (AAVE) has some patterns that differ from SE. Grammar instruction then focuses on the rules of each such that students can see them (see Figure 10.3 for a few examples). If this reminds you of morphological awareness instruction about affixes, we agree! Understanding patterns equips a student with ways to analyze the language structures.

Figure 10.3 Patterns in English

Possessive	
AAVE Pattern	**SE Pattern**
Owner + thing owned	*Owner + s + thing owned*
Her mom name is Rita.	Her mom's name is Rita.

Am/Is/Are	
AAVE Pattern	**SE Pattern**
I + am *Any other subject + is* My team and I is playing in the tournament.	*I + am* *he/she/it + is* *plural subject + are* My team and I are playing in the tournament.

Past Tense	
AAVE Pattern	**SE Pattern**
Time word + phrase Last night, we walk to the store.	*verb + -ed* Last night, we walked to the store.

Source: Wheeler and Swords (2006, p. xvii).

Young children can be deeply influenced by the unintended messages of school. If the implication is that their home dialect is "not as good," they can in turn begin to devalue themselves and their community. Rather than viewing language structures through a reductive model of eliminating dialects to replace them with SE, contrastive analysis seeks to expand the patterns that students can use to match the context. Wheeler et al. (2012) suggest a simple but innovative way for beginning discussions about language structures using places and greetings as examples (see Figure 10.4).

Figure 10.4 Contrasting Places and Greetings

Informal Places	Formal Places
Your home A picnic A sports event Visiting with friends outside a church, mosque, or synagogue	The president's home A fancy restaurant A live theater performance A church, mosque, or synagogue
Informal Language to Greet a Friend	**Formal Language to Greet a Teacher**
What up, bro?	Good morning, Mr. Johnson.

Syntax. This has been described by Scott as the "workhorse of meaning" (2009, p. 185). Syntax refers to the ways in which words are ordered in a sentence. As an exercise in syntax, we often use this example with older students. Take a look at how the placement of the word *only* in the following sentences affects the meaning:

She *told him that she loved him.*

She **only** told him that she loved him.

She told **only** him that she loved him.

She told him **only** that she loved him.

She told him that **only** she loved him.

She told him that she **only** loved him.

She told him that she loved **only** him.

Syntax is the "workhorse of meaning."

It comes as no surprise that there is a relationship between syntactical knowledge and reading comprehension for young children (Lesaux et al., 2007). Syntax is often taught through sentence-level instruction, and especially through varying the types of sentences used, such as subject-relative clause sentences: *I am helping my friend who gave me some help last week* (*who gave me some help* is the relative clause). Not only is the ordering of the words more difficult, but there is also a relative pronoun in there (*me*) that the reader or listener has to keep track of. Whew!

Even more complex sentences show up frequently in written language, compared with spoken language. Consider the complexity of language structures, including grammar and syntax, in these sentences from five books for children:

- "Wemberly worried about spilling her juice, about shrinking in the bathtub, even about snakes in the radiator." (*Wemberly Worried*, Henkes, 2000, p. 1)
- "Some people won't understand about your hijab, but if you understand who you are, one day they will too." (*The Proudest Blue*, Muhammad & Ali, 2019, p. 4)
- "The most important reason for going from one place to another is to see what's in between, and they took great pleasure in doing just that." (*The Phantom Tollbooth*, Juster, 1961, p. 117)
- "Jim Thorpe looked ridiculous and he knew it—like a scarecrow dressed for football, he'd say later." (*Undefeated: Jim Thorpe and the Carlisle Indian School Football Team*, Sheinkin, 2017, p. 1)
- "You ain't never had to live on nobody's place but your own and long as I live and the family survives, you'll never have to." (*Roll of Thunder, Hear My Cry*, Taylor, 1976, p. 7)

The importance is not in the labeling (we don't believe that most of us need to be able to label a subject-relative clause) but rather in how it can be understood. It is crucial for students to be able to comprehend the ways in which words, phrases, and clauses work in sentences.

Using Cloze and Maze Procedures to Gauge Knowledge of Language Structures

The cloze procedure was originally developed as a measure of readability of text (Taylor, 1953), but it was soon being used to determine students' levels of comprehension (e.g., Shanahan et al., 1982). The tool can be used to identify several aspects of students' language comprehension skills as well as their knowledge of grammar, syntax, semantics, and vocabulary.

A cloze procedure, so-named because of the closure effect prompted by the task, uses a teacher-selected passage of up to 250 words. The length, of course, should be adjusted to meet the developmental level of the students. Every fifth word is deleted except in the first and last sentences, which are preserved in their entirety so that the reader can draw on context. This means that a variety of words end up being deleted—articles like *a* and *the*, pronouns—as well as content vocabulary. Students read the passage and fill in the missing words. Scoring is straightforward as well, with most sources recommending that a word be marked as correct only if it is an exact match. This may seem counterintuitive, but it really does make scoring easier and consistent across students.

In terms of reading comprehension, students who get 60% or more of items correct are considered able to generally read at the grade level represented by the passage. For example, if you selected a fourth-grade passage and followed the cloze procedure, you would know which students generally comprehended texts at that level. But for our purposes, it's interesting to look at which items are completed and how. In analyzing student responses, you can theorize about their knowledge of grammar and syntax, as well as content knowledge. Consider the following passage presented to third graders in advance of a reading about the solar system.

> The Sun is the center of our solar system. We live on planet _____. It is the fourth _____ from the Sun. Our _____ travels around the Sun _____ a year. The Moon _____ around the Earth. The _____ orbit takes 27 days _____ go around the _____. The Moon looks different _____ the light from the _____ changes the way the _____ appears to us on _____. These are called the phases of the Moon.

A maze procedure is quite similar, but in this case students are provided a word bank from which to select options. Traditionally, a maze assessment consists of selected passages in which words are periodically deleted (usually every seventh word) and replaced with one of three word choices, only one of which fits in the sentence (Wiley & Deno, 2005). There is a free maze assessment generator here: www.interventioncentral.org/teacher-resources/test-of-reading-comprehension. One of the incorrect choices is a *near distractor*, meaning that it preserves the syntax, but not the meaning, of the sentence. The other incorrect choice is a *far distractor*, meaning that it does not make sense syntactically or semantically (Shinn & Shinn, 2002). Both maze and cloze procedures allow you to observe how it is that your students are applying their knowledge of language structures to understand at the sentence level.

NOTICE AND WONDER

Knowledge of language structures moves beyond the single word or phrase to the comprehension of a sentence. Reflect on your own experiences as a child with grammar instruction. What elements of grammar and syntactical learning are similar to your own childhood experiences? What elements are different?

Similarities Between Your Learning and Your Current Teaching Practices	Differences Between Your Learning and Your Current Teaching Practices

Instruction About Language Structures

A major principle of language structure instruction is that it should be embedded in meaningful tasks, not drills that isolate the skill from its application. Always consider how production, through oral and/or written language, will occur. These experiences with instruction on language structures benefit all readers, regardless of age, because they impact their ability to communicate verbally and in writing.

TEACHING REFERENTS AND DETERMINERS

A referent is a person, thing, or idea that a word or expression denotes or stands for. At a very basic level, the word represents a concrete or abstract idea. Consider the sentence: "The painted wall brought joy to many." The *painted wall* refers to a concrete object. *Joy* is more abstract. But you can see the challenge with referents in this sentence? Which painted wall are we talking about? Many what? To whom? Did you infer people? What if the painted wall brought joy to the birds? If that is the case, the author assumes that birds can experience joy.

Readers use referents so that they can maintain understanding while reading a text, and track who or what is being referred to in it. In addition, many sentences contain determiners, which are words placed in front of a noun to specify the quantity. The first word of the sentence about the painted wall is *the,* which signals that it is one specific wall. Determiners clarify what the noun is referring to. Determiners fall into the following categories:

- An article, such as *a/an, the*
- A demonstrative (*that, these, this, those*)
- An ordinal, such as *first, second, third,* as so on
- A possessive (*her, his, its, my, our, their, your*)
- A quantifier (*few, many, more, most, much, some*)

Instruction in the use of referents and determiners needs to extend across the elementary grade levels because as students read increasingly complex texts, both may become less obvious. The kindergarteners in Eliza Sellier's class knew the articles *a, an,* and *the* by sight. They were reading a book that focused on *-ug* endings, and each page followed a pattern: *I see. . . .* The students had read the book before, but Ms. Sellier wanted to focus on the determiners that help students infer using referents. For example, one page said, "I see a bug," and another page said, "I see the rug."

Ms. Sellier projected an image of the bug page on her smartboard and asked, "Which bug are they talking about?" The page had several images, including several distractors such as a bed, a mug, and bag. In addition, the page had several different types of bugs. Ms. Sellier said, "Josiah, can you help? Can you come point for me? Class, let's read the sentence again together." They did, and Josiah pointed to one of the bugs.

Ms. Sellier said, "Well done. I see the bug that you are pointing to. Is there another option? Natalia, can you come up and point? Yes, that bug also works for the sentence 'I see a bug.' And now can you point to the bed?" Natalia does.

Ms. Sellier continues, "There is only one bed, so we can say 'the bed,' because it's more specific. It's okay to say 'a bed,' but usually when we use *a* or *an,* it's not specific to one."

Ms. Sellier is introducing her students to the idea that the definite article *the* (as well as demonstrative determiners such as *this* and *that*) often refer to a specific item, whereas the indefinite articles *a* and *an* refer to one member of a class (as in the case of the bugs).

Fourth-grade teacher Antonio Silas focuses some of his instructional time on interpreting pronouns as referents. Often, pronouns are used in place of the original referent to increase sentence variety, and it's the way we talk. Consider the pronoun referents in the following sentences:

- Jordan, Taylor, and their children left when he became sleepy.
- Jordan, Taylor, and their children left when they became sleepy.
- Jordan, Taylor, and their children left when she became sleepy.

The first referent *their* is likely to be inferred to be Jordan and Taylor's children. But, if the sentence before focused on a different group of people, then *their* might be something else. In terms of the gendered pronoun *he* in the first sentence, who is that? The same is true for the gendered pronoun *she*. *They* is even more complex. Is it Jordan and Taylor or the children who became sleepy? Readers are required to make a lot of inferences based on these pronouns.

Mr. Silas intentionally selects books with pronoun referents in them so that his students can practice applying this skill. In the past, there was agreement in terms of gender and number, but that has changed, and *they/them* is increasingly common and can be used for an individual. Older texts tend to use *he/his* and *she/her* for singular and *they/them* for plural. As students read these texts, they need to make inferences and develop that particular noticing skill. This is not a single lesson, but rather should be integrated into teacher modeling and student practice. For example, while reading *Pocahontas* (Gourse, 1996), Mr. Silas read aloud, "Pocahontas rubbed her stomach and pretended to be eating. She then pointed at his stomach and mouth. Captain Smith realized that Pocahontas knew the English were hungry, that they needed food to stay alive" (p. 50).

He asked Partner A to share with Partner B the answer to who is pointing in that excerpt. In his class, students know their partners and which letter they are. The teacher then asked Partner B to tell Partner A who is the "his" that Pocahontas pointed to. Several students answered incorrectly.

Mr. Silas said, "Isn't this interesting? The person that the author is talking about comes after, in the next sentence. The author just assumes we know but doesn't tell us until the next sentence." Then he asks Partner A to tell Partner B who *they* are in the last sentence. Most students said Captain Smith and Pocahontas, whereas a few said, "the English." Mr. Silas invited students to think aloud for their peers so that they could all hear the inferences. Mr. Silas then had students read the next few pages together, stopping at pronouns to talk with their partners about who was being referenced, taking notes on their graphic organizers.

In another classroom, sixth-grade teacher Gabriela Molina noticed that her students were not always able to infer when the author used a relative pronoun. These pronouns, such as *who*, *which*, and *that*, have two roles. They are part pronoun and part conjunction. Consider the patterns in the following sentences:

- The runner *who* won the marathon trained hard.
- It was a happy memory *that* came to mind.
- Lasagna, *which* we eat at least weekly, is one of the family's favorite meals.

Did you note that the referent is mentioned in the same clause as the relative pronoun, which is not the case with other pronouns such as *they* (as in, "they ate all of the cake")?

Ms. Molina has students generate sentences that include these relative pronouns as part of her writing instruction. She then asks peers to review the sentences and identify who or what is being referenced. For example, Leilani created the following sentence:

I walked in the park that was open for people who had dogs.

Her partner Mia was confused by this sentence. Mia asked, "Who had dogs?"

Leilani said, "The people."

Mia said, "Which people?"

Leilani responded, "Read it again. No, I will." She read the sentence slowly emphasizing the word *for.*

Mia said, "Oh, I get it now. The people with dogs can walk in the park. Is that right?"

Leilani said "Yes! But now think about me."

"What about you?"

"I'm in the park, so what do you know about me?"

"OMG. You have a dog!"

FIND THE MISTAKES

Be on the lookout for common grammar errors that elementary students (and older ones, too) make in their written and verbal language. Directly teach (and reteach and teach yet again) to address these errors:

1. Confusing *there/their/there.*
2. Confusing *two/to/too.*
3. *Then* versus *than. Then* refers to time, space, or order. *Than* is a contrastive.
4. Putting apostrophes in plural words.
5. Unclear antecedents. *Jamie and Robby went back to the playground to get his ball.* Who's ball—Jamie's or Robby's?

NOTES

Close Reading of Sentences

What makes reading hard? Most children will tell you it's the words. However, we would argue that the arrangement of the words is an important factor. Phrases and clauses contain subtleties of meaning that can be easily lost on the reader. We don't believe there's much value to teaching students lots of technical grammar terms (really, when was the last time you needed to furnish a definition of an infinitive phrase?), but rather to assisting children in being able to detect what a sentence has to offer.

Juicy sentences is a close reading process developed by Fillmore and Fillmore (n.d.) to parse and slice complex sentences. The purpose is to assist students in unlocking the meaning of individual sentences and therefore the meaning of the longer text itself. Fillmore and Fillmore note that juicy sentences should be selected from texts students are reading, in order to support them more completely in understanding the reading itself. In other words, these exercises are not isolated but are used to provide guidance on how language structures are used to make meaning in the sentences of the text. Student Achievement Partners, a nonprofit dedicated to educational supports in literacy and mathematics for students and their teachers, offers guidance on selecting a juicy sentence. It notes that it is not necessary for all of these conditions to be met (Student Achievement Partners, n.d.):

- ☐ Comes from grade-appropriate complex text.
- ☐ Comes from a text that is conceptually connected to content being discussed in class already. STEM, history, social studies, and ELA texts all make great candidates! This allows students to build on and reinforce the knowledge and vocabulary they've acquired from other texts.
- ☐ Has high informational density. That is, multiple pieces of information are contained in the sentence and/or can be construed from its subtext.
- ☐ Is "chunkable." You can break it apart into smaller sections for focused discussion. There isn't a rule about the exact right number of chunks, or the right number of words or phrases that constitute a chunk, but think strategically about the ideas each chunk is conveying—don't leave students hanging by splitting apart an idea into two chunks!
- ☐ Features language related to complex thought, where readers are asked to interpret motivation, rationale, time, place, contingencies related to actions, et cetera.
- ☐ Features grade-level academic language.
- ☐ Contains complex noun phrases (nouns that are modified or expanded by other phrases).
- ☐ Contains adverbial clauses.
- ☐ Uses passive voice.
- ☐ Includes linking phrases.
- ☐ Introduces a metaphor or simile.

Third-grade teacher Amir Douglas looks for juicy sentences in his students' readings to unpack meaning. Many of Mr. Douglas's students are multilingual learners, although he has said that "this works to support all my kids." He locates a complex sentence and, with the help of his students, parses the components into bite-size slices. Using what they have found in the juicy sentence, they map information to extend these concepts.

Their science text on animal groups contained this sentence: "Being part of a group helps animals find food, defend themselves, and adjust to changes in their environment." The teacher chose this sentence because the paragraphs that follow discuss the concepts it contains in more detail about several animal groups. He began by projecting the sentence on the smartboard and worked with his students to perform some "sentence surgery" to parse it. In a few minutes, he and the class had identified the major ideas by examining the phrases and clauses. In addition, they named questions they would need to keep in mind as they read further. Together they co-constructed a table:

Being part of a group	Whose group?
helps animals	How does it help?
find food	What kind of food?
defend themselves	Defend against what?
adjust to changes	What changes?
in their environment	What is an environment?

Each phrase was then underlined with a different colored marker to designate the individual concepts; for example, the first phrase was blue, while the second was green. Working in small groups, the students then read the next paragraphs and wrote concepts they learned on corresponding colored sentence strips. One group read about rabbits and composed these sentences:

- Rabbits live in groups called a fluffle.
- They live in warrens so they can be safe from predators.
- Rabbits forage for food like green plants.
- They defend themselves by running or staying very still.
- In the winter they eat tree bark, twigs, and pine needles.

"It's so useful to deconstruct a juicy sentence and read it closely to really interrogate what that sentence is offering," said Mr. Douglas. "It sets up my students for what they need to learn from the text. By extracting information and writing it on sentence strips, they get more actively involved in the reading itself."

NOTES

Sentence Combining

Fourth-grade teacher Marla O'Campo writes sentences for her students to combine. Sentence combining provides students with an opportunity to utilize syntactic knowledge to create more sophisticated sentences. During sentence combining, students take simple sentences and build them into more complex ones that make use of conjunctions, rearrange words to modify phrases, and develop dependent clauses. For example,

> **Before combining:** The tree is tall. The tree is old. The tree gives shade on a sunny day.
>
> **After combining:** The tall, old tree gives shade on a sunny day.

One reviewer for this playbook had a brilliant analogy for the purpose of sentence combining, noting that taking sentences apart and putting them back together is much like Legos—you learn to build by taking them apart and reassembling them. Saddler and Graham (2005) compared traditional grammar instruction with sentence combining instruction and found significantly better results for sentence combining.

There are a number of ways to combine sentences, including these:

- **Punctuation.** Students learn that some punctuation marks end sentences (period, question mark, exclamation mark) and others allow for sentences to be combined. It is important that students know that the comma is not powerful enough to combine sentences. Simply using a comma to combine two sentences will likely result in a run-on sentence or comma splice. The punctuation marks that do allow for sentence combining are the dash (—), colon (:), and semicolon (;).
- **Compound Sentences.** Another way to combine sentences is through the use of compound sentences. Students learn to use specific words to create compound sentences when the ideas are equal to one another. The words that connect ideas, or clauses, in this way are called *coordinating conjunctions,* and the most common ones are *and, or, but, so,* and *because.*
- **Subordination.** Combining sentences to make one sentence more important than another is done through subordination. These complex sentences have a main clause or independent clause and one or more subordinate clauses or dependent clauses. The words *when, although,* and *if* (called *subordinating conjunctions*) or words such *as who, what,* and *that* (called *relative pronouns*) are commonly used in subordination.
- **Reduction**. A way to combine sentences even further is to change one of the sentences to a phrase. This reduction results in a few words added to the main sentence such that the new sentence contains important details from the sentence being reduced to a phrase.
- **Apposition.** An appositive is like a parenthetical statement surrounded by commas, not by parentheses. This final way for teaching students sentence combining results in students understanding how to take a word or phrase and place it in a parallel position to a noun in the sentence.

These main approaches to sentence combining require sophisticated knowledge of syntax and not simply memorized grammar rules.

In one lesson, Ms. Ocampo's class developed 12 statements during a discussion about their recent visit to the Museum of Us. She then distributed scissors and copies of the sentences for each of the students to cut apart, challenging them to rewrite the sentences as a summary that contained no more than six sentences. Together they performed sentence surgery, cutting unnecessary words out of the disjointed statements. Using the sentence strips as manipulatives, the students moved them around on the table until they were satisfied that they had created a smoother sounding document. In addition, they had blank sentence strips to add new words not in the original list. Here are the 12 original statements:

1. Fourth graders went to the Museum of Us.
2. The students were amazing.
3. We went on Tuesday.
4. We were impressed with area that explained Indigenous people.
5. It described daily life 100 years ago.
6. We met people from different tribes.
7. We enjoyed meeting the people.
8. The people told us interesting stories.
9. The stories were about their ancestors.
10. We liked eating tortillas.
11. The tortillas were handmade.
12. Eating tortillas was the best part of the day.

Jaban's table group composed a new six-sentence summary using sentence combining to support their writing:

> On Tuesday, the most amazing class of fourth graders visited the Museum of Us. We were most impressed with the native peoples area because it described daily life 100 years ago. We enjoyed meeting different people, all from different tribes. They told us interesting stories about their ancestors. However, the best part of the day was eating a handmade tortilla.

WHAT'S YOUR ADVICE?

Most states, provinces, and territories have specific language standards for grade levels. These typically include grammar, such as pronoun-antecedent agreement, verb tenses, and varying sentence patterns. Other language standards emphasize syntactical knowledge to place phrases and clauses in sentences. Importantly, there is a standard for students to recognize variations from standard English in their own and others' writing and speaking. Your school district is forming a committee to study how to strengthen instruction in language structures, and you've been invited to serve. You have been given some materials to prepare for the first meeting, and you have been asked to chronicle your thoughts. What are key considerations you want to bring forward to the committee?

Topics	Your Key Points to Bring to Your First Committee Meeting
Grammar Instruction	
Syntax Instruction	
Variations in Language	

Generative Sentences

One easy and quick way to assess students' understanding of syntax (and vocabulary) is through generative sentences, an extension of the given word approach described by Fearn and Farnan (2001). Students are given a word and then provided the conditions necessary to construct a sentence, which may include the placement of the word in a sentence (e.g., in the third position, final position, etc.) and the overall length of the sentence (e.g., more than seven words or exactly 11 words). In doing so, they must use knowledge of language structures to compose a sentence that is grammatically, syntactically, and semantically correct. See Figure 10.5 for ways to engage students in this assessment task.

Figure 10.5 Prompts for Generative Sentence Activities

Letter Placing	• Word that begins with ___________. • Word that contains ___________. • Word that contains ___________ in the ___________ position.
Structure Sentences	• Begin a sentence with ___________. • End a sentence with ___________. • Create a sentence with ___________in the ___________ position.
Word Limiting	• Provide a range (e.g., eight to ten words in length). • Provide a minimum (e.g., at least five words in length). • Provide a maximum (e.g., no more than 11 words in length). • Provide a specific length (e.g., exactly eight words in length).
Sentence Patterning **(Parts of Speech)**	• Begin a sentence with a noun. • Use a proper noun in a sentence. • Use a noun and a pronoun in a sentence. • Include an adjective with a target word. • Use an adverb in the third position in the sentence. • Include a preposition in your sentence. • Use ___________ as a gerund. • Use a noun infinitive to make an interesting sentence.
Sentence Patterning **(Punctuation)**	• Write a sentence that ends with an exclamation mark. • Ask a question using the word ___________. • Write a sentence with an independent clause and a semicolon. • Use a colon with a list. • Include a parenthetical expression in a sentence.

Sentence Patterning (Elements of Style)	• Write an imperative using the word ________. • Create a sentence with a prepositional phrase. • Use a possessive with the target word ________. • Begin a sentence with a dependent clause. • Write a sentence that uses alliteration. • Use ________ as a simile. • Include an appositive in a sentence with the word ________.

Source: Fisher and Frey (2007).

Sixth-grade teacher Lena Pritchard uses generative sentences to foster her students' ability to move from content vocabulary knowledge through the development of sentences and paragraphs. In doing so, they must apply their knowledge of language structures. They had targeted vocabulary they had been learning during a unit of instruction about the San Francisco earthquake disaster of 1906. During the first few minutes of class, she gave them these generative sentence challenges, saying, "I'd like for you to develop these sentences in the context of what you have been learning about this event."

- Write a sentence that is at least 10 words in length with the word *inadequate* in the ninth position.
- Write a sentence that is between seven and nine words in length with the word *catastrophe* in the ending position.
- Use the word *genuine* in a sentence that has a dependent clause.
- Write a sentence with the word *evaluated* and include a parenthetical expression.

Kylie wrote the following generative sentences:

1. The response of the military was heroic but inadequate, so the city burned.
2. Newspapers across the country called it a catastrophe.
3. After the earthquake, the people had genuine concerns about going back into buildings.
4. Experts evaluated the disaster and made many improvements to the building code (no more wood structures, stronger materials.)

The teacher uses generative sentences about once a week to reinforce knowledge of previously taught words and to strengthen students' application of language structures. "I've found it's not enough for them to learn to identify grammatical and syntactical elements. They need to apply them to their writing and understand them in their reading," said Ms. Pritchard.

Near the end of their English class, Ms. Pritchard reminded them of the exit ticket. "Please go back to the generative sentences you wrote today. Choose one of those as the topic sentence for a summary of what we have been learning today from our readings from the National Archive." Kylie wrote the following:

> The response of the military was heroic but <u>inadequate</u>, so the city burned. They were the first responders, but they couldn't fight the fire. It burned for three days and destroyed 500 city blocks. The military fed people, treated injuries, and gave people shelter.

"I like using this technique because there's some scaffolding that happens," the teacher explained. "We go from the word level, to the sentence level, to the paragraph level. I get to see what they know about vocabulary, comprehension, and language structures, all at once."

TAKE ACTION

What do the generative sentences about the San Francisco earthquake tell you about students' knowledge of language structure? How might you use this technique with your students?

____

____

____

TEXT-TO-SELF CONNECTION

What are key reasons for making instruction of language structures explicit in your classroom? Consider the grade level of your students as you articulate a rationale for doing so.

____

____

____

Using the traffic light scale, with red being not confident, yellow being somewhat confident, and green indicating very confident, how confident are you in your ability to

- Integrate instruction of language structures into reading, discussion, and writing?

- Use comparative analysis to teach students about language variations and patterns?

- Use techniques outlined in this module (close reading of sentences, sentence combining, generative sentences) in your classroom?

Takeaways

- Contemporary grammar instruction adopts a descriptive approach to understanding the patterns that appear in English and its dialects, as well as in other languages.
- Languages and dialects have rules (grammar) that impact understanding. Word order, (syntax), is a subset of grammar that also impacts comprehension.
- Instruction on language structures doesn't need to be didactic and limited to worksheets and drills. In fact, authentic integration of techniques fosters learning and is beneficial for students throughout their school careers.
- Sentence-level work fosters understanding and application of language structures.

PS: The answers to the anticipation guide are F, T, F, T.

online resources

Visit the companion website at
resources.corwin.com/teachingreading
for this module's downloadable resources.

MODULE

11

Literacy and Text Knowledge

In this module, we will

- **Examine the behaviors associated with print and digital print concepts.**
- **Identify the role of text features and text structures in language comprehension.**
- **Explore the ways in which understandings of genre aid readers.**

Photo by iStock.com/STEEX

Look at the hands of the child in the picture. Notice how the book is held and the position of the book. Think about yourself holding a book, turning a page, starting to read. Where did you start? Did you read to the end of the line? Where do your eyes go next? These are all print concepts, and you know them well. But how did you learn them? How do you teach them?

Print concepts are an entry point into the world of literacy knowledge. The recognition of print, including directionality and spatial displays, is just one element of literacy knowledge.

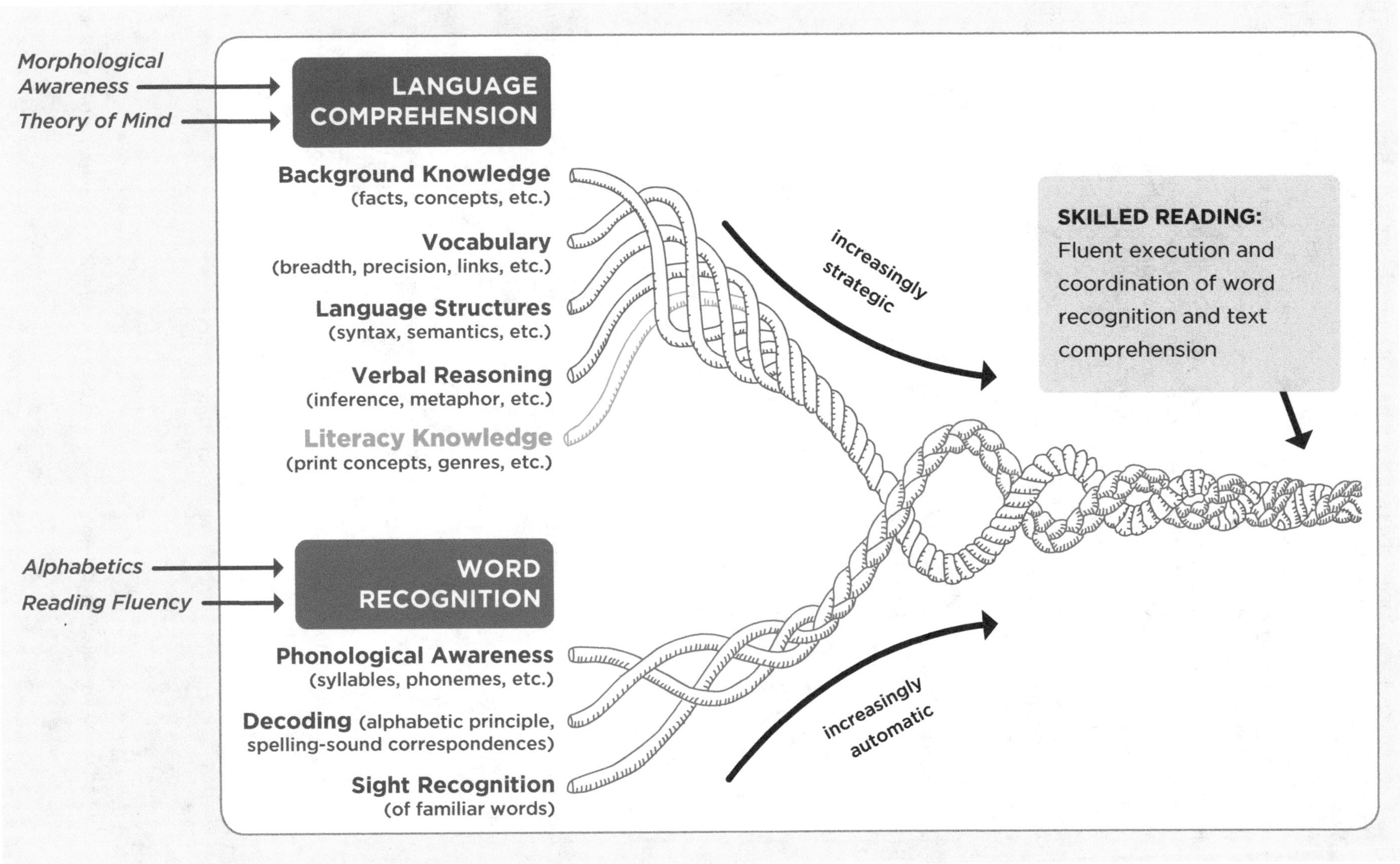

Source: Adapted from Scarborough, H. S. (2001). Connecting early language and literacy to later reading (dis)abilities: Evidence, theory, and practice. In S. Neuman & D. Dickinson (Eds.), *Handbook for research in early literacy* (pp. 97–110). Guilford Press.

Did you notice, for instance, the text features that were designed to help you process the information? We use headings, for example, to signal the organizational structure. We include features to help you reflect on, process, and evaluate the content and consider the application of ideas. We provide you with an advance organizer with some statements that you can later evaluate. We use images to illustrate some of the ideas and figures to highlight others. You were likely able to use the information in these features because of the knowledge you have about how they work.

In addition to your knowledge of text features, your knowledge of text structures and genres likely aided your understanding. Further, your knowledge about teaching and learning (which is your background knowledge; the focus of Module 7) was supplemented by your knowledge about informational texts and the structures that authors commonly use to convey information.

Read each statement and mark **T** if you think the statement is true and **F** if you think the statement is false. As you read through the module, you might change your responses. Be prepared to explain your responses and use the text for evidence.

Before Reading	Statements	After Reading
T **F**	1. Literacy knowledge is primarily print awareness.	**T** **F**
Why did you indicate true or false?		Has your thinking changed after reading?
T **F**	2. Digital print concepts are taught in grades 3 and above.	**T** **F**
Why did you indicate true or false?		Has your thinking changed after reading?
T **F**	3. Genres are easily defined, and there is widespread agreement about which texts belong to which genres.	**T** **F**
Why did you indicate true or false?		Has your thinking changed after reading?
T **F**	4. Text feature instruction should be focused on use, not just identification.	**T** **F**
Why did you indicate true or false?		Has your thinking changed after reading?

What Are Print Concepts?

Children who understand print concepts know how to handle a text while reading, because they know how the print in the text works. These understandings are the foundations for their developing knowledge about literacy. To support successful reading experiences, students must learn that what can be said can also be written. And what can be read can also be spoken. Importantly, there is permanence to the print, as the message remains the same.

Some children begin their school careers already knowing print concepts, because they have sat on the laps of adults who have modeled how to hold a book, how to read from left to right by pointing to words, and how to pause when they come to a punctuation mark. Others may not have had these experiences. Thus, the focus on print concepts is strongest in prekindergarten and kindergarten classrooms but tapers off as other aspects of reading become the focus.

Of course, there are older students who still need to develop these skills, such as a speaker of Arabic (which is organized from right to left) who is learning to read English or a student with interrupted formal education who has not had many opportunities to handle books. These physical book-handling skills shift as students read texts digitally. Fortunately, print concepts, which are early foundational skills, can be taught once children are at school. The following list of 10 print concepts supports early learning about text handling and how the print inside a text works (Johns, 1980; Lomax & McGee, 1987).

10 PRINT CONCEPTS

1. **Print Carries Meaning**. The black marks on this page are letters that make words, and those words mean something to you. Students need to learn that markings on a page carry meaning for them, too!
2. **Book Handling**. Since we are not born with a book in our hands, children must learn how to hold a book the correct way rather than upside down. They also must learn how to turn the pages from right to left without tearing them.
3. **Directionality of Text on a Page**. Students need to be taught where their eyes should start reading on a page. Teaching students to look from top to bottom, left to right will help them understand this early reading skill.
4. **Directionality Within Words**. Just as we read several words, sentences, and paragraphs from left to right, so too must we read letters within the words from left to right.
5. **Return Sweeps**. It is a habit for you that when you read to the end of a line, your eyes sweep back to the left and continue reading on the next line. For a student who doesn't know this, comprehension is sure to quickly break down.
6. **1:1 Correspondence**. Knowing that every word that is read in the text is represented by a printed word is an understanding that needs to be taught.
7. **Word Boundaries and Spacing**. It sure would be difficult to read words without knowledge of word boundaries and spacing. Try it! readingisdifficultwithout spacesasyouareunsurewherewordsstartandstop.
8. **Beginning and Ending of Text.** Why are words put together in a sentence? Why are sentences put together in a paragraph? What does it mean when I no longer see print at the end of the book? Although this is obvious to you as a proficient reader, students need to be taught this print concept.

9. **Identification of the Title and Author**. A frequent sentence a child will hear in school is "The title of this book is ________." It is important for students to understand that just as they have names, so do books.

10. **Identification of Punctuation**. To sound like fluent readers, students need to learn what the little black dots (periods, full stop) mean along with other punctuation marks, such as question marks, quotation marks, commas, and exclamation marks.

DIGITAL PRINT CONCEPTS

Of course, printed books are not the only sources of reading material. Students also read digitally and need to understand how these texts work. They come to understand that they can engage with text online in different ways. For example, they may be able to tap, drag/slide, free rotate, drag and drop, pinch, spread, and flick. The technology tools are changing rapidly; a fundamental understanding of print concepts assists children in bridging print and e-books. Javorsky (2014) explored the comparisons between print concepts and digital print concepts, noting their similarities and differences (see Figure 11.1).

Figure 11.1 Observed Differences Between Paper-Based and Mobile Digital Stories

Description	With a Paper-Based Text	With a Mobile Device
Starting a Story	Locate front of the book and open the cover.	Activate the device, adjust volume, make onscreen selections, and activate story application.
Rereading a Story From the Beginning	Close the book and reopen it.	May need to use an icon, navigate a settings menu, "swipe" repeatedly to return to the first screen, or close the application and reopen it.
Turning Pages	Learn to hold paper corners and turn from right to left.	Recognize that a "virtual page" on the screen has turned from right to left, or has flipped over from the bottom to the top, because the text, or the illustration, or both, suddenly changed.
Maintaining a Sense of Place	Reader enters and stays within the story.	Reader can unknowingly leave the story through external links embedded in the mobile app.
Receiving Sensory Input	Visuals.	Frequently simultaneous input from visuals and auditory.
Processing Visual Information	Static illustrations.	Animated illustrations that may be automatic or reader-activated; text that may change size, be highlighted, or be underlined.

Description	With a Paper-Based Text	With a Mobile Device
Processing Auditory Information	Story could be read aloud by another person sitting with the child.	Disembodied text narration presented automatically or when user-activated, background music, sound effects that typically connect to illustrations.
Option to Read Aloud	Child may ask another person sitting with them to read the book aloud.	May have choice to activate narration option by using an icon or a settings menu or by touching speech bubbles onscreen.
Visually Matching Narration to the Text	Physical finger pointing initiated by the person who is reading or by the child who is listening.	Text may be automatically highlighted or underlined while audio plays, and this match may be illustrated word for word, sentence by sentence, or page by page.

Source: Javorsky (2014).

A study of 200 preschoolers that compared digital and print highlights the fact that both digital and print concepts are important to develop (Reich et al., 2019). The children were randomly assigned to be read the same book, half with auto-narration on a tablet and the others by a researcher from a print book. Engagement with both versions was the same. The children vocalized more about the e-book but scored higher on comprehension and vocabulary on the print book. While there is some research showing that digital reading interferes with comprehension, the fact is that e-books are used daily in elementary classrooms. (See Fisher & Frey, 2018, for a review of studies on digital reading.) In addition, students in grades 3 and above participate in state standards-based tests that are administered digitally, and these tests require them to read and manipulate texts.

A study of 200 preschoolers that compared digital and print highlights the fact that both digital and print concepts are important to develop.

NOTICE AND WONDER

When I inventory my classroom to identify materials to teach print and digital print concepts, I note the following needs:

____

____

____

Text Types

As students engage with texts, they come to understand the structures that authors use, such as the difference between narrative and expository texts. And they learn specifics within these two broad categorizations, such as story grammar or cause-and-effect structures. (See Figure 11.2 for information about aspects of story grammar and Figure 11.3 for common informational text structures.) They learn that nonfiction, informational, and expository texts have certain characteristics. And they learn that stories, poems, and plays have their own unique structures.

Figure 11.2 Narrative Text Structure Based on Story Grammar

Element	Definition
Setting	The physical location used to tell the story.
Point of View	The perspective from which the story is told (first person, third person, omniscient).
Plot	The sequence of events, especially how the characters interact with the setting through dialogue.
Characters—Antagonist	A character or group of characters who represent the opposition against which the hero(es) or protagonist(s) must contend.
Characters—Protagonist	The leading character, but not always a hero. Typically, the protagonist changes or evolves during the story.
Dialogue	The language that the characters use to convey their ideas and feelings.
Rising Action	A series of events that lead to the climax of the story. Action typically relates to the conflicts or struggles of the protagonist.
Climax	The point of greatest tension and the turning point in the action; also signals the change from rising action to falling action.
Conflict	The struggle between the opposing forces, of which there are five basic forms: person versus person, person versus self, person versus nature, person versus society, and person versus God.
Falling Action	The events that follow the climax and end in the resolution.
Resolution	The point in the story where the conflict has been settled or worked out.

Figure 11.3 Common Informational Text Structures and Signal Words

Text Structure	Definition	Signal Words
Compare/Contrast	A text that describes the similarities and differences among two or more things, places, events, ideas, and so on	although, as well as, as opposed to, both, but, by contrast, compared with, different from, either . . . or, even though, however, in common, in comparison, instead of, like, on the other hand, otherwise, similar to, similarly, still, unlike, whereas, yet
Problem/Solution	A text that identifies an issue and how the issue is solved; often the solution becomes another problem	because, consequently, despite, dilemma is, if . . . then, problem is, puzzle is solved, question/answer, resolved, result, so that, thus
Cause/Effect	A text that explains how or why something happened	accordingly, as a result of, because, begins with, consequently, effects of, for this reason, if . . . then, in order to, is caused by, leads/led to, may be due to, so that, steps involved, thereby, therefore, thus, when . . . then
Chronological/ Sequence/ Temporal	A text that presents information in order of time, sequence, or as a process	additionally, after, afterward, another, as soon as, before, during, finally, first, following, immediately, initially, last, later, meanwhile, next, not long after, now, on (date), preceding, second, soon, then, third, today, tomorrow, until, when, yesterday
Descriptive	A text that provides details that could be a list or outline	above, across, along, appears to be, as in, behind, below, beside, between, down, for example, for instance, in back of, in addition, in front of, in particular, looks like, near, on top of, onto, outside, over, specifically, such as, to the right/left, under

NOTES

Text Features

Readers also need to develop an understanding of text features. We define text features as design elements used in a text to provide a structure to the reading. These features include titles, headings, charts, and illustrations. We can broaden the definition as we consider graphic and typographical design elements such as color, illustrations, diagrams, boldfaced or italicized words, and fonts. Other text features that further organize longer texts include conventional book elements such as a table of contents, chapters, page numbers, and indexes. These are guideposts in the truest sense, because they allow the reader to locate information quickly without getting lost in a sea of words. Some common text features are described in Figure 11.4.

Figure 11.4 Common Text Features

Type of Element	Text Features
Elements That Organize	Chapters Titles Headings Subheadings List of figures
Elements for Locating Information	Table of contents Indexes Page numbers
Elements for Explanation and Elaboration	Diagrams Charts and tables Graphs Glossary
Elements That Illustrate	Photographs Illustrations
Elements That Notify	Bolded words Italics and other changes in font

FIND THE MISTAKES

Too often, intentional and direct instruction of text features occurs in isolation, or not at all. A study of modeling during shared reading of teachers in grades 3 to 8 revealed that text features ran a distant fourth in frequency, with most modeling attention devoted to comprehension, vocabulary, and text structures (Fisher et al., 2008). Avoid these mistakes as they relate to text features:

1. **Teaching text features in isolation.** The goal isn't for students to label them, but rather to understand how they support a reader's understanding of a text. Demonstrate how these features work within the text. For instance, headings and subheading allow the reader to predict what will happen next. As students read to the end of a text passage, have them develop a habit of checking back to the heading at the beginning to see if their predictions were realized.
2. **Assuming that students already know how to navigate text features.** Students may be able to label a text feature but fail to use it when needed. When a student is stuck and a text feature might help, prompt them. (For example, "Would now be a good time to look at the glossary?")
3. **Failing to require the use of text features in their own writing.** Text features are designed by the author to support the comprehension of their readers. Make sure that you require students to use text features in their own writing.

Text Genres

Beyond the broad literacy knowledge of narrative and informational texts, students grow in their reading-specific knowledge as it relates to genre. Students learn about genres and the ways in which text types are used to organize them. They learn the difference between realistic fiction and fantasy, for example. And they know how biographies, opinion essays, and reports of information differ. Although there are debates about what makes a genre and how to define a specific genre, most people agree that texts within the same genre have similarities in form and style.

Some literary genres are unfamiliar and need to be explicitly taught.

Some literary genres are unfamiliar and need to be explicitly taught; poetry comes to mind as a common example. Another form is the graphic novel, in which text and images are intertwined to tell a complicated narrative. The *Bone* series of graphic novels is aimed at a young audience, but its thousand-plus pages arch over a series of adventures that rival the *Lord of the Rings* trilogy. This genre requires a specialized kind of reading, in which meaning is conveyed through movement, color, and placement on the page as well as the written text. As is the case with many of the literary and informational texts cited in this module, multiple qualitative factors are in play, in this case levels of meaning (e.g., *Bone* follows the heroic cycle) and visual elements as well as genre. We have organized a range of text types into a genre wheel (see Figure 11.5).

Figure 11.5 Genre Wheel

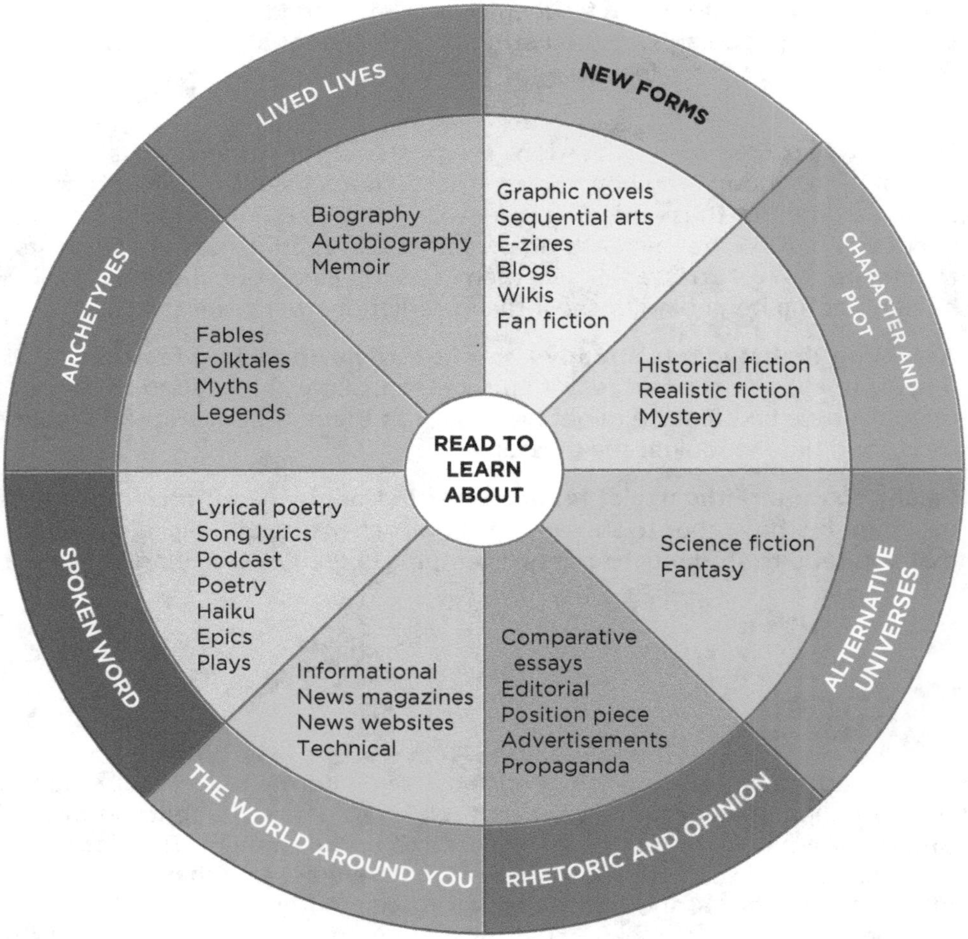

Source: Wiseman et al. (2020).

NOTES

Instruction in Literacy Knowledge

PRINT REFERENCING

Young children rarely ask questions about print (Yaden et al., 1989); their attention is on the story and its illustrations, not on how it is encoded. Eye-gaze research with preschoolers has demonstrated that less than 5% of their visual fixations are on print, and their knowledge of alphabetics does not correlate to time with eyes on print (Justice et al., 2005). In other words, although some children had early literacy skills, that didn't predict whether they would spend time noticing the print itself. And it turns out that teachers don't spend much time pointing out the print representations. However, when teachers of young children are taught how to reference print during shared readings, their students' literacy knowledge improves. Teachers in one study learned how to use four domains of print referencing during reading: print organization, print meaning, letters, and words (see Figure 11.6). As one example, they would point out dialogue, saying, "On this page the lion says, 'Help me!' to the mouse. Here are the lion's words [pointing]." Their students, in turn, saw significant gains in print concept knowledge, alphabet knowledge, and name-writing ability compared with students who were not in print-referencing classrooms (Justice et al., 2009). Explicit instruction that draws children's attention to print has a positive impact. We are reminded, yet again, of Scarborough's reminder that the individual strands of the reading rope can impact the entire bundle.

When teachers of young children are taught how to reference print during shared readings, their students' literacy knowledge improves.

Figure 11.6 Four Print-Referencing Domains

Instructional Domain 1: Print Organization	
Objectives	**Sample Print Reference**
1. **Page Order:** Knows the order in which pages are read in a book.	I am going to read this page first and then this page over here next.
2. **Author:** Knows the role of the author.	The author, Eric Carle, wrote all the words in this book.
3. **Page Organization:** Knows that reading occurs from the top of the page to the bottom of the page.	This is the top of the page. This is where I begin reading.
4. **Title of Book:** Knows the role of the title of the book.	This is the title of the book. It tells is the name of the book.
5. **Print Direction:** Knows that reading must occur from left to right.	I start reading here and I read this way.
Instructional Domain 2: Print Meaning	
Objectives	**Sample Print Reference**
1. **Print Function:** Understands the relationship between meaning and print.	Here are the penguin's words. He says, "Thank you."
2. **Environmental Print:** Knows the purpose of print embedded within the environment.	This is a box of cereal. It says "Corn Flakes."
3. **Metalinguistic Concept of Reading:** Understands the meaning behind reading and the contexts in which reading occurs.	We're going to read these words what will these words tell us?

(Continued)

(Continued)

Instructional Domain 3: Letters	
Objectives	**Sample Print Reference**
1. **Upper- and Lowercase Letters:** Knows that letters come in two forms, one of which is the uppercase letter.	This M in red block is an uppercase letter. See how this uppercase letter is bigger than these lowercase letters?
2. **Names of Letters:** Knows the names of the majority of uppercase letters.	What is this letter?
3. **Metalinguistic Concept of Letter:** Knows that letters are a symbols used in written language.	Do you see a letter that is in your own name?

Instructional Domain 4: Words	
Objectives	**Sample Print Reference**
1. **Word Identification:** Identifies some written words in familiar contexts.	This word is "the." This word is in this book all the time, can you help me find it?
2. **Short vs. Long Words:** Knows that the number of letters in words can vary from many to few.	This word is "lollapaloosh." It is a long word. It has a lot of letters in it! Let's count all the letters.
3. **Letters vs. Words:** Knows that letters are different than words.	This is the letter K. K is in the words kangaroo and kick.
4. **Concept of Word in Print:** Represents the systematic relationship between spoken words and written words.	Let's point to each word as I read it. Ready?

Source: Justice et al. (2009, p. 80).

INTEGRATED INSTRUCTION IN PRINT CONCEPTS AND TEXT HANDLING

In addition to the direct instruction of print concepts and text handling, teachers should integrate information about these skills into their interactions with students, whether that be whole-class, small-group, or individual instruction. For teachers of older students with unfinished learning or who are new to the conventions of English, print concepts are likely taught during intervention or individualized instruction time.

A few examples of the ways in which teachers integrate instruction about print concepts and text handling include the following:

- During a reading conference with a kindergarten student, the teacher says, "Show me which way you would read the words."

  The student indicates left to right. The teacher then invites the student to read the line, which ends with a period.

  The student correctly reads the sentence, and the teacher asks, "Where do we start to read next?"

  The student points to the first word on the next page.

The teacher responds, "There's a lot of information on each page. Let's take a look at this page again (pointing to the original page). You read this sentence, but look, there's more! Let's keep reading. We move to the next line on the page. Let me show you." And they continue working through the page.

- A first-grade teacher asks the students in a small-group lesson to point to the words as she reads the text aloud. She is specifically looking for their flow and whether their fingers start the words as she does. She notices that two students' fingers are way ahead of her voice and invites them to all try again. She reads a little more slowly to observe closely. She notes that two of her students do not understand 1:1 correspondence and plans another lesson with them.

  When she meets with them later that day, she asks the students to point to the first letter of the first word. They do so correctly.

  She asks them to point the last letter of the word. Both do so correctly.

  She then reads the word and has them follow with their finger. She then reads the next word, and they follow her voice. They get each word right and track exactly with her voice.

  She then reads the next sentence, and the students' fingers are way ahead of her, and she realizes that they are reading ahead of her voice. She asks them to show her the spaces between words and where several words start.

  She realizes that these two students have made significant progress and need more challenging reading instruction.

- After reading and discussing the text, second-grade students are asked to write about it. The teacher asks them, "What do we start with?"

  The students respond: Capitals! The teacher replies, "Great. And what do we end with?" The students respond: Periods!

  The teacher continues, "Remember the writing rules. We also indent the first word and write to the end of the line and then start all the way to the left on the next line. Ready?"

- A fifth-grade teacher is meeting with an emergent multilingual learner whose heritage language is Farsi, a language whose print is read right to left. The teacher uses Language Experience Approach (Dorr, 2006), in which the teacher scribes the student's words, usually following a discussion, and the student reads these transcriptions aloud back to the teacher. For example, a line of the transcription reads as follows:

  > I saw the man. The man was mad. Very mad. Because when he sat on the bus seat it was wet. What do you think it was?

  When the student reads this aloud, they read through all the periods as if it were a single sentence.

  The teacher focuses them on the full stops, saying, "Remember, these periods tell us to stop. There's an idea there, and we need a little pause, maybe to think and reflect or visualize. Not a long one, but a short one. Let's read the first sentence on the line."

  The lesson continues through the remaining sentences and lines, with the focus on sentences. After reading, the student and teacher count the number of words in each sentence and revisit the experience that the student had on the bus.

WHAT'S YOUR ADVICE?

An instructional coach at your school is surveying teachers about print and digital print concepts in your school. They are seeking advice about what these concepts should look like in each grade level. Consider your own students' needs. What would you advise is useful in your grade level, either for teaching all students or for intervention purposes? Keep students with disabilities and multilingual learners in mind.

Print and Digital Print Concepts for All Students in My Grade Level	Print and Digital Print Concepts for Intervention in My Grade Level

Modeling Text Structures and Text Features

Authors often present information through graphs, charts, and tables, and these text features typically have a great deal of information and are open to a number of interpretations. Interpreting graphs, charts, and tables is not simply a school task; it's something that people do nearly every day. Information presented in graph or chart form is often critical to understanding the text. It's not an extra added for visual stimulation. Interestingly, test makers often require that students interpret information found in graphs, charts, and tables if students are to be scored as proficient.

Modeling and thinking aloud provides students with examples that they can try on as they read. When teachers model, they make their thinking visible for students. It's a cognitive apprenticeship approach in which students start to notice aspects of texts that they may have missed. Over time, and with practice, students try on the behaviors of their teachers and begin to incorporate these behaviors as their own. Of course, modeling is not limited to text structures and text features, and students also need direct instruction in the ways in which text works, as might occur when a teacher is introducing various genres or signal words that suggest a specific structure. But modeling provides students with examples of thinking on the run and opportunities to notice specific aspects of written language.

Sixth-grade science teacher Rebecca Jessop showed her students information from the National Oceanic and Atmospheric Administration (NOAA) website on carbon dioxide measures taken at the Mauna Loa Observatory (see Figure 11.7). As she talked, she explained her thinking about the chart on emissions for the last five years.

> I see this trend line, and it's not slowing down. I know that this is a positive trend, as I can read the scale on the left side of the chart. The red lines seem to imply that there is an up and down trend within the year. But I notice that each year has four small tick marks—do you see them? I bet that's an indicator for each season: fall, spring, summer, and winter. It makes sense that the carbon dioxide concentration would change during the year, based on the seasons, but I can easily see that the overall trend is increasing concentration. If I were asked a question about the overall trend, I'd know the answer. I'd also be able to discuss the idea that there is a carbon dioxide cycle; there are times when the concentration is lower or higher than the average for the year. What other trends do you see? Take a minute and construct a question about this graph with your partners, and we'll see if we can use the graph to answer the questions.

Figure 11.7 Recent Monthly Mean CO_2 at Mauna Loa Observatory

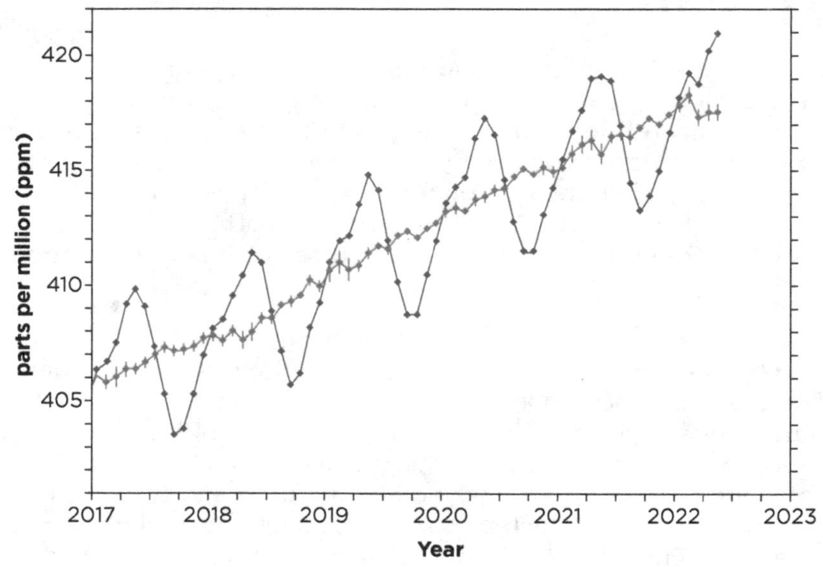

Source: National Oceanographic and Space Administration (2022).

NOTES

Genre Studies

Genres continue to expand and blur, much to the delight of most readers! Classroom libraries typically have many genres of text, but students can get stuck in reading a narrow range. One approach for teaching about the unique characteristics of a group of texts and expanding students' reading diets is through genre studies. Fourth-grade teacher Naomi Winters introduced the fantasy genre to her students, noting that "it's undertaught. Lots of kids don't get much exposure to this genre." She said the inspiration came from a group of her students who had watched the movie *Howl's Moving Castle* and kept talking about it. Using the characteristics of the fantasy genre outlined by Cruz and Pollock (2004), Ms. Winters's students developed a running class chart of evidence they found in the picture books, short stories, and books they read:

- Connection to another world
- A quest
- Magic or magical creatures
- Heroic change
- Good versus evil

They started with a few picture books to analyze for the fantasy genre characteristics, such as *Sector 7* by David Weisner, *Mufaro's Beautiful Daughters* by John Steptoe, and *The Star People: A Lakota Story* by S. D. Nelson. She then moved them into a targeted text for all the students to read: *The Phantom Tollbooth* by Norton Juster. In addition, students chose a book from the following list to utilize in collaborative literature circles:

- *Inkworld,* the first book in the *Inkheart* series by Cornelia Funke
- *Fantastic Beasts and Where to Find Them* by J. K. Rowling
- *The Girl Who Drank the Moon* by Kelly Barnhill
- *Malice in Ovenland* by Micheline Hess
- *Dragons in a Bag* by Zetta Elliott

"I selected the last two titles because they feature children of color in contemporary settings," said the teacher. "I want my students to see that the fantasy genre exists in places throughout the world and across time."

Using a comparative approach, the class added items to the chart to call out specific examples of the identified characteristics in each book. "Using an immersive approach to learn about an unfamiliar genre proved to be an effective way to analyze the texts. It will also set them up for exploring the hero's cycle in literature, which they'll be learning more formally in sixth grade."

TAKE ACTION

Inventory your own class library to examine the genres of texts available for students. Are some genres underused? Identify two that you would like to see being read by more students. How might you profile underused genres in your curriculum?

Genre Type	Titles You Have	Possible Curriculum Connections

TEXT-TO-SELF CONNECTION

What are the key reasons for teaching literacy knowledge in my classroom? What are the areas of emphasis I will use with my students?

____

____

____

Using the traffic light scale, with red being not confident, yellow being somewhat confident, and green indicating very confident, how confident am I in my ability to

- Teach print concepts?
- Teach digital print concepts?
- Teach text types?
- Teach text features?
- Teach text genres?

Takeaways

- Literacy knowledge focuses on how texts work. This includes print concepts, text types and genres, and text features. These provide texts with structures that aid in comprehension.
- Start teaching digital text concepts in the primary grades. Given the widespread use of digital texts in classrooms, this dimension of literacy knowledge assists students in understanding e-books, and older students use it in digitally based assessments.
- Genres continue to be redefined as newer formats are introduced. Having said that, students' knowledge and use of genres can assist them in comprehending the texts they read.
- Text features are woefully undertaught compared with other dimensions of literacy knowledge. Integrate text feature instruction such that it moves beyond simple identification. Encourage students to use the text features to support their understanding of the text.

PS: The answers to the anticipation guide are F, F, F, T.

online resources

Visit the companion website at
resources.corwin.com/teachingreading
for this module's downloadable resources.

MODULE

12

Verbal Reasoning

In this module, we will

- Explain and explore the concept of verbal reasoning.
- Differentiate between forward and backward inferences.
- Analyze various literary devices that authors use.
- Identify question protocols that allow students to use textual evidence.

Photo by Guy Basabose on Unsplash

Spend just a short amount of time with young children, and you'll almost certainly hear questions like this: *Why? Why not? How come?* They are curious about the social, biological, and physical worlds around them. Their questions help them to locate a logic in what they experience and see. That's verbal reasoning at work. Some of you may have looked at the module title and immediately thought about your SAT or GRE scores, which report verbal reasoning. But verbal reasoning is definitely not something that we should wait until adolescence to teach. Verbal reasoning is fundamental to how it is that we as humans understand the world and ourselves.

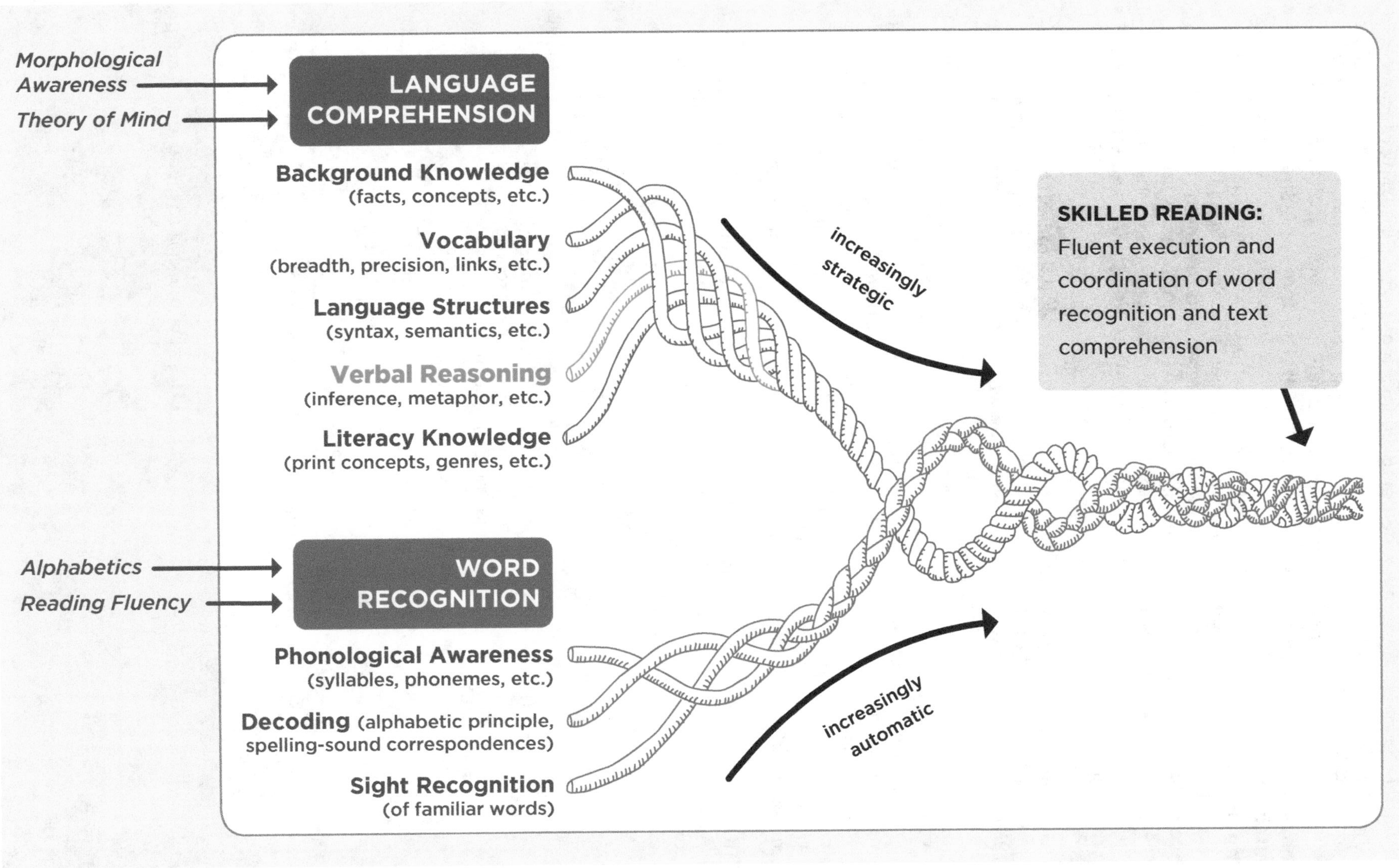

Source: Adapted from Scarborough, H. S. (2001). Connecting early language and literacy to later reading (dis)abilities: Evidence, theory, and practice. In S. Neuman & D. Dickinson (Eds.), *Handbook for research in early literacy* (pp. 97–110). Guilford Press.

Verbal reasoning underpins the comprehension of texts, too. Think of the verbal reasoning skills we associate with reading. The reader pictured in the opening of this module is humored by what he is reading. The ability to infer a character's actions and motivations and to track written dialogue among multiple speakers are just two examples. Readers apply their verbal reasoning when they transform a metaphor used by an author to explain a complex idea. They locate the figurative language that a poet uses to describe the emotional or visual representations in the piece. Older readers sense the mood, the tone, and the theme of a text. Emergent and early readers use verbal reasoning to make predictions about what will happen next in a story. A student's verbal reasoning skills, which emerge when they are toddlers, continue to be applied and strengthened through reading instruction.

Verbal reasoning is definitely not something that we should wait until adolescence to teach.

But students need to be intentionally taught to use verbal reasoning skills. Jacqueline, a first grader, used to stare at other children when they read, rather than look at her own book. One day we asked her what she was doing, and she said, "I'm watching their heads."

When we asked her to explain, she told us that she didn't understand how everyone else knows what the characters were thinking when "it didn't say so in the book." At that moment we realized that Jacqueline hadn't yet figured out what others seemed to do so easily. She thought that looking at the heads of her peers might give her a clue about how they understand what they read. Jacqueline and other young readers need to be taught that the author doesn't tell you explicitly everything you need to know. A solid understanding of a text comes from applying the verbal reasoning needed to infer.

Read each statement and mark **T** if the statement is true and **F** if the statement is false. As you read through the module, you might change your responses. Be prepared to explain your responses and use the text for evidence.

<table>
<tr><th>Before Reading</th><th colspan="2">Statements</th><th>After Reading</th></tr>
<tr><td>**T** **F**</td><td colspan="2">1. As students get older, verbal reasoning plays an increasingly dominant role in their reading comprehension.</td><td>**T** **F**</td></tr>
<tr><td colspan="2">Why did you indicate true or false?</td><td colspan="2">Has your thinking changed after reading?</td></tr>
<tr><td>**T** **F**</td><td colspan="2">2. Teaching literary devices begins in sixth grade.</td><td>**T** **F**</td></tr>
<tr><td colspan="2">Why did you indicate true or false?</td><td colspan="2">Has your thinking changed after reading?</td></tr>
</table>

Before Reading		Statements	After Reading	
T	F	3. Inferencing is a demonstration of verbal reasoning.	T	F
Why did you indicate true or false?			Has your thinking changed after reading?	
T	F	4. Inferences need to be correct in order to be valid.	T	F
Why did you indicate true or false?			Has your thinking changed after reading?	

What Is Verbal Reasoning?

Verbal reasoning is the ability to infer in order to find logical coherence in a text. Verbal reasoning involves understanding concepts as they are framed in words, especially in terms of making inferences and understanding figurative language such as metaphors and idioms. For some students, it's a piece of cake. Others get by by the skin of their teeth. Notice what you just did? You used your verbal reasoning, not isolated word meaning, to understand our point.

Verbal reasoning is essential for reading comprehension. Further, it follows a developmental trajectory that shifts as reading ability grows. There was an interesting study of third-, seventh-, and tenth-grade students in Florida. The researchers wanted to look at the contributory role of skills associated with the simple view of reading (SVR) as well as those associated with verbal and nonverbal reasoning. Their findings were instructive. It should come as no surprise that factors associated with SVR, especially fluency, were important. But they also found that the relative influence of verbal reasoning grew across the grades, becoming increasingly predominant. They reported that "inferential reasoning skills become an important contributor to reading comprehension at increasing grade levels" (Tighe & Schatschneider, 2014, p. 101).

A solid understanding of a text comes from applying the verbal reasoning needed to infer.

Similarly, Hoover and Gough (1990) reported that the impact of SVR changes as readers mature and that there is a gradual decline of the relative amount of influence decoding has in third grade as language comprehension exercises an increasingly dominant role. The message here is not an either/or: Children need to develop word recognition skills, but not at the expense of language comprehension skills. Verbal reasoning is an essential part of language comprehension, and its importance grows as they progress through their school careers. Investment in verbal reasoning with young readers can equip them for a lifetime of reading of complex texts.

How a Reader Uses Verbal Reasoning

We use verbal reasoning to understand what's happening in a sentence. Consider these sentences from *Jabari Jumps* (Cornwall, 2017, p. 9) as the young boy watches other children climb a diving board ladder and jump off.

"'Looks easy,' Jabari said. But when his dad squeezed his hand, Jabari squeezed back."

There's a lot of verbal reasoning that needs to occur to understand these two sentences. The first is the referent *his* used twice in the same sentence. They are possessive referents, but the first refers to the boy's dad, while the second refers to the boy's hand. Young children benefit from instruction about how pronouns are used to refer to characters, as noted in Module 10 on language structures.

Investment in verbal reasoning with young readers can equip them for a lifetime of reading of complex texts.

The second level of inferencing has to do with filling in a gap in information. The author doesn't explicitly say that Jabari is feeling a bit nervous about jumping off the diving board. The word *but* at the beginning of the second sentence sets up a contrastive. While Jabari's words sound confident, his action may be telling us something else. Take *but* out of the sentence, and there's no longer a reason to question how Jabari is feeling. The author chose that word carefully to signal that the protagonist's words and actions might not be completely aligned. (By the way, you did your own inferencing as you read this. We never explicitly told you he was at a swimming pool, but you filled in that gap anyway.)

NOTES

Using Backward and Forward Inferences

Now we'll complicate it a bit more. There are potentially two other kinds of inferences that are needed at this moment to understand those sentences from *Jabari Jumps*. Trabasso and Magliano (1996) called these forward and backward inferences.

Forward inferences encourage the reader to draw a conclusion or make a prediction based on what has been discussed so far. A forward inference in this case is drawing the conclusion that Jabari has been excited about using the diving board now that he has passed his swimming test, discussed in the previous pages, but now his action suggests that he might be having some second thoughts. When we ask students to summarize what they know so far, we are inviting them to draw a conclusion and perhaps make a prediction. "Do you believe that Jabari will jump?" (Keep the title in mind.) But there might also be a backward inference needed, too.

A *backward inference* happens when "you spot the gap and realize that you don't know how to fill it; then you must be vigilant for the needed info when it arises" (Shanahan, 2021, ¶ 9). A backward inference, in this case, might be to ask the question, "Will it be easy or hard for Jabari when he does jump?"

NOTICE AND WONDER

Some students may be narrowly oriented on getting the "right" answer and therefore feel that they are wrong when they need to change a prediction or inference when new information is revealed. How do you assist students who are reluctant to change their minds?

NOTES

Literary Devices Are Inferencing "Shortcuts"

Authors rely on several ways to support the inferring of their readers. One example is through literary devices, which are cognitive shortcuts to convey a concept. Flashback and foreshadowing are ready examples of times when backward and forward inferencing are required. However, these extend to other devices. For instance, authors often use metaphors to convey an otherwise unstated condition. *The Other Side* (Woodson, 2001) features a fence that serves as a literal and figurative barrier between white and Black children, until they decide to do something about it. Another example is *What Do You Do With an Idea?* (Yamada, 2014), which relies on personification in the form of a child's idea that grows and reshapes itself. Common literary devices can be found in Figure 12.1.

Figure 12.1 Common Literary Devices for K–6

Term	Definition	Example
Allegory	Story used to teach something, usually long and requiring analysis to find the intention	• The parables in the Bible • Aesop's Fables
Alliteration	Occurs when the author uses the same letter or sound to start each word in a string; used frequently in books for emergent readers, in part to foster phonemic awareness	*Peter Piper picked a peck of pickled peppers.*
Allusion	Reference to a well-known person, myth, or historical event	• *Bobby's personal Kryptonite was fudge candy.* • *It's as bad as the sinking of the Titanic.*
Flashback	Pauses the action to comment or portray a scene that took place earlier in order to provide more detail about the present character, setting, or plot	During a scene in which a person walks through a dark alley, the author pauses to relate a story about another time the character was scared.
Foreshadowing	Hint of things to come—usually, but not always, an unpleasant event	In the beginning of *Where the Red Fern Grows*, there is a dog fight that hints of future conflict.
Hyperbole	An overstatement or exaggeration that is used for effect and is not meant to be taken literally	*As he looked with disappointment at the ten candles on his birthday cake, Andrew said, "It will take forever before I can drive a car."*

Term	Definition	Example
Irony	Uses sophisticated humor in relaying a message, often saying what something is when the opposite or reverse could be true; authors use irony to say one thing when they mean another.	*James looks at the shark bite out of his surfboard and says, "Great! Now I finally have the short board I always wanted."*
Metaphor	Comparison in which one thing is said to be another; in contrast with similes, metaphors make a direct statement and do not use "like" or "as" to make the comparison.	*The dog's fur was electric, standing on end.*
Onomatopoeia	A word that makes the sound that it represents	boing, buzz, clank, crack, grunt, hiccup, hoot, pitter-patter, screech, splat, tick-tock, whir, zap
Personification	Animals, ideas, or actions possess the qualities of humans.	*Worry had Matty trapped in its arms.*
Point of View—First Person	Told from the perspective of the narrator, and we readers cannot know or witness anything the narrator does not tell us.	*I walked down the dusty lane, listening to the lazy sound of cicadas carried on the warm breeze.*
Point of View—Second Person	The narrator speaks directly to the reader.	*You will likely know by now that Andre is a bad guy.*
Point of View—Third Person	Narrator can convey different perspectives at different times and often shifts to different characters' perspectives (third person omniscient or all-knowing), or narrator tells the story as an outsider but from only one person's perspective (third person limited).	*He walked to the store, not looking for anything in particular. Once inside, James waited for a sign.*
Simile	Statement in which two things are compared and said to be like or as another	*Like a rain-filled cloud, Anna cried and cried when she learned of her lost fortune.*
Symbolism	Object or action that means something more than its literal meaning	A white dove in a poem conveys peace or life.
Tone and Mood	An author presents an attitude and manner of a subject or character as related through dialogue, settings, or descriptions	Hateful, serious, humorous, sarcastic, solemn, objective

WHAT'S YOUR ADVICE?

Memorizing a list of literary devices is not very useful. Rather, noticing when literary devices are used helps students infer to create deeper comprehension. Your grade-level team brings up literary devices during a meeting. They want to revise some of their approaches to make their instruction more effective. What advice do you have for them? Use the categories below to spark your thinking. Remember that you can return to this chart later in the module to add more ideas.

Research on verbal reasoning	
Literary devices to focus on	
Curriculum and materials to support application of verbal reasoning through literary devices	
Instruction about literary devices	

Word Games for Verbal Reasoning

One element of verbal reasoning is word associations. These are often done in the form of games that offer students the opportunity to build schema and vocabulary. These logic puzzles engage students in reasoning and give you an opportunity to observe their thinking. Many of these lend themselves to short sponge activities that "soak up" those extra few minutes between the end of a lesson and the start of recess.

- Spotting the "odd ones out" in a list of words. (In the list *chair/soccer/table/couch, soccer* would be the odd one.)
- Finding the words that mean the same from two lists. (In the two lists *money/hungry/tired* and *currency/angry/hotel, money* and *currency* would mean about the same thing.)
- Finding antonyms (opposites) from two lists of words. (In the two lists *up/over/on* and *through/down/out, up* and *down* would be the opposites)

Mark Jackson plays Odd One Out with his first-grade students when they have a few extra minutes before dismissal. Several items are presented, one of which is not related to the others. This activity requires deductive reasoning skills, and students must apply rules for information to identify the logical conclusion. Or, in some cases, there are many valid responses, and the teacher is looking for the logical inferences that the student makes.

"I have a file folder of word games for just such occasions," he explained (see Figure 12.2). He writes a list of items on the whiteboard and asks students not only to identify the correct answer but also to explain their reasoning. "I try to chart all the good reasons they have for the odd one out," he said. "They're pretty creative. I really like it when they debate about the reason they selected compared to a different person's reason."

Figure 12.2 Odd One Out Assessment

Odd One Out: Circle the one that does not belong.			
apple	banana	potato	pear
red	blue	green	three
twenty	ten	thirty	forty-one
nose	elbow	finger	arm
March	August	Tuesday	December
knee	chin	mouth	nose
Monday	Thursday	Saturday	February
cat	blue	dog	bird
one	tree	four	two

Notice that this task requires word knowledge in addition to the ability to reason through and select the logical choice. Talking with students helps identify their reasoning. When asked about the *nose* question, one student said they selected *arm* because it was so big and the others were small. For the *knee* response, two said they chose *nose* because you could not move your nose, but you could move all the other body parts listed. "Interesting logic and useful information for me," said Mr. Jackson.

Noticing Students' Use of Verbal Reasoning

Verbal reasoning relies on deep knowledge of vocabulary, understanding of logic and literary devices, and the ability to make inferences. Students utilize their verbal reasoning every time they read, discuss, and write about text. Students who read widely tend have stronger verbal reasoning and inferencing strategies at their disposal. It's difficult to teach verbal reasoning if you don't recognize when it does and doesn't happen. Figure 12.3 contains some reflective questions to ask yourself about a student. Consider a student you currently have who is not yet making expected progress. Which of these are they doing well, intermittently, or not at all? Not all of these will apply, of course, depending on your student's developmental level. However, use of these questions can shine a light on where a student might be struggling as it relates to language comprehension.

Students who read widely tend have stronger verbal reasoning and inferencing strategies at their disposal.

Figure 12.3 Questions to Consider in Verbal Reasoning

Does the student . . .	Can the student . . .
Understand story elements?	• Explain why identifying the initiating event can help a reader understand the story? • Describe the beginning, middle, and end of a story? • Identify the basic elements of the story (characters, plot, setting, problem, and solution)? • Use these elements to retell? • Use the contents page to keep track of story events? • Use a chapter title to make predictions and keep track of story events?
Identify and understand literary devices?	• Identify words or ideas that signal personification? • Recognize alliteration? • Recognize a pun? • Recognize onomatopoeia? • Recognize when authors contrast images? • Recognize understatement? • Use similes and metaphors in their oral and written language? • Relate the use of flashback and foreshadowing to the author's craft?

Does the student . . .	Can the student . . .
Understand and analyze characters?	• Discuss the relationships between characters? • Identify who is speaking in a dialogue? • Identify ways to infer the relationships between and among characters? • Use a character's words and actions to make inferences about the character? • Use dialogue to infer characters' feelings toward one another? • Identify a character's plan for solving a problem? • Relate character to plot? • Explain how the problem and solution affect the character's actions?
Understand and analyze plot and setting?	• Identify the plot? • Recognize how characters influence the plot? • Identify the setting? • State why the setting is essential to the story? • Relate plot and setting to one another?
Understand and analyze theme?	• Identify the theme of the story? • Discriminate between plot and theme? • Name other stories with similar themes? • Recognize the universality of major themes? • Relate the author's purpose to the theme?

NOTES

Noticing Verbal Reasoning Through Retelling

Retellings have been used as an assessment tool for many years with narrative and expository texts (e.g., Lucero, 2018; Moss, 2004). Conventional retellings typically attend to a student's ability to accurately recount the events in the texts using the story grammars of plot, character, and so on. But retellings can also be used with a specific focus on inferring, which provides insight into a student's verbal reasoning. Figure 12.4 contains a holistic rubric for evaluating an inference retelling.

Figure 12.4 Retelling Rubric

6	• Develops thoughtful predictions, interpretations, and/or conclusions about the text with depth and understanding • Identifies meanings, clues, and details that are not explicitly stated (inferred) • Includes connections between the text and the reader's background knowledge (schema) or ideas and beliefs
5	• May develop predictions, interpretations, and/or conclusions about the text • May identify meanings, clues, and/or details that are not explicitly stated (inferred) • Includes connections between the text and the reader's background knowledge (schema) or ideas and beliefs
4	• Makes a prediction and/or draws a conclusion about the text • Includes details that are not explicitly stated • Includes a connection between the text and the reader's background knowledge (schema)
3	• Makes a prediction or draws a conclusion about the text • May include details that are not explicitly stated • May include details, predictions, or conclusions that are inaccurate or unsubstantiated based on text information
2	• Attempts to make a prediction or draw a conclusion about the text • Includes some inaccuracies, such as details, conclusions, or predictions that are inaccurate or unsubstantiated based on text information
1	• No evidence of inference (making a prediction, interpreting information, or drawing a conclusion) about the text • Conveys a minimum amount of information about the text • May include information that is off topic

Source: Developed by the Hill Middle School Staff, Long Beach Unified School District (2000). Accessed (12/20/2021) via MiddleWeb .com https://www.middleweb.com/6917/

FIND THE MISTAKES

In previous modules, this feature has focused on the avoidance of errors. But verbal reasoning and inferencing require critical thinking. The challenge is that critical thinking is rarely a linear process. We explore lines of reasoning that don't always pan out, and at times we have to reverse course, change a prediction, and test whether our new thinking holds up. In other words, it's necessary to make mistakes along the way. But do we create a "mistake-friendly classroom" that allows students opportunities to develop their verbal reasoning? (Laslocky, 2021). Use the checklist below to evaluate the extent to which you are a "mistake-friendly teacher." How often did these occur in the last 30 days of learning?

	Never (0)	Sometimes (1-5 times)	Frequently 5+ times
Anticipated "good mistakes" (e.g., using an anticipation guide in advance of a lesson)			
Recognized and engaged in a "good mistake" when it happened			
Asked students to generate "good mistakes" on purpose (e.g., developing three good but incorrect answers to a question that might trick someone)			
Asked students which wrong answer is "more right" (e.g., comparing two incorrect reasons for a character's actions, then asking which one is closer to being right)			

NOTES

Instruction in Verbal Reasoning

What does verbal reasoning instruction look like in the classroom? How can we teach students about reasoning while they are developing other aspects of literacy? In this section, we discuss techniques for using questions, retellings, and sequential art to foster verbal reasoning and inferencing in your classroom.

UNDERSTANDING EVIDENCE AND LINKING QUESTIONS: QAR

When confronted with a question, especially one that challenges them to apply critical thinking, many elementary students have difficulty locating a source for answers. At times, they incorrectly search the text in a fruitless effort to locate an answer that requires them to form an opinion. At other times, they may rely strictly on what they recall to answer a literal-level question, failing to return to the text to support a more nuanced answer. The question-answer relationship (QAR) strategy focuses on four types of questions used to interrogate a text (Raphael et al., 2006). A goal of QAR is for students to develop the ability to recognize where the source of an answer is likely to be found. The four types of answer sources are

- Right there
- Think and search
- Author and you
- On your own

QAR allows students to move beyond literal, recall questions and think about text-explicit ways (book questions) and text-implicit ways (book-and-brain questions; see Figure 12.5) to understanding their readings. These questions allow students to practice using evidence from the text as well as their inferences to respond.

Figure 12.5 Question-Answer Relationships

Question Type	Description	Question Stems
In the Text (Book Questions)		
Right There	Words in the question and answer are directly stated in the text. It is explicit, and the words or phrases can be found within one sentence.	How many . . . ? Who is . . . ? Where is . . . ? What is . . . ?
Think and Search	Information is in the text, but readers must think and make connections between passages in the text.	What is the main idea of . . . ? What caused . . . ?

Question Type	Description	Question Stems
In My Head (Book-and-Brain Questions)		
Author and You	Readers need to think about what they already know, what the author tells them in the text, and how it fits together.	What is the author implying by . . . ? What is suggested by . . . ? What is the author's attitude toward . . . ?
On Your Own	These questions require the reader to use prior knowledge to answer. The text may or may not be needed.	In your own opinion, . . . ? Based on your experience, . . . ? What would you do if . . . ?

"What did the author tell you that can help you answer the question?" asks fourth-grade teacher Amy Martin. "Remember, authors imply, and readers infer."

The students were learning about the ways in which physical geography, including climate, influenced how the local native people and their nations adapted to their natural environment. These students were stuck on the question Ms. Martin raised: How did the environment or location of the Tongva influence the food that they ate? "

"We've been working on QAR this month," said the teacher. "Have a talk with your table group, and use these book-and-brain questions to see if you can develop a good answer. I'll be coming around to your tables to listen to your reasoning."

The teacher went to one group just as David was saying, "You can't find that in a book, you have to think about that on your own. I looked and there isn't a place that says it."

"I bet we can find part of it in the book," Mariah said. "Like, we know what they ate, right?"

"Yeah, we got that part. I think this is more like a think-and-search question. Can we reread the first part that talks about the location?" Destini asked.

The group took a minute or two to reread the passage in their social studies textbook.

David interrupts. "They lived by rivers, creeks and other sources of water. So that's why they ate clams!"

The conversation continued with an exploration of the impact of the environment on the diet of this group of people. Later in the class, Ms. Martin asked a different question about the climate that a person favors and why "you" live where you do. David repeated, "This one is on your own. The author doesn't help you, but you know that there are different choices of environments. I don't get to choose because my parents live here."

Understanding Evidence and Linking Questions: QtA

Questioning the author (QtA) is a text-based strategy that invites the reader to interact with the information and make inferences from the content by analyzing the author's purpose and craft (Beck et al., 1997). One of the reasons students don't question the text is because they don't view reading as a transactional activity between themselves and the author. Using QtA, we can teach them to imagine that the author of the text is sitting next to them, and they can ask them questions. Young readers find this concept liberating, since they may not have previously thought about the person behind the words.

The questions in QtA are meant to serve as discussion prompts that invite students to develop ideas rather than restate information directly from the text. These questions require that students take responsibility for their thinking and for constructing understanding. QtA focuses on five main questions:

1. What is the author trying to tell you?
2. Why is the author telling you that?
3. Does the author say it clearly?
4. How could the author have said things more clearly?
5. What would you say instead?

These can be expanded to include questions that extend students' ability to make inferences through discussion (see Figure 12.6).

During their peer-led book club discussion about *Because of Winn-Dixie* (DiCamillo, 2021), a group of fifth-grade students used Question the Author to make inferences about the text. They finished Chapter 7 and were discussing a notable event that occurred in the story. After talking about the details, they shifted to some QtA questions their teacher provided for them to discuss. The conversation started when Sitha asked, "Why did the author tell us that story about the librarian fighting off the bear with a book?"

The group talked about the fact that the librarian was brave, and, as Riley noted, "Librarians think books are the most powerful thing they have!"

"I think the author wanted us to see that Opal is kinda different, and for sure the dog is, too," Jameer said. "She tells us that story so that we can see Miss Franny [the librarian] was sorta different, too. So, then it makes sense that Miss Franny is Opal's first friend in town."

After several minutes of discussion in which students analyzed the author's message, Randi corrected Jameer. "Miss Franny is her first *human* friend. Winn-Dixie is her first friend no matter what."

Figure 12.6 Examples of Queries to Drive Verbal Reasoning in QtA

- What is the author trying to say here?
- What is the author's message?
- What is the author talking about?
- What does the author mean here?
- Did the author explain this clearly?
- Does this make sense with what the author told us before?
- How does this connect with what the author has told us before?
- Does the author tell us why?
- Why do you think the author tells us this now?
- How do things look for this character now?
- How has the author let you know that something has changed?
- How has the author settled this for us?
- Given what the author has already told us about this character, what do you believe he's up to?

Source: Beck et al. (1997). Used with permission.

TAKE ACTION

QAR and QtA are two evidence-based instructional techniques useful for fostering verbal reasoning and inferring. How might you use each of these techniques? Use the planning grid below to guide your thinking about how you would apply these approaches.

Getting Started	Question-Answer Relationships	Question the Author
How might I introduce this technique? (e.g., small group, large group)		
What texts or passages could I use to introduce this technique?		
Who are students who may initially struggle with this technique?		
How might I accommodate these students to reduce barriers to learning this technique?		

Inferencing With Sequential Art

Teachers have long used a series of visual images that tell a story to teach students about sequencing. For example, four panels from a comic strip are cut apart and then reassembled by the student in a logical order. A child who is doing this is drawing on their ability to infer about a logical sequence of events. However, this instructional practice can be deepened by drawing students' attention to what is happening between the panels.

First, a bit of vocabulary instruction about sequential art. Comics are distinguished from other literary forms because of their use of images and words to tell a story. The words may be contained in speech bubbles of characters or in captions that comment on the scene. Longer episodic stories are called comic books. A series of comic books may be assembled as a graphic novel, or the graphic novel may be a single story.

The story, whether a short comic strip or a long graphic novel, is told through a series of panels that frame the images. Each panel contains any number of visual images that the reader draws upon to infer what's happening. The term *emanata* is used to describe the sweat beads, motion lines, and other symbols that signal the emotions of the character. The white spaces between the panels are called the *gutters* and are used to separate the action into a sequence. The layout of the panels also transmits the story. A full-page image is called a *splash page* and is intended to pause the narration to emphasize a point. Narrow panels stacked across the page speed up the pace.

The gutter is where much of the inferring happens. It is here where the author and reader meet.

The gutter is where much of the inferring happens. It is here where the author and reader meet. How did the action move forward from one panel to the next? This is the place of transition, and the reader must actively participate in order to make sense of the story. Comic book artists call this *closure*, but teachers call this inference.

Sequential art can be used to teach far more than sequencing. Blum et al. (2020) developed three-panel sequential art to gauge verbal reasoning and inferencing with 8- to 12-year-old students. To do so, they developed questions that aligned with the question-answer relationship model discussed earlier in this module. One example, shown in Figure 12.7, is a short visual narrative about the interactions of two children.

Figure 12.7 Sample Comic With Questions

Source: Blum et al. (2020, p. 1984). Used with permission.

They asked children the following questions (Blum et al., 2020, p. 1984):

1. Why do you think Tom let Jimmy keep the toy car?
2. What made you think of that answer?
3. What is the most important lesson someone can learn from this comic?
4. What made you think of that answer?

While their goal was to develop an assessment that accurately measured reasoning and inferences within a QAR framework, its foundation underpins the findings of others that verbal reasoning and inferencing play an important role in reading comprehension and word recognition for younger and older elementary students (Oakhill & Cain, 2012; Segers & Verhoeven, 2016).

Inspired by the book *99 Ways to Tell a Story* (Madden, 2005), Jaylen Foster decided to use a similar approach with his sixth-grade students. Madden's book features an eight-panel wordless story that is reassembled again and again to tell 99 different stories. Mr. Foster used a different set of wordless panels and challenged his students to assemble them in any order they liked to provide a coherent story.

The teacher set up a cork board so that students could pin their story panels in their chosen order and then write a title for the story on a sentence strip at the top. He set up a video camera for them to record their storyboard in the frame. "I asked them to video record their story first using the cells, and then to go back again and describe the action happening in each of the gutters. It gave me a great way to be able to see how they inferred and what they wanted their readers to infer." Each student then took a screenshot of their completed storyboard, and Mr. Foster edited these efforts together into a class digital diary. "We called it, '*31 Ways to Tell a Story*,'" he chuckled.

TEXT-TO-SELF CONNECTION

What are key reasons for making verbal reasoning instruction explicit in your classroom? Consider the grade level of your students as you articulate a rationale for doing so.

____

____

____

Using the traffic light scale, with red being not confident, yellow being somewhat confident, and green indicating very confident, how confident are you in your ability to

- Promote verbal reasoning and inferencing in your reading instruction?

- Notice when students are and are not using verbal reasoning and inferencing in their reading?

- Use techniques outlined in this module (Question-Answer Relationships, Question the Author, and sequential art to teach inferencing) in your classroom?

Takeaways

- Verbal reasoning is an important factor in reading from the onset, and its importance deepens as readers advance through the grades.
- Literary devices are used in texts for the youngest readers. Developmentally appropriate instruction about literary devices and the ways authors use them should begin in primary school.
- Students demonstrate their verbal reasoning in many ways. They make forward and backward inferences, discuss their inferences in retelling, make associations between words, and make inferences using visual texts.
- Inferences do not need to be correct to be valid. Ensure that students understand that "good mistakes" are valued in your classroom as a pathway to making inferences. Allow students to provide different reasons to support their inferences.

PS: The answers to the anticipation guide are T, F, T, F.

online resources

Visit the companion website at
resources.corwin.com/teachingreading
for this module's downloadable resources.

MODULE

13

Theory of Mind

Photo by Andrew Ebrahim on Unsplash

In this module, we will

- **Examine the research on theory of mind and its influence on reading comprehension.**
- **Consider perspective taking and point of view in reading through the lens of theory of mind.**
- **Describe the use of familiar instructional strategies for fostering theory of mind in reading.**

The two third-grade students in the photo appear to be collaborating. They are sharing a book and might be in close conversation about the story. One student is gesturing to the illustration while the other student seems to be writing. But as adults we also know that although they are working together, they don't have the exact same thoughts. The student on the left might be making a point that the one on the right doesn't agree with. Or maybe he is ignoring his classmate's idea and moving forward with his own. Further, the perspectives they hold about the situation will impact what each believes about the other's motivations. Based on the limited information, we can't know for sure. But we

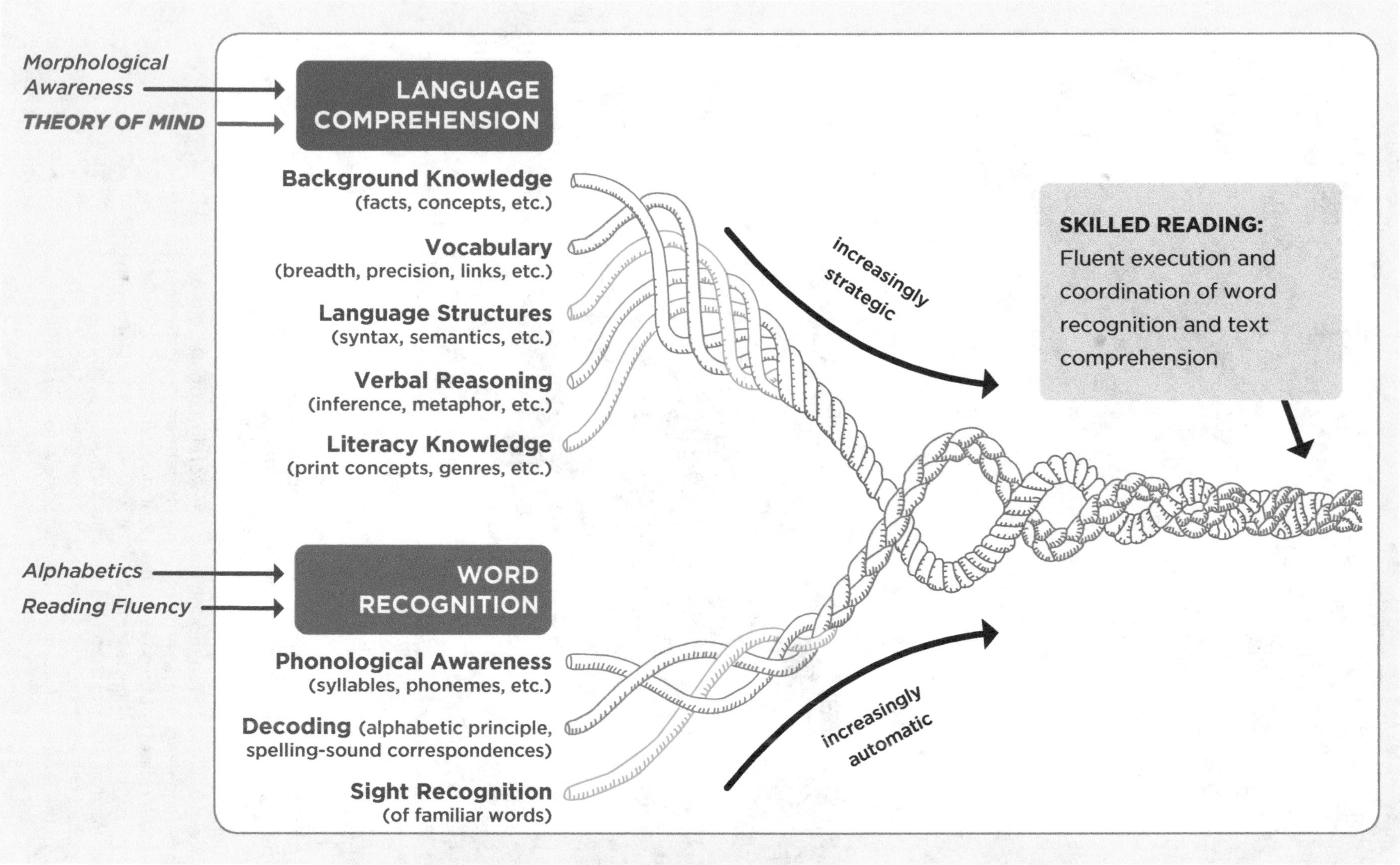

Source: Adapted from Scarborough, H. S. (2001). Connecting early language and literacy to later reading (dis)abilities: Evidence, theory, and practice. In S. Neuman & D. Dickinson (Eds.), *Handbook for research in early literacy* (pp. 97–110). Guilford Press.

are readily able to speculate about the potentially different perspectives each might have adopted. Our ability to do so speaks to our theory of mind.

If verbal reasoning is the ability to infer in order to find logical coherence in the story, then theory of mind speaks to the social reasoning necessary to understand it. A theory of mind is the understanding that other people's thoughts and feelings are different from your own. The perceptions of others shape their motivations, beliefs, desires, and actions. Readers use a theory of mind to understand the real and imagined characters in texts by assigning different mental states to them.

A theory of mind is the understanding that other people's thoughts and feelings are different from your own.

Take as an example a story of two characters. One character unintentionally does something that gets their friend in trouble. The reader uses a theory of mind (ToM) to predict that the first character feels guilty about their actions, while the second feels betrayed and disappointed about their relationship. If we had told you that the first character intentionally got their friend in trouble, we would immediately shift the perspective. The first character is untrustworthy, while the second character is angry. Your ToM made that logical shift possible.

The relationship between theory of mind and reading comprehension is still new in the field and represents a leading edge of literacy research. And that's how it should be. Reading comprehension is the oldest realm of educational research, dating back to studies from 1865. Our understanding of how these complex skills and concepts work together—what Thorndike called a "cooperation of forces"—continues to evolve.

You probably didn't learn about ToM in your teacher preparation program. However, it has taken on an increasingly important dimension in this decade, as it is associated with deep levels of reading comprehension. One study found that reasoning, perspective taking, and academic language were responsible for a significant variance in deep reading scores (LaRusso et al., 2016). Another study of reading comprehension of students in grades 4 to 8 noted that ToM alone explained 12% of the variance (Dore et al., 2018). (In statistics, variance is a measure of the spread of the scores). These and other findings about the role of theory of mind in fostering reading comprehension point to the need to devote more attention to its instruction. And that's precisely why we are dedicating a module to this topic.

Read each statement and mark **T** if the statement is true and **F** if the statement is false. Be prepared to explain your reasoning. As you read through the module, you might change your responses. Be prepared to explain your responses and use the text for evidence.

Before Reading	Statements	After Reading
T **F**	1. Theory of mind has been documented to directly impact reading comprehension.	**T** **F**
Why did you indicate true or false?	Has your thinking changed after reading?	

(Continued)

(Continued)

Before Reading	Statements	After Reading
T **F**	2. Children who do not have a developmentally appropriate level of theory of mind may experience reading comprehension difficulties.	**T** **F**
Why did you indicate true or false?	Has your thinking changed after reading?	
T **F**	3. Elementary students who can take perspective into account score higher on measures of textual comprehension.	**T** **F**
Why did you indicate true or false?	Has your thinking changed after reading?	
T **F**	4. Textual discussion routines can foster theory of mind.	**T** **F**
Why did you indicate true or false?	Has your thinking changed after reading?	

NOTES

What Is Theory of Mind?

Theory of mind first emerged several decades ago in two distinct channels: developmental psychology and research on autism. The trajectory of an emerging ToM among infants and children as a developmental phenomenon is well understood. Infants begin to attend to the facial expressions and movements of caregivers and soon begin to imitate them. As their language develops, toddlers begin to recognize that others have emotions, and they use words to label other people as feeling *happy* or *sad* or *mad*. Two- and three-year-olds understand that they like some things that others don't and can discern that others take action to get what they want. (Think of the delight expressed by a giggling toddler who watches the family dog take food off the kitchen counter.) They engage in imaginative play, such as pretending to be a truck driver or a mail carrier, and they may recognize when someone is joking. Overall, these are called first-order perspectives, because these children have an overall awareness of their own mental state and that of the speaker (Baron-Cohen et al., 2001).

One study found that reasoning, perspective taking, and academic language were responsible for a significant variance in deep reading scores.

Four- and five-year-olds make significant strides in ToM, such as being able to look at a person's eye gaze to predict what they may want or think. These emerge in the following order (Lowry, 2016, ¶ 3):

- **Understanding "wanting"**—Different people want different things, and to get what they want, people act in different ways.
- **Understanding "thinking"**—Different people have different, but potentially true, beliefs about the same thing. People's actions are based on what they think is going to happen.
- **Understanding that "seeing leads to knowing"**—If you haven't seen something, you don't necessarily know about it. If someone hasn't seen something, they will need extra information to understand.
- **Understanding "false beliefs"**—Sometimes people believe things that are not true, and they act according to their beliefs, not according to what is really true.
- **Understanding "hidden feelings"**—People can feel a different emotion from the one they display.

These second-order skills include false beliefs. One well-known test involves showing a child a closed box of candy. When asked, the child will predict that it contains candy, but when it is opened, they discover instead that it holds pencils. A child who has not developed this skill will answer that when another child is shown the same box, they will answer that it has pencils. A child with second-order skills understands that another person will be bluffed as well. This skill seems to have implications for early literacy. An imaginative study of children between three and six years of age found that "overall, [those] who were better at understanding their own and other's mental states were better at producing and reading their own written marks," leading the researchers to speculate that these children had a better sense of audience in their writing (Leyva et al., 2012, p. 711).

Higher-order ToM skills emerge throughout the elementary years and are notable for a child's ability to embed multiple perspectives. For instance, a third grader reading a passage about the hidden and stated perspectives of two characters is probably able to glean

- The perspectives of each character (first order).
- The perspectives that each character holds about the others (second order).
- The internal reflections about what each character believes the other holds about them (third order).

These abilities have implications for how a student understands the stated and hidden beliefs of characters. Consider this example:

> A burglar mistakenly confesses because a policeman noticed the burglar dropped a glove. Children are asked why the burglar confessed, given that the policeman just wanted to give him back his glove. Children under six have difficulty explaining this situation, even when they recognize that the policeman was surprised by the burglar's actions. It is not until about 9 years of age that children describe the mental states behind the burglar's behavior, explaining that the burglar *thought* that the policeman *knew* that he had robbed the store. (Dore et al., 2018, p. 1071)

Theory of mind remains a relatively new construct as a contributor to reading comprehension. Having said that, instruction about point of view and perspective taking in reading has a broader scope of research.

NOTICE AND WONDER

Educational research is informed by and informs other fields. In the case of ToM, the fields of psychology, linguistics, and disability are animating reading research discussions.

■	What is squaring with you? How does ToM confirm what you know about reading instruction?	
●	What is circling in your mind? What are your speculations about ToM and reading?	
?	What questions do you have about ToM going forward?	

NOTES

Point of View and Perspective Taking in Reading

As students read narrative texts, most will adopt a point of view similar to the protagonist's, even as they recognize that their beliefs and views may differ. You've probably witnessed this firsthand while reading a story aloud to a child. Say you're reading Little Red Riding Hood, and the moment in the story comes when the unsuspecting heroine opens the door to a disguised Big Bad Wolf. Children will often howl out loud to dissuade Little Red Riding Hood from doing the inevitable. They are adopting her point of view even as they recognize they wouldn't do the same thing. In other words, they can hold both a character-centered and a reader-centered perspective at the same time. These dual perspectives are not always mutually exclusive. At times during a narrative, they converge and are in close alignment.

Texts that are rich in social and emotional content help to foster perspective taking in narrative works.

Texts that are rich in social and emotional content help to foster perspective taking in narrative works. Many social-emotional learning curricula use stories for exactly that purpose, especially as a means to foster empathetic thinking.

There is also mounting evidence that perspective taking and point of view have a spillover effect on other dimensions of the school day. For instance, the ability to communicate effectively in academic discussions is predicated on a growing understanding that two speakers are at times imperfect in sharing their thoughts and ideas with one another. Children who are more skilled are likely to persist in making themselves understood while also accounting for what another child is misunderstanding. This has direct implications for deep reading comprehension. Research on perspective taking found that elementary students who were able to take perspective into account scored higher on measures of textual comprehension (LaRusso et al., 2016). Perspective taking has been associated with a higher degree of comprehension in social studies as well, especially in understanding nuances of historical events (Gehlbach, 2004).

NOTES

Instruction in Theory of Mind

While theory of mind does have a developmental component, the experiences we create in our classrooms can assist students in their reading by applying perspective taking, point of view, and an understanding of what others do or do not know.

TEACHING THEORY OF MIND THROUGH INTERACTIVE READ-ALOUDS

Reading instructional practices for young children include interactive read-alouds, which allow for the use of more complex texts that emergent and early readers would not be able to read independently. This practice is an essential part of comprehension instruction, as it provides opportunities to highlight the use of vocabulary, language structures, and dimensions of literacy knowledge, to name but a few. But narrative texts in particular allow for teachers to teach about the social knowledge needed to make inferences. The ability to draw inferences is essential for developing verbal reasoning skills and is crucial for reading comprehension (Oakhill & Cain, 2012).

Narrative texts offer readers real and imagined stories that mirror the human condition and support the social development of young children. Kelly and Taboada Barber developed a framework for teachers in prekindergarten through second grade to use in fostering ToM and verbal reasoning during interactive read-alouds (2021; see Figure 13.1). They advise

- Choosing narrative texts that offer "an abundance of opportunities for inference making about mental states" that require inferencing to identify a character's mental state (p. 109).
- Make note of three instances when these opportunities occur in the story. These can be direct inferences, such as when the text specifically labels a feeling (e.g., "Olivia was mad at herself because she made an embarrassing mistake") as well as indirect inferences (e.g., "Her eyes filled up with tears"). These are the key mental states you want students to attend to.
- To teach toward a ToM for inferring in social dynamics, introduce a story students have read before with the purpose of identifying how the character is responding to events and situations.
- Before reading the story, teach key vocabulary that describes mental states, and stop at points during the story where students need to draw a direct or indirect inference.
- Ask questions about how students understand the character's emotions, prompting them as needed to attend to the written language as well as illustrations.
- As a culminating activity, map the story grammar using the inferences drawn to chronicle how the character's reactions propel the events in the story and to identify the theme.

Figure 13.1 Theory of Mind and Narrative Structure

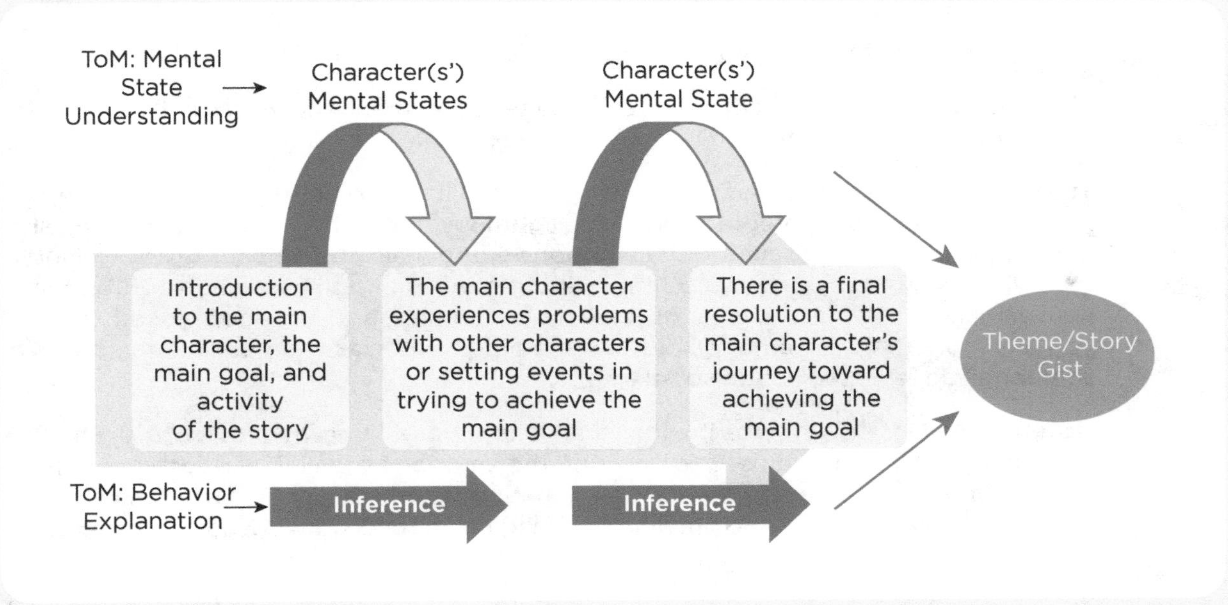

Source: Kelly and Taboada Barber (2021, p. 108).

First-grade teacher Melanie Booth revisited the picture book *Hello Lighthouse* (Blackall, 2018) with her students to discuss the complex emotions the main character, a lighthouse keeper, experiences throughout the story. The teacher identified three key mental states she wanted her students to notice: loneliness, joy, and the sadness that comes from saying goodbye to a place you love. She began the lesson by teaching about these emotions that come from saying goodbye, charting ideas from students about their own feelings. Several students talked about having to move and feeling "sad." Keith talked about "having a stomachache."

Ms. Booth then asked the children how they might feel if they got to see a favorite place again. This time the emotion words changed, and they added phrases such as "jumping for joy" and "being excited and silly."

She paused at times during the reading to ask questions. Early in the story, the lightkeeper is lonely in his isolation. While the students readily recognized that, she pressed them for lines in the text that helped them understand this emotion. Liam pointed out that a sentence reads that the lighthouse keeper "sets the table and hums a tune and wishes he had someone to talk to."

On the following page, Riley said, the lighthouse keeper "writes her a letter" and "waits for her reply."

Ms. Booth added, "So let's talk about that. Is he only lonely?"

She and her students discussed the fact that he is also hoping that something good will happen. She introduced the word *hopeful* to them, and they added that to a chart detailing the emotions the character goes through as the story progresses. After reading a few more pages, they discussed how his emotions change because of two events: marriage to the woman he wrote to, and the birth of their child. "That's joy, just like the movie!" exclaimed Sadie, in a reference to the film *Inside Out*.

The story progresses, and soon the lightkeeper receives "an unexpected letter with the coast guard's seal" foreshadowing another event—he will be replaced by an electric lamp.

"What words are telling us how he might be feeling now?" asked Ms. Booth.

They found further evidence in the text: "He tends the light and writes in the logbook but knows it's not for long."

The ending two-page spread is wordless, with an illustration of the lighthouse keeper, his wife, and their daughter looking at the lighthouse from their new house on the shore. Once again, the class discussed the emotions of the main character, this time linking their discussion to the earlier discussion about moving and then seeing your former house again. This time, the feelings were more complex, and Ms. Booth asked, "Can you feel more than one emotion at the same time?" Her class then talked about how someone can feel "sad" but also "okay."

"Hmm . . . let's use a new word, rather than 'okay.' Here's a new word: *wistful*." She explained that it's a word used to describe the emotion as feeling sad for something that is gone but also accepting of a new situation. As the teacher brought the story to a close, the class finished the timeline they had developed showing how the character's emotions change because of the events in the story.

WHAT'S YOUR ADVICE?

A colleague in your grade level asks about how to increase the level of metacognitive challenge for their students during interactive read-alouds. You've been learning more about ToM. What advice would you offer regarding the following questions they have?

What should I consider in selecting a text?	
What qualities should I be looking for as I identify the discussion points during the story?	
What are some good questions to ask?	
What follow-up activities could I use?	

ACCOUNTABLE TALK

Discussions about text can be difficult for some students to follow. As well, a discussion during small-group or whole-class instruction can quickly wander away from the intended points you planned. The moves a teacher enacts during discussion provide a scaffold for organizing the information that emerges. In addition, skillful use of conversational moves by the teacher can propel the discussion, evoke reasoning, refocus attention on citing textual evidence, and clarify understanding. Taken together, these form the heart of accountable talk (Michaels et al., 2010). Over time, and with consistent daily opportunities to practice, these principles mark the way students engage in peer-led collaborative conversations.

Accountable talk is an instructional approach designed to foster the meaningful conversation, respectful debate, and academic discourse needed to build the collective knowledge of its participants (Michaels et al., 2010). Accountability is threefold. Everyone is accountable to

- The classroom community
- The knowledge base
- And to reasoned logic

Accountable talk is an instructional approach designed to foster meaningful conversation, respectful debate, and academic discourse.

These discourse habits are built through teacher modeling and facilitation, with the intent of fostering application during peer-led academic discussion. One of the ways that we help students learn the language of accountable talk is through sentence frames. For example, the following frames are used to provide students with examples they can use when talking with their group members:

- I agree that ____.
- I don't agree that ____, but I do understand ____.
- The text says that ____.
- I have a different opinion, that ____.

Begin working on this habit during the first week of school, emphasizing ways that we report on the ideas of others and extend them with our own. You might make a list of ways to do so, such as, "Can you put the author's ideas into your own words?" and "Tell me more about that."

Then give students a discussion prompt and ask them to carry on a conversation with a partner where they encourage one another to elaborate on an idea. Pull the whole group back together, and invite students to restate their partner's ideas. You can then discuss the importance of listening, not just formulating one's own responses.

During the second week, spotlight lessons on accountability to the knowledge base. Use a short piece of text, and analyze it for the author's main points and key details. Then ask partners to work similarly with a second short reading and encourage them to provide examples from the text.

By the end of the month, you are focused on the need to be able to present a reasoned argument without simply being argumentative. You might list ways in which their younger siblings argue ("ah huh"/"na uh") and the pointlessness of such an approach. Then list ways that students can voice disagreement without shutting down the conversation. Introduce another topic for discussion; then ask partners to list the pros and cons. This gives them a chance to apply some of the strategies we discussed about voicing disagreement.

Routines to Promote Accountable Talk

Group work routines that promote discussions focused on sharing include TTYPA ("turn to your partner and . . ."), as well as variations of Think-Write-Pair-Share that invite students to contemplate their perspectives and take into account the views of others.

"Telling the other person 'your answer is wrong' isn't enough. Explain your thinking, and find out about how they figured it out," sixth-grade teacher Sabrina Ye says to her students. "If it's different than yours, dig even deeper."

After a few minutes of paired discussion, students are primed for whole-class sharing. "They're often so unsure of their own thinking. They don't trust themselves yet. This gives them a chance to check in with someone else before we talk about it as a class," Ms. Ye said.

Other routines require students to assemble into temporary groups for the purpose of sharing ideas and concepts. Fifth-grade teacher Greg Swanson uses Opinion Stations so that like-minded students can clarify their understandings and then engage with others who have opinions different from their own. He has posted four statements spaced far apart around his classroom: Strongly Agree, Agree, Disagree, and Strongly Disagree. ("No neutrals in this class," he said. "Have an opinion, defend it, and listen to the opinions of others.")

During a unit on governance during social studies, he displayed a statement that read, "All fifth graders in our state should be given an allowance of $10.00 per week."

Without further discussion, he asked his students to move to the poster that best described their opinion. In the first round, the assembled groups discussed their shared point of view. After a few minutes, he moved them to a second round of discussion, this time with members of another group with an opposing opinion. "I usually group the Strongly Agrees with the Disagrees, so they are not so far apart," he said later.

After the second round of discussion, students can change their opinions. "This sets us up for our social studies readings on establishing new rules," he offered. "Open debate about the issues, with opportunities to change one's opinion based on discussion."

Modeling Accountable Talk

Students aren't the only ones who should engage in accountable talk. As teachers, we model, even when we don't think we are, how interactions take place. If we want accountable talk to happen in our classrooms, then it must begin with how we use it ourselves. Michaels et al. (2010) recommend that teachers use the following conversational moves to promote accountable talk:

- **Marking:** "That's an important point." Throughout a discussion, important turning points occur, as when a speaker makes a pivotal observation that matches the learning goals of the teacher. Such a remark ensures that the point is sufficiently emphasized.
- **Challenging students:** "What do you think?" At times students may regress and direct questions to you that are better answered by other members of the class. Acknowledge the question, and then re-pose it to the group to increase involvement.
- **Keeping the channels open:** "Did everyone hear that?" Statements such as this assist other students in building on the remarks of others.
- **Keeping everyone together:** "Who can repeat . . . ?" Invite group members to restate important points in their own words. This emphasizes a key point, engages other students, and allows the original speaker to hear how their words are interpreted by another.
- **Linking contributions:** "Who wants to add on . . . ?" Questions like this encourage cognitive connections within the conversation and foster investment in the discussion by recalling ideas put forth by earlier speakers.
- **Verifying and clarifying:** "So, are you saying . . . ?" While the point may be apparent to the speaker, that may not be the case for other participants. Asking for verification provides all students with evidence or reasoning and can expose a gap in logic for the speaker.

- **Pressing for accuracy:** "Where can we find that?" This probe refocuses students on the text and can be useful when the discussion begins to drift.
- **Building on prior knowledge:** "How does this connect?" Link the concepts and texts under current discussion to those that have been read and discussed in previous lessons.
- **Pressing for reasoning:** "Why do you think that?" The intent of a question like this is to move the conversation from opinion to argument. This encourages the speaker to provide facts, cite textual evidence, or identify when the circumstance is ambiguous.
- **Expanding reasoning:** "Take your time; say more." This is a key probe in the teacher's cadre of discussion tools because it accomplishes so much. The most obvious is that it encourages the speaker to extend their response, but it also signals to the rest of the class just how much every member is valued. This deceptively simple move assures every student in the class that their ideas are worthy of the group's collective patience.
- **Recapping:** "What have we discovered?" Longer discussions yield ideas that evolve, and the questions that invite summary provide group members with succinct statements that heighten understanding. (pp. 27–32)

FIND THE MISTAKES

Are your students using a theory of mind when discussing texts? How might you know if your students are developing and using a ToM in their reading? Your observations and noticings are invaluable. Here are some informal look-fors and listen-fors as your students interact with one another.

IN DISCUSSIONS AND PEER INTERACTIONS

- Does the child engage directly with others to communicate?
- Does the child notice and repair communication when their point is not understood by another?
- Does the child attempt to persuade others?
- Does the child make shared plans with others during small-group work?
- Does the child gain and share a focus or topic of attention with others?

WHEN READING TEXTS

When talking about texts with students, ask questions that are designed to surface a ToM as it relates to reading comprehension. We drew inspiration for these questions from the theory-of-mind test (Muris et al., 1999).

- Ask about the emotions of the characters.
- Ask about the characters' intentions.
- Ask about characters' beliefs.
- Ask how the child's opinion is similar to or different from the character's.
- Listen for the child's use of words that describe thoughts, emotions, and beliefs.

CHARACTER MAPS

Getting inside the mind of characters, especially those who have conflicting opinions, forms the heart of any good story. Character maps can assist students in understanding the motives, perspectives, and beliefs of the main characters of a narrative. These graphic organizers provide a visual representation of the impact of other story elements on the characters, such as the setting and the plot. They are used during and after readings.

Character maps are widely available and are likely already in your curricular materials. We've used ones that are shaped like the outline of a head. Sonya Henderson uses the one in Figure 13.2 with her kindergarten students. She programmed a template of it into her smartboard so that she can pull it up. Students co-construct the character map as she reads so that they can chronicle the evolution of the main characters in a text. "Once we've developed these, we can have a conversation about what's happening in the story. Sometimes I have them return to their tables to write and draw about one of the elements," she said.

Figure 13.2 Kindergarten Character Map

Feels	Thinks
Says	Acts
Wants	Doesn't Want

Sixth-grade teacher Marcus Jackson uses character maps to help his students understand historical figures. During a unit on ancient societies, Mr. Jackson curated online resources for teams of students to develop a character study of an assigned prominent person of the time. Groups of students analyzed material related to Aristotle, Enzana Axum, Alexander the Great, Endubis, Cleopatra, Hammurabi, Hatshepsut, Siddartha, and Dido. The teacher used questions inspired by Facing History and Ourselves (https://www.facinghistory.org/resource-library/teaching-strategies/character-maps) and added questions about evidence to bring his students back to the texts they were reading.

- **Head:** What does this person think about their society? What is our evidence?
- **Mouth:** What is this person saying? What is our evidence?
- **Heart:** What is this person feeling? Or who is at the center of this person's universe of obligation? What is our evidence?
- **Hands:** What actions has this person taken; what choices have they made? What is our evidence?

- **Feet:** What might be some consequences of this person's choices? What is our evidence?

"I gave them some license about how they would develop their projects," said Mr. Jackson. "Some students did this as a paper-and-pencil task, and others used art materials to build a display. Several of them went all out and used multimedia to show their findings."

Once they had completed their projects, each group developed an augmented reality presentation using Aurasma.

"All the students then viewed the other groups' work before we had an extended discussion about the similarities and differences among them. These historical figures didn't all live at the same time, and they didn't necessarily know each other. But we imagined what a dinner with all these people might be like," said Mr. Jackson. "It was a hit with families, too, for our school's Open House night. Families got to see and hear how wise and insightful their young people are."

TAKE ACTION

Review your curriculum materials to locate tasks and resources that can be used to highlight ToM in reading comprehension. What resources can you use as is? What materials could be revised to better address ToM?

Existing curricular materials I can use as currently designed.	
Existing curricular materials I could revise.	

READING ACROSS TEXTS

Theory of Mind in reading can be further developed through book-related activities that cause the reader to consider information that may conflict. These conflicting viewpoints can be further explored through interrogating the possible purposes and motives of each major character, the narrator, or the author.

The idea of understanding a narrator's or author's purpose is not a new one. Although often not specifically stated, there is a purpose for each text. Sometimes, the genre or the text type helps the reader understand the author's purpose. Was the specific text written to convey an experience, inform, or persuade? Other times, the way in which the author constructs the text—the point of view—helps readers determine the purpose. First-person texts tell the reader one thing, while third-person limited versus omniscient tell the reader something else. Further, texts are told from a specific vantage point, and readers want to know whose story is not represented. Ask students about the author's purpose, including the choice of narrator. As students discuss this, note their understanding of the difference between first person and third person and the influence that point of view has on understanding and perspective.

Second-grade teacher Helena Georgiou uses some of her texts to support her efforts at fostering critical literacy skills. Critical literacy has gained wide acknowledgment for the role it plays in reading comprehension. Critical literacy "views readers as active participants in the reading process and invites them to move beyond passively accepting the text's message to question, examine, or dispute the power relations that exist between readers and authors" (McLaughlin & DeVoogd, 2004, p. 14). These include questioning the commonplace in a text and seeking alternative perspectives.

Critical literacy has gained wide acknowledgment for the role it plays in reading comprehension.

Primary teachers everywhere use *The True Story of the Three Little Pigs* (Scieszka, 1996) to encourage students to reconsider the traditional fairy tale. The wolf's explanation that "the real story is about a sneeze and a cup of sugar" (p. 6) is slyly humorous and invites readers to notice when the wolf seems to protest too much. However, it is less common to read it first—most lessons are a compare-and-contrast of the original fairy tale followed by a reading of Scieszka's book.

Ms. Georgiou does it the opposite way. She and her class read and discuss *The True Story of the Three Little Pigs* first. She sets up a two-column language chart to write down her students' insights. One column is labeled as the Wolf's Actions, while the other is The Pigs' Actions.

"Let's look for evidence and characteristics of the wolf and the pigs," she begins. After recording their observations, she says, "What if the wolf was not so bad? What are some things we think the pigs did wrong?" The children made a list:

- Why did the pigs not help each other with building better houses? Maybe they are selfish.
- Why did the pigs assume the wolf was bad? Maybe he just wanted to play.
- The pigs let the wolf fall into the fire. Even if they were mad at him, they didn't have to hurt him.

"Now we're going to read *The Three Little Wolves and the Big Bad Pig* by Eugene Trivizas. But let's do something different. Let's say that the wolves were right. and it's the pig that's the bad character. Can you listen and look for evidence that the wolves were right, and the pig was wrong?"

After reading the second book, the teacher starts a new language chart. "What are some things you noticed in this version?"

- The wolves helped each other.
- The big bad pig did his best to destroy the houses, but he couldn't.
- The wolves found a way to make friends with the big bad pig.

Satisfied that her students had stretched their imaginations, she asked them to work together in their groups to write a letter of apology from the pigs to the wolf. One group wrote.

> Dear Mr. Wolf,
>
> We are saying we are sorry because we didn't give you a chance. You could be a friend. We didn't let you. You can be in our neighborhood.
>
> We are sorry.
>
> Signed,
>
> The Pigs

"When I do a lesson like this," Ms. Georgiou later said, "it isn't really to get them to write about the book. We do that with lots of other texts. But what I do want them to be able to do is to see that sometimes what we read is only focused on one viewpoint. I hope they continue to challenge ideas," she said. "That means that sometimes they have to imagine the opposite of what they think they know."

TEXT-TO-SELF CONNECTION

What are the key reasons for teaching theory of mind in my classroom?

Using the traffic light scale, with red being not confident, yellow being somewhat confident, and green indicating very confident, how confident am I in my ability to

- Teach theory of mind to my students?

- Teach perspective taking in reading?

- Use accountable talk in my classroom?

Takeaways

- Theory of mind is a relatively new dimension of reading comprehension instruction. While it is not yet a proven dimension of reading, research on its use is promising.
- Some children who have comprehension difficulties may be impacted by a less-developed sense of how to apply a theory of mind in their reading.
- Students who excel at perspective taking in reading score at higher levels on comprehension assessments.
- Use routines such as accountable talk, interactive read-alouds, and texts that present different perspectives to foster ToM in reading.

PS: Answers to the anticipation guide are F, T, T, T.

online resources

Visit the companion website at
resources.corwin.com/teachingreading
for this module's downloadable resources.

Appendices

Appendix A

Yopp-Singer Test of Phoneme Segmentation

Student's Name: ______________________ Date: __________________ Grade: ____________

Score (number correct) ______________________

Directions: Today we're going to play a word game. I'm going to say a word, and I want you to break the word apart. You are going to tell me each sound in the word in order. For example, if I say "old," you should say */o/ - /l/ - /d/. (Administrator: Be sure to say the sounds, not the letters, in the word.)* Let's try a few together.

Practice items: *(Assist the child in segmenting these items as necessary.)*

ride (3) ***go (2)*** ***man (3)***

Test items: *(Circle those items that the student correctly segments; incorrect responses may be recorded on the blank line following the item.)*

1. dog ________________	12. lay ________________
2. keep ________________	13. race ________________
3. fine ________________	14. zoo ________________
4. no ________________	15. three ________________
5. she ________________	16. job ________________
6. wave ________________	17. in ________________
7. grew ________________	18. ice ________________
8. that ________________	19. at ________________
9. red ________________	20. top ________________
10. me ________________	21. by ________________
11. sat ________________	22. do ________________

Source: The author, Hallie Kay Yopp, California State University, Fullerton, grants permission for this test to be reproduced. The author acknowledges the contribution of the late Harry Singer to the development of this test.

Appendix B

Letter Recognition Assessment

LETTER/SOUND IDENTIFICATION SCORE SHEET

Student Name: ____________________ Date: ______________ Grade: _____________

Directions:

Check in the "N" column for the correct letter name.

Check in the "S" column for correct letter-sound response.

If the student says a word with or for the letter, record that word in the "Word" column for word response.

Record any incorrect responses in the "I.R." column.

	N	I.R.		N	S	Word	I.R.
A			a				
F			f				
K			k				
P			p				
W			w				
Z			z				
B			b				
H			h				
O			o				
J			j				
U			u				
			a				
C			c				
Y			y				
L			l				
Q			q				
M			m				
D			d				

Observations

Note such things as:

Speed of response

Confusions (e.g., b/d)

Patterns of response

	N	I.R.		N	S	Word	I.R.
N			n				
S			s				
X			x				
I			i				
E			e				
G			g				
R			r				
V			v				
T			t				
			g				
26			28		/26		

Letter Name Total Score	/54

Letter Sound Total Score	/26

Source: Macomb Intermediate School District (2001); adapted from Clay (2019).

Appendix C

Dolch Sight Word Assessment: Preprimer

Name: ______________________________ Teacher: ______________________________

Directions: Present the student each Dolch sight word on an index card. Highlight or circle each correct response using the color code at the bottom of the page.

DOLCH SIGHT WORDS: PREPRIMER

a	funny	look	see
and	go	make	the
away	help	me	three
big	hers	my	to
blue	I	not	two
can	in	one	up
come	is	play	we
down	it	red	yellow
find	jump	run	you
for	little	said	

Coding for sight words:

1st administration: red (Date:)

2nd administration: blue (Date:)

3rd administration: green (Date:)

4th administration: yellow (Date:)

Appendix D

Dolch Sight Word Assessment: Primer

Name: ______________________________ Teacher: ______________________________

Directions: Present the student each Dolch sight word on an index card. Highlight or circle each correct response using the color code at the bottom of the page.

DOLCH SIGHT WORDS: PRIMER

all	four	out	this
am	get	please	too
are	good	pretty	under
at	has	ran	want
ate	he	ride	was
be	into	saw	well
black	like	say	went
brown	must	she	what
but	new	so	white
came	no	soon	who
did	now	that	will
do	on	there	with
eat	our	they	yes

Coding for sight words:

1st administration: red (Date:)

2nd administration: blue (Date:)

3rd administration: green (Date:)

4th administration: yellow (Date:)

Appendix E

Dolch Sight Word Assessment: First Grade

Name: ______________________ Teacher: ______________________

Directions: Present the student each Dolch sight word on an index card. Highlight or circle each correct response using the color code at the bottom of the page.

DOLCH SIGHT WORDS: FIRST GRADE

after	from	let	some
again	give	live	stop
an	going	may	take
any	had	of	thank
as	has	old	them
ask	her	once	then
by	him	open	think
could	how	over	walk
every	just	put	where
fly	know	round	when

Coding for sight words:

1st administration: red (Date:)

2nd administration: blue (Date:)

3rd administration: green (Date:)

4th administration: yellow (Date:)

Appendix F

Dolch Sight Word Assessment: Second Grade

Name: ______________________________ Teacher: ______________________________

Directions: Present the student each Dolch sight word on an index card. Highlight or circle each correct response using the color code at the bottom of the page.

DOLCH SIGHT WORDS: SECOND GRADE

always	fast	pull	use
around	first	read	very
because	five	right	wash
been	found	sing	which
before	gave	sit	why
best	goes	sleep	wish
both	green	tell	work
buy	its	their	would
call	made	these	write
cold	many	those	your
does	off	upon	
don't	or	us	

Coding for sight words:

1st administration: red (Date:)

2nd administration: blue (Date:)

3rd administration: green (Date:)

4th administration: yellow (Date:)

Appendix G

Dolch Sight Word Assessment: Third Grade

Name: ______________________________ Teacher: ____________________________

Directions: Present the student each Dolch sight word on an index card. Highlight or circle each correct response using the color code at the bottom of the page.

DOLCH SIGHT WORDS: THIRD GRADE

about	fall	kind	seven
better	far	laugh	shall
bring	full	light	show
carry	got	long	six
clean	grow	much	small
cut	hold	myself	start
done	hot	never	ten
draw	hurt	only	today
drink	if	own	together
eight	keep	pick	try
			warm

Coding for sight words:

1st administration: red (Date:)

2nd administration: blue (Date:)

3rd administration: green (Date:)

4th administration: yellow (Date:)

online resources

Visit the companion website at
resources.corwin.com/teachingreading
for downloadable appendices.

References

Adams, M. J. (1990). *Beginning to read: Thinking and learning about print.* Massachusetts Institute of Technology.

Adlof, S. M., & Patten, H. (2017). Nonword repetition and vocabulary knowledge as predictors of children's phonological and semantic word learning. *Journal of Speech, Language & Hearing Research, 60*(3), 682–693.

Afflerbach, P., Pearson, P., & Paris, S. (2008). Clarifying differences between reading skills and reading strategies. *The Reading Teacher, 61,* 364–373.

Agar, M. (1995). *Language shock: Understanding the culture of conversation.* William Morrow.

Al Otaiba, S., Allor, J., Werfel, K., & Clemens, N. (2016). Critical components of phonemic awareness instruction and intervention: Recommendations for teacher training and for future research. In R. Schiff & R. Joshi (Eds.), *Interventions in Learning Disabilities: Literacy Studies* (Vol. 13). Springer.

Alemagna, B. (2017). *On a magical do-nothing day.* Thames Hudson.

Allington, R. A., & Johnston, P. H. (2002). *Reading to learn: Lessons from exemplary fourth-grade classrooms.* Guilford.

Anders, P. L., & Bos, C. S. (1986). Semantic feature analysis: An interactive strategy for vocabulary development and text comprehension. *Journal of Reading, 29,* 610–616.

Anderson, R. C., Hiebert, E. H., Scott, J. A., & Wilkinson, I. A. G. (1985). *Becoming a nation of readers. The report of the Commission on Reading.* Center for the Study of Reading and National Academy of Education.

Anderson, R. C., Wilson, P. T., & Fielding, L. G. (1988). Growth in reading and how children spend their time outside of school. *Reading Research Quarterly, 23,* 285-303.

Anthony, J. L., Lonigan, C. J., & Burgess, S. R. (2002). Structure of preschool phonological sensitivity: Overlapping sensitivity to rhyme, words, syllables, and phonemes. *Journal of Experimental Child Psychology, 82*(1), 65–92.

Apel, K., Petscher, Y., & Henbest, V. S. (2021, February 3). *Morphological awareness test for reading and spelling (MATRS).* Technical report. psyarxiv.com/ty2pe. https://doi.org/10.31234/osf.io/ty2pe

Apel, K., Wilson-Fowler, E. B., Brimo, D., & Perrin, N. A. (2012). Metalinguistic contributions to reading and spelling in second and third grade students. *Reading and Writing, 25,* 1283–1305.

Ash, G. E., Kuhn, M. R., & Walpole, S. (2009). Analyzing "inconsistencies" in practice: Teachers' continued use of round robin reading. *Reading & Writing Quarterly, 25*(1), 87–103.

Ashman, L. (2011). *No dogs allowed!* Sterling.

Asimov, I. (1950). *I, robot*. Doubleday.

Atkinson, R. K., Catrambone, R., & Merrill, M. M. (2003). Aiding transfer in statistics: Examining the use of conceptually oriented equations and elaborations during subgoal learning. *Journal of Educational Psychology, 95*, 762–773.

Baron-Cohen, S., Wheelwright, S., Hill, J., Raste, Y., & Plumb, I. (2001). The "Reading the Mind in the Eyes" test revised version: A study with normal adults, and adults with Asperger syndrome or high-functioning autism. *Journal of Child Psychology and Psychiatry, and Allied Disciplines, 42*(2), 241–251.

Barnes, W. G. W. (1989). Word sorting: The cultivation of rules for spelling in English. *Reading Psychology, 10*(3), 293–307.

Baumann, J. F., Edwards, E. C., Boland, E. M., Olejnik, S., & Kame'enui, E. J. (2003). Vocabulary tricks: Effects of instruction in morphology and context on fifth-grade students' ability to derive and infer word meanings. *American Educational Research Journal, 40*(2), 447–494.

Baumann, J. F, Kame'enui, E. J., & Ash, G. E. (2003). Research on vocabulary instruction: Voltaire redux. In J. Flood, D. Lapp, J. R. Squire, & J. M. Jensen (Eds.), *Handbook on teaching the English language arts* (2nd ed., pp. 752–785). Erlbaum.

Bear, D. R., Invernizzi, M., Templeton, S., & Johnston, F. (1996). *Words their way: Word study for phonics, vocabulary, and spelling instruction*. Merrill.

Bear, D. R., Invernizzi, M., Templeton, S., & Johnston, F. (2000). *Words their way: Word study for phonics, vocabulary, and spelling instruction* (2nd ed.). Prentice Hall.

Bear, D. R., Invernizzi, M., Templeton, S., & Johnston, F. (2008). *Words their way: Word study for phonics, vocabulary, and spelling instruction* (4th ed.). Prentice-Hall.

Bear, D. R., Templeton, S., Invernizzi, M., & Johnston, F. (2016). *Words their way. Word study for phonics, vocabulary, and spelling instruction* (6th ed.) Pearson.

Beck, I. L., McKeown, M. G., Hamilton, R. L., & Kucan, L. (1997). *Questioning the author: An approach for enhancing student engagement with text*. International Literacy Association.

Beck, I. L, McKeown, M. G., & Kucan, L. (2002). *Bringing words to life: Robust vocabulary instruction*. Guilford Press.

Berry, A. (2020). Disrupting to driving: Exploring upper primary teachers' perspectives on student engagement. *Teachers and Teaching, 26*(2), 145–165. https://doi.org/10.1080/13540602.2020.1757421

Bishop, R. S. (1990). Mirrors, windows, and sliding glass doors. *Perspectives, 1*(3), ix–xi.

Blachman, B. A. (2000). Phonological awareness. In M. L. Kamil, P. B. Mosenthal, P. D. Pearson, & R. Barr (Eds.), *Handbook of reading research* (Vol. 3, pp. 483–502). Lawrence Erlbaum Associates Publishers.

Blachowicz, C. L. Z., & Fisher, P. (2000). Vocabulary instruction. In M. L. Kamil, P. B. Mosenthal, P. D. Pearson, & R. Barr (Eds.) *Handbook of reading research* (Vol. 3, pp. 502–523). Erlbaum.

Blackall, S. (2018). *Hello lighthouse*. Little, Brown Books for Young Readers.

Blevins, W. (2006). *Phonics from A to Z: A practical guide*. Scholastic.

Blevins, W. (2017). *A fresh look at phonics: Common causes of failure and 7 ingredients for success*. Corwin.

Blevins, W. (2022). 10 common causes of phonics instruction failure and how to avoid them. *William H. Sadlier*. https://go.sadlier.com/school/10-common-causes-of-phonics-instruction-failure-masterclass-register

Bloodgood, J. W. (1999). What's in a name? Children's name writing and literacy acquisition. *Reading Research Quarterly, 34*(3), 342–367.

Bluemle, E. (2017). *Tap tap boom boom* (illustrated by G. Brian Karas). Candlewick.

Blum, A. M., Mason, J. M., Kim, J., & Pearson, P. D. (2020). Modeling question-answer relations: The development of the integrative inferential reasoning comic assessment. *Reading & Writing, 33*(8), 1971–2000.

Bolaños, D., Cole, R. A., Ward, W. H., Hasbrouck, J., Tindal, G. A., & Schwanenflugel, P. J. (2013). Human and automated assessment of oral reading fluency. *Journal of Educational Psychology, 105*(4), 1142–1151.

Bos, C. S., & Anders, P. L. (1990). Effects of interactive vocabulary instruction on the vocabulary learning and reading comprehension of junior-high learning disabled students. *Learning Disability Quarterly, 13*(1), 31–42.

Bottari, M. (2021). Transitioning from word wall to sound walls. *Reading Rockets.* https://www.readingrockets.org/article/transitioning-word-walls-sound-walls

Bowyer-Crane, C., & Snowling, M. J. (2005). Assessing children's inference generation: What do tests of reading comprehension measure? *British Journal of Educational Psychology, 75*(2), 189–201.

Brown, E. K., & Copple, M. T. (2018). Constructing two phonological systems: A phonetic analysis of /p/, /t/, /k/ among early Spanish–English bilingual speakers. *International Journal of Bilingualism, 22*(1), 51–68.

Bruyère, J., & Rusk-Carter, D. (2022, February 7). Using sounds walls in early elementary classrooms. *Edutopia.* https://www.edutopia.org/article/using-sound-walls-early-elementary-classrooms

Burnford, S. (2018). *The incredible journey.* Delacorte Press. (Original work published 1961)

Carle, E. (2008). *The very hungry caterpillar.* Philomel.

Carlisle, J. F., & Feldman L. B. (1995). Morphological awareness and early reading achievement. In L. B. Feldman (Ed.), *Morphological aspects of language processing* (pp. 189–209). Lawrence Erlbaum Associates.

Carr, E., & Ogle, D. (1987). K-W-L Plus: A strategy for comprehension and summarization. *Journal of Reading, 30,* 626–631.

Carroll, J. B., Davies, P., & Richman, B. (1971). *Word frequency book.* Houghton Mifflin.

Carroll, L. (2021). *Alice in wonderland: The original 1865 edition with complete illustrations by Sir John Tenniel.* Amazon.

Cartwright, K. B. (2007). The contribution of graphophonological-semantic flexibility to reading comprehension in college students: Implications for a less simple view of reading. *Journal of Literacy Research, 39*(2), 173–193.

Cartwright, K. B., Bock, A. M., Clause, J. H., Coppage August, E. A., Saunders, H. G., & Schmidt, K. J. (2020). Near- and far-transfer effects of an executive function intervention for 2nd to 5th grade struggling readers. *Cognitive Development, 56,* Article 100932. https://doi.org/10.1016/j.cogdev.2020.100932

Chall, J. (1996). *Stages of reading development* (2nd ed.). Harcourt.

Chall, J. (1983). *Stages of reading development.* McGraw-Hill.

Chapman, J. W., & Tunmer, W. E. (2003). Reading difficulties, reading-related self-perceptions, and strategies for overcoming negative self-beliefs. *Reading and Writing Quarterly, 19*(1), 5–24.

Cirino, P. T., Miciak, J., Ahmed, Y., Barnes, M. A., Taylor, W. P., & Gerst, E. H. (2019). Executive function: Association with multiple reading skills. *Reading and Writing, 32*(7), 1819–1846.

Clay, M. (2019). *An observation survey of early literacy achievement* (4th ed.). Heinemann.

Cornwall, G. (2017). *Jabari jumps.* Candlewick.

Crosson, A. C., McKeown, M. G., Moore, D. W., & Ye, F. (2019). Extending the bounds of morphology instruction: Teaching Latin roots facilitates academic word learning for English learner adolescents. *Reading & Writing, 32*(3), 689–727.

Cruz, M. C., & Pollock, K. B. (2004). Stepping into the wardrobe: A fantasy genre study. *Language Arts, 81*(3), 184–195.

Cunningham, A., & Stanovich, K. (1998). What reading does for the mind. *American Educator, 22,* 8–15.

Cunnings, I., & Clashen, H. (2007). The time-course of morphological constraints. Evidence from eye-movements during reading. *Cognition, 104*, 476–494.

Dempsey, L. (2020). Building pre-readers' background knowledge: The impact of a play-based event exposure on children's comprehension of stories read aloud. *Early Child Development and Care, 190*(9), 1371–1381.

DiCamillo, K. (2021). *Because of Winn-Dixie.* Candlewick.

Dolch, E. W. (1936). A basic sight vocabulary. *The Elementary School Journal, 36,* 456–460.

Dole, J. A., Nokes, J. D., & Drits, D. (2009). Cognitive strategy instruction. In S. E. Israel & G. G. Duffy (Eds.), *Handbook of research on reading comprehension* (pp. 347–372). Routledge.

Dore, R. A., Amendum, S. J., Golinkoff, R. M., & Hirsh-Paske, K. (2018). Theory of mind: A hidden factor in reading comprehension? *Educational Psychology Review, 30*(3), 1067–1089.

Dorr, R. E. (2006). Something old is new again: Revisiting Language Experience. *The Reading Teacher, 60*(2), 138–146.

Duke, N. K., & Cartwright, K. B. (2021). The science of reading progresses: Communicating advances beyond the simple view of reading. *Reading Research Quarterly, 56*(1), 25–44.

Dunne, A. (2017). *Magnetism.* Capstone Press.

Ehri, L., & Nunes, S. (2002). The role of phonemic awareness in learning to read. In A. E. Farstrup & S. J. Samuels (Eds.), *What research has to say about reading instruction* (pp. 110–140). International Reading Association.

Ehri, L. C. (2004). Teaching phonemic awareness and phonics: An explanation of the National Reading Panel meta-analyses. In P. McCardle & V. Chhabra (Eds.), *The voice of evidence in reading research* (pp. 153–186). Brookes.

Ehri, L. C. (2005). Learning to read words. *Scientific Studies of Reading, 9*, 167–188. https://doi .org/10.1207/s1532799xssr0902_4

Ehri, L. C. (2014). Orthographic mapping in the acquisition of sight word reading, spelling memory, and vocabulary learning. *Scientific Studies of Reading, 18*(1), 5–21.

Ehri, L. C. (2020). The science of learning to read words: A case for systematic phonics instruction. *Reading Research Quarterly, 55,* S45–S60.

Ehri, L. C., Nunes, S. R., Willows, D. M., Schuster, B. V., Yaghoub-Zadeh, Z., & Shanahan, T. (2001). Phonemic awareness instruction helps children learn to read: Evidence from the national reading panel's meta-analysis. *Reading Research Quarterly, 36*(3), 250–287.

Ehri, L. C., & Wilce, L. S. (1985). Movement into reading: Is the first stage of printed word learning visual or phonetic? *Reading Research Quarterly, 20*(2), 163–179.

Elleman, A. M. (2017). Examining the impact of inference instruction on the literal and inferential comprehension of skilled and less skilled readers: A meta-analytic review. *Journal of Educational Psychology, 109*(6), 761–781. https://doi.org/10.1037/edu0000180

Endo, A. (2021). Optimizing literacy instruction with oral reading fluency assessments. *Houghton Mifflin Harcourt.* https://www.hmhco.com/blog/oral-reading-fluency-assessment

Ericsson, K. A., Krampe, R. T., & Tesch-Römer, C. (1993). The role of deliberate practice in the acquisition of expert performance. *Psychological Review, 100*(3), 363–406.

Farndon, J. (2007). *Weather.* Scholastic Nonfiction.

Farrall, M. (2018, October). Understanding reading fluency: Research implications for assessment and instruction [Paper presentation]. Session presented at the Annual International Dyslexia Association's Reading, Learning, & Literacy Conference, Mashantucket, CT.

Farrell, L., Hunter, M., Davidson, N., & Osenga, T. (2019). The simple view of reading. *Reading Rockets.* https://www.readingrockets.org/article/simple-view-reading

Farrell, L., Hunter, M., & Osenga, T. (2019). A new model for teaching high-frequency words. *Reading Rockets.* https://www.readingrockets.org/article/new-model-teaching-high-frequency-words

Fearn, L., & Farnan, N. (2001). *Interactions: Teaching writing and the language arts.* Allyn & Bacon.

Fillmore, L. W., & Fillmore, C. J. (n.d.). What does text complexity mean for English learners and language minority students? *Understanding Language Project.* Stanford University. https:// ell.stanford.edu/sites/default/files/pdf/academic-papers/06-LWF%20CJF%20Text%20 Complexity%20FINAL_0.pdf

Fisher, D., & Frey, N. (2007). *Scaffolded writing instruction: Teaching with a gradual-release framework.* Scholastic.

Fisher, D., & Frey, N. (2009). *Background knowledge: The missing piece of the comprehension puzzle.* Heinemann.

Fisher, D., & Frey, N. (2016). Designing quality content area instruction. *The Reading Teacher, 69*(5), 525–529.

Fisher, D., & Frey, N. (2018). Reading and writing on screen and paper. *Journal of Adolescent & Adult Literacy, 62*(3), 349–351.

Fisher, D., Frey, N., & Hattie, J. (2020). *The distance learning playbook, grades k-12: Teaching for engagement and impact in any setting.* Corwin.

Fisher, D., Frey, N., & Lapp, D. (2008). Shared readings: Modeling comprehension, vocabulary, text structures, and text features for older readers. *The Reading Teacher, 61*(7), 548–556.

Fisher, D., Frey, N., & Law, N. V. (2021). *Comprehension: The skill, will, and thrill of reading.* Corwin.

Flavell, J. H. (1979). Metacognition and cognitive monitoring. A new area of cognitive-development inquiry. *American Psychologist, 34*(10), 906–911.

Flood, J., Lapp, D., & Fisher, D. (2005). Neurological impress method plus. *Reading Psychology, 26*, 147–160.

Forster, K. I. (2012) A parallel activation model with a sequential twist. In J. S. Adelman (Ed.), *Visual word recognition: Vol. 1. Models and methods, orthography and phonology* (pp. 52–69). Psychology Press.

Frey, N., & Fisher, D. (2009). *Learning words inside and out: Vocabulary instruction that boosts achievement in all subject areas.* Heinemann.

Frey, N., Fisher, D., & Hattie, J. (2018). *Developing assessment-capable visible learners: Maximizing skill, will, and thrill.* Corwin.

Frey, N., Fisher, D., & Ortega, S. (2021, April). See it, say it. *Language Magazine*. https://www.languagemagazine.com/2021/04/13/see-it-say-it/

Frost, R. (1998). Toward a strong phonological theory of visual word recognition. True issues and false trails. *Psychological Bulletin, 123*(1), 71–99.

Fry, E. (2004). Phonics: A large phoneme-grapheme frequency count revised. *Journal of Literacy Research, 36*(1), 85–98.

Gaertner, M. (2019). *Magnets.* ABDO Publishing Company.

Galloway, A. M. (2003). *Improving reading comprehension through metacognitive strategy instruction: Evaluating the evidence for the effectiveness of the reciprocal teaching procedure* (Publication No. AAI3092542) [Doctoral dissertation, University of Nebraska-Lincoln]. ProQuest Dissertations and Theses.

Gambrell, L., Palmer, B., Codling, R., & Mazzoni, S. (1996). *Motivation to read profile (MRP).* National Reading Research Center.

Ganske, K. (2000). *Word journeys: Assessment-guided phonics, spelling, and vocabulary instruction.* Guilford Press.

Gartland, L. B., & Smolkin, L. B. (2016). The histories and mysteries of grammar instruction. *Reading Teacher, 69*(4), 391–399.

Gehlbach, H. (2004). Social perspective taking: A facilitating aptitude for conflict resolution, historical empathy, and social studies achievement. *Theory and Research in Social Education, 32*(1), 39–55.

Gillon, G. T. (2017). *Phonological awareness: From research to practice* (2nd ed.). Guilford.

González, N., Moll, L. C., & Amanti, C. (2005). *Funds of knowledge: Theorizing practices in households, communities, and classrooms.* Lawrence Erlbaum Associates.

Goodwin, A., Lipsky, M., & Ahn, S. (2012). Word detectives: Using units of meaning to support literacy. *Reading Teacher, 65*(7), 461–470.

Gough, P., & Tunmer, W. (1986). Decoding, reading, and reading disability. *Remedial and Special Education*, *7*(1), 6–10.

Gourse, L. (1996). *Pocahontas*. Aladdin.

Graves, M. F., & Slater, W. H. (1996). Vocabulary instruction in content areas. In D. Lapp, J. Flood, & N. Farnan (Eds.), *Content area reading and learning: Instructional strategies* (2nd ed., pp. 261–275). Allyn & Bacon.

Greutman, H. (2017). *Basics of fine motor skills: Developmental activities for kids*. CreateSpace Independent Publishing Platform.

Guthrie, J. T., Hoa, A. L. W., Wigfield, A., Tonks, S. M., Humenick, N. M., & Littles, E. (2007). Reading motivation and reading comprehension growth in the later elementary years. *Contemporary Educational Psychology, 32*(3), 282–313.

Guthrie, J. T., Wigfield, A., Barbosa, P., Perencevich, K. C., Taboada, A., Davis, M. H., Scafiddi, N. T., & Tonks, S. (2004). Increasing reading comprehension and engagement through Concept-Oriented Reading Instruction. *Journal of Educational Psychology, 96*(3), 403–423.

Harn, B. A., Stoolmiller, M., & Chard, D. J. (2008). Measuring the dimensions of alphabetic principle on the reading development of first graders: The role of automaticity and unitization. *Journal of Learning Disabilities*, *41*(2), 143–157.

Hasbrouck, J., & Tindal, G. (2017). *An update to compiled ORF norms* (Technical report no. 1702). Behavioral Research and Teaching, University of Oregon.

Hasbrouck, J., & Tindal, G. A. (2006). Oral reading fluency norms: A valuable assessment tool for reading teachers. *Reading Teacher, 59*(7), 636–644.

Hays, A. J. (2004). *Here comes silent e!* Random House.

Heckelman, R. G. (1966). Report on neurological impress method. *Academic Therapy, 1*, 235–239.

Heckelman, R. G. (1969). A neurological-impress method of remedial-reading instruction. *Academic Therapy, 4*, 277–282.

Henderson, E. H. (1985). *Teaching spelling*. Houghton Mifflin.

Henk, W. A. (1983). Adapting the NIM to improve comprehension. *Academic Therapy, 19*, 97–101.

Henkes, H. (2000). *Wemberly worried.* Greenwillow Books. (Original work published 1900)

Hesse, K. (1999). *Come on, rain!* (illustrated by Jon Muth). Scholastic Press.

Hill Middle School, Long Beach Unified School District. (2000). Inference rubric. *MiddleWeb.* http://www.middleweb.com/wp-content/uploads/2013/04/InferRubric2.pdf

Hoover, W. A., & Gough, P. B. (1990). The simple view of reading. *Reading and Writing, 2*(2), 127–160.

Hu, S., Torphy, K. T., & Opperman, A. (2019). Culturally relevant curriculum materials in the age of social media and curation. *Teachers College Record, 121*(14), 1–8.

Huang, J., & Chen, G. (2019). From reading strategy instruction to student reading achievement: The mediating role of student motivational factors. *Psychology in the Schools, 56*(5), 724–740.

Hudson, A., Koh, P. W., Moore, K. A., & Binks-Cantrell, E. (2020). Fluency interventions for elementary students with reading difficulties: A synthesis of research from 2000–2019. *Education Sciences*, *10*(3), 52–80.

Hudson, R. F., Lane, H. B., & Pullen, P. C. (2005, May). Reading fluency assessment and instruction: What, why, and how? *The Reading Teacher, 58*(8), 702–714.

International Literacy Association. (2019). *Position statement and research brief: Phonological awareness in early childhood literacy development.* https://www.literacyworldwide.org/docs/default-source/where-we-stand/ila-phonological-awareness-early-childhood-literacy-development.pdf

Iowa Reading Research Center. (2018). *Reading racetrack sight word activity.* https://iowareadingresearch.org/sites/iowareadingresearch.org/files/reading_racetrack_sight_word_activity.pdf

Iris Center. (n.d.). *What components comprise high-quality reading instruction?* https://iris.peabody.vanderbilt.edu/module/rti03/cresource/q3/p07

Javorsky, K. H. (2014). *Digital print concepts: Conceptualizing a modern framework for emerging knowledge.* [Doctoral dissertation, University of Nebraska-Lincoln]. Digital Commons. https://digitalcommons.unl.edu/cgi/viewcontent.cgi?article=1043&context=teachlearnstudent

Johns, J. L. (1980). First graders' concepts about print. *Reading Research Quarterly, 15*(4), 529–549.

Johnson, E. J., & Johnson, A. B. (2016). Enhancing academic investment through home-school connections. *Journal of Language & Literacy Education, 12*(1), 104–121.

Jones, C. D., Clark, S. K., & Reutzel, D. R. (2012). Enhancing alphabet knowledge instruction: Research implications and practical strategies for early childhood educators. *Teacher Education and Leadership Faculty Publications, Paper 404.* https://digitalcommons.usu.edu/teal_facpub/404

Jones, C. D., Clark, S. K., & Reutzel, D. R. (2013). Enhancing alphabet knowledge instruction: Research implications and practical strategies for early childhood educators. *Early Childhood Education Journal, 41,* 81–89.

Jones, C. D., & Reutzel, D. R. (2012). Enhanced alphabet knowledge instruction: Exploring a change of frequency, focus, and distributed cycles of review. *Reading Psychology, 33*(5), 448–464.

Jones, C. F. (1999). *Yukon gold: The story of the Klondike Gold Rush*. Holiday House.

Juster, N. (1961). *The phantom tollbooth*. Scholastic.

Justice, L. M., Skibbe, L., Canning, A., & Lankford, C. (2005). Pre-schoolers, print and storybooks: An observational study using eye movement analysis. *Journal of Research in Reading, 28*(3), 229–243.

Justice, L. M., Sofka, A. E., Sutton, M., & Zucker, T. A. (2006). *Project STAR: Fidelity coding checklist*. Preschool Language and Literacy Lab, University of Virginia.

Justice, R. M., Kaderavek, J. N., Fan, X., Sofka, A., & Hunt, A. (2009). Accelerating preschoolers' early literacy development through classroom-based teacher–child storybook reading and explicit print referencing. *Language, Speech, and Hearing Services in Schools, 40*, 67–85.

Karlsson, J., van den Broek, P., Helder, A., Hickendorff, M., Koornneef, A., & van Leijenhorst, L. (2018). Profiles of young readers: Evidence from thinking aloud while reading narrative and expository texts. *Learning & Individual Differences, 67,* 105–116.

Katz, W. (n.d.). *Manners of articulation.* https://cpb-us-e2.wpmucdn.com/labs.utdallas.edu/dist/7/128/files/2021/06/manners_of_artic.jpg

Kearns, D. M. (2020). Does English have useful syllable division patterns? *Reading Research Quarterly, 55*(S1), S145- S160.

Keesey, S., Konrad, M., & Joseph, L. M. (2015). Word boxes improve phonemic awareness, letter-sound correspondences, and spelling skills of at-risk kindergartners. *Remedial and Special Education, 36*, 167–180. https://doi.org/10.1177/0741932514543927

Kelly, J., & Taboada Barber, A. (2021). Interactive read-aloud instruction with narratives: Teaching inferencing using Theory of Mind. *Teaching Exceptional Children, 54*(2), 106–115.

Kilpatrick, D. (2016). *Equipped for reading success: A comprehensive, step-by-step program for developing phonemic awareness and fluent word recognition.* Casey & Kirsch Publishers.

Kilpatrick, D. A. (2015). *Essentials of assessing, preventing, and overcoming reading difficulties.* John Wiley and Sons.

Kim, S. Y., Yap, M. J., & Goh, W. D. (2019). The role of semantic transparency in visual word recognition of compound words: A megastudy approach. *Behavior Research Methods, 51*, 2722–2732.

Kuhn, M. R. (2020). Whole class or small group fluency instruction: A tutorial of four effective approaches. *Education Sciences, 10*(5), 145–156.

Kuhn, M. R., Schwanenflugel, P. J., Morris, R. D., Morrow, L. M., Woo, D., Meisinger, B., Sevcik, R., Bradley, B., & Stahl, S. A. (in memoriam). (2006). Teaching children to become fluent and automatic readers. *Journal of Literacy Research, 38*(4), 357–387.

Kupetz, B. N. (1993). Shared responsibility: Nurturing literacy in the very young. *School Library Journal, 39*, 28–31.

LaBerge, D., & Samuels, S. J. (1974). Toward a theory of automatic information processing in reading. *Cognitive Psychology, 6*, 293–323.

Lapp, D., Wolsey, T. D., & Wood, K. (2015). *Mining complex text, grades 2–5: Using and creating graphic organizers to grasp content and share new understandings.* Corwin.

LaRusso, M., Kim, H. Y., Selman, R., Uccelli, P., Dawson, T., Jones, S., Donovan, S., & Snow, C. (2016). Contributions of academic language, perspective taking, and complex reasoning to deep reading comprehension. *Journal of Research on Educational Effectiveness, 9*(2), 201–222.

Laslocky, M. (2021). The mistake-friendly classroom. *Edutopia.* https://www.edutopia.org/article/mistake-friendly-classroom

Lee, J., & Yoon Yoon, S. (2017). The effects of repeated reading on reading fluency for students with reading disabilities: A meta-analysis. *Journal of Learning Disabilities, 50*(2), 213–224.

Leon, V. (2001). *Uppity women of the new world.* Conari Press.

Lesaux, N. K., Rupp, A. A., & Siegel, L. S. (2007). Growth in reading skills of children from diverse linguistic backgrounds: Findings from a 5-year longitudinal study. *Journal of Educational Psychology, 99*(4), 821–834.

Lewkowicz, N. K. (1980). Phonemic awareness training: What to teach and how to teach it. *Journal of Educational Psychology, 72*(5), 686–700.

Leyva, D., Hopson, S., & Nichols, A. (2012). Reading a note, reading a mind: Children's notating skills and understanding of mind. *Reading & Writing, 25*(3), 701–716.

Liebfreund, M. D. (2021). Cognitive and motivational predictors of narrative and informational text comprehension. *Reading Psychology, 42*(2), 177–196.

Lomax, R. G., & McGee, L. M. (1987). Young children's concepts about print and reading: Toward a model of word reading acquisition. *Reading Research Quarterly, 22*(2), 237–256.

Lonigan, C. J., & Shanahan, T. (2008). *Developing early literacy: Report of the National Reading Panel. Executive Summary: A scientific synthesis of early literacy development and implications for intervention.* National Institute for Literacy.

Lowry, L. (2016). "Tuning in" to others: How young children develop theory of mind. *Hanen Centre.* http://www.hanen.org/helpful-info/articles/tuning-in-to-others-how-young-children-develop.aspx

Lucero, A. (2018). The development of bilingual narrative retelling among Spanish-English dual language learners over two years. *Language, Speech & Hearing Services in Schools, 49*(3), 607–621.

Lupo, S. M., Berry, A., Thacker, E., Sawyer, A., & Merritt, J. (2020). Rethinking text sets to support knowledge building and interdisciplinary learning. *The Reading Teacher, 73*(4), 513–524.

Macomb Intermediate School District. (2001). Letter/sound identification. *Michigan Literacy Progress Profile.* https://www.misd.net/mlpp/assessments/letterSoundidentify/letter-sound-A.pdf

Madden, M. (2005). *99 ways to tell a story: Exercises in style.* Chamberlain.

Manguel, A. (1996). *A history of reading.* Penguin.

Manyak, P. C., Baumann, J. F., & Manyak, A. (2018). Morphological analysis instruction in the elementary grades: Which morphemes to teach and how to teach them. *Reading Teacher, 72*(3), 289–300.

Martinez, M., Roser, N. L., & Strecker, S. K. (1998–1999). "I never thought I could be a star": A reader's theatre ticket to fluency. *The Reading Teacher, 52*, 326–334.

Masonheimer, P. E., Drum, P. A., & Ehri, L. C. (1984). Does environmental print identification lead children into word reading? *Journal of Reading Behavior, 16*, 257–271. https://doi.org/10.1080/10862968409547520

McCandliss, B. D., & Posner, M. I. (2003). Fostering literacy through understanding brain mechanisms. *Education Canada, 43*(2), 4–7.

McCarthy, P. (2008). Using sound boxes systematically to develop phonemic awareness. *The Reading Teacher, 62*(4), 346–349.

McCraw, B. (2014). *There's an app for that: Uses of print and digital materials in the lives of three preschoolers* [Unpublished doctoral dissertation]. University of South Carolina.

McEwan, E. K. (2007). *40 ways to support struggling readers in the content classrooms, grades 6–12*. Corwin.

McGee, L. M., & Morrow, L. M. (2005). *Teaching literacy in kindergarten.* Guilford Press.

McGee, L. M., & Richgels, D. J. (1989). "K is Kristen's": Learning the alphabet from a child's perspective. *The Reading Teacher, 43*, 216–225.

McGill-Franzen, A., Lanford, C., & Adams, E. (2002). Learning to be literate: A comparison of five urban early childhood programs. *Journal of Educational Psychology, 94*(3), 443–464.

McLaughlin, M., & Devoogd, G. (2004). Critical literacy as comprehension: Expanding reader response. *Journal of Adolescent & Adult Literacy, 48*(1), 52–62.

Meisinger, E. B., Bradley, B. A., Schwanenflugel, P. J., Kuhn, M. R., & Morris, R. D. (2009). Myth and reality of the word caller: The relation between teacher nominations and prevalence among elementary school children. *School Psychology Quarterly, 24*(3), 147–150. https://doi.org/10.1037/a0017191

Mesmer, H. (2001). Examining the theoretical claims about decodable texts: Does text decodability lead to greater application of letter/sound knowledge in first-grade readers? *Yearbook: National Reading Conference, 50*, 444–459.

Mesmer, H. A. (2019). *Letter lessons and first words: Phonics foundations that work*. Heinemann.

Metcalfe, J. (2017). Learning from errors. *Annual Review of Psychology, 68*, 465-489.

Michaels, S., O'Connor, C., & Resnick, L. B. (2008). Deliberative discourse idealized and realized: Accountable talk in the classroom and in civic life. *Studies in Philosophy and Education, 27*(4), 283–297.

Michaels, S., O'Connor, M. C., Hall, M. W., & Resnick, L. B. (2010). *Accountable talk sourcebook: For classroom conversation that works* (v.3.1). University of Pittsburgh Institute for Learning. Retrieved from ifl.lrdc.pitt.edu/ifl/index.php/download/ index/ats/

Moats, L. C. (1995). *Spelling: Development, disability, and instruction.* York Press.

Moore, D., Alvermann, D., & Hinchman, K. (2000). *Struggling adolescent readers: A collection of teaching strategies.* International Reading Association.

Moss, B. (2004). Teaching expository text structures through information trade book retellings. *The Reading Teacher, 57*(8), 710–718.

Muhammad, I., & Ali, S. K. (2019). *The proudest blue: A story of hijab and family*. Little, Brown Books for Readers.

Muris, P., Steerneman, P., Meesters, Merckelbach, C., Horselenberg, R., van den Hogen, T., & van Dongen, L. (1999). The TOM Test: A new instrument for assessing theory of mind in normal children and children with pervasive developmental disorders. *Journal of Autism and Developmental Disorders, 29*(1), 67–78.

Muter, V., Hulme, C., Snowling, M., & Taylor, S. (1998). Segmentation, not rhyming, predicts early progress in learning to read. *Journal of Experimental Child Psychology, 71*, 3–27.

Nagy, W., & Townsend, D. (2012). Words as tools: Learning academic vocabulary as language actuation. *Reading Research Quarterly, 47*(1), 91–108.

Nagy, W. E., & Anderson, R. C. (1984). How many words are in printed school English? *Reading Research Quarterly, 19*(3), 304–330.

National Assessment of Educational Progress (NAEP). (2021a). *Illustrative student oral reading.* https://nces.ed.gov/nationsreportcard/studies/orf/illustrative_audio.aspx

National Assessment of Educational Progress (NAEP). (2021b). *NAEP oral reading fluency passage reading expression scoring rubric.* https://nces.ed.gov/nationsreportcard/studies/orf/scoring.aspx

National Early Literacy Panel. (2008). *Developing early literacy: Report of the National Early Literacy Panel.* https://lincs.ed.gov/publications/pdf/NELPReport09.pdf

National Institute of Child Health and Human Development. (2000). *Report of the National Reading Panel. Teaching children to read: An evidence-based assessment of the scientific research literature on reading and its implications for reading instruction* (NIH Publication No. 00-4769). U.S. Government Printing Office.

National Oceanographic and Space Administration. (2022, June 22). *Monthly average Mauna Loa CO^2*. https://gml.noaa.gov/ccgg/trends/mlo.html

National Reading Panel. (2000). Teaching children to read: An evidence-based assessment of the scientific research literature on reading and its implications for reading instruction. *National Institute of Child Health and Human Development.* https://www.nichd.nih.gov/sites/default/files/publications/pubs/nrp/Documents/report.pdf

National Research Council. (2000). *How people learn: Brain, mind, experience, and school.* Committee on developments in the science of learning. In J. D. Bransford, A. L. Brown, & R. Cocking (Eds.), *Commission on behavioral and social sciences and education.* National Academy Press.

Naylor, P. R. (2000). *Shiloh.* Atheneum.

Neuman, S. B., Kaefer, T., & Pinkham, A. (2014). Building background knowledge. *Reading Teacher, 68*(2), 145–148.

Neuman, S. B., & Roskos, K. (2012). Helping children become more knowledgeable through text. *The Reading Teacher, 66*(3), 207–210.

Nunes, T., Bryant, P., Pretzlik, U., & Hurry, J. (Eds.). (2006). *Improving literacy by teaching morphemes.* Routledge.

Nuthall, G. (2007). *The hidden lives of learners.* NZCER Press.

O'Connor, R. E., & Vadasy, P. F. (Eds.). (2011). *Handbook of reading interventions.* Guilford.

Oakhill, J. V., & Cain, K. (2012). The precursors of reading ability in young readers: Evidence from a four-year longitudinal study. *Scientific Studies of Reading, 16*(2), 91–121.

Ogle, D. (1986). K-W-L: A teaching model that develops active reading of expository text. *The Reading Teacher, 39*(6), 564–570.

Optiz, M. F., & Rasinski, T. V. (2008). *Good-bye round robin: 25 effective oral reading strategies* (updated ed.). Heinemann.

Padak, N., Rasinski, T., & Newton, J. (2020). *Building vocabulary with Greek and Latin roots: A professional guide to word knowledge and vocabulary development* (2nd ed.). Shell Education.

Paige, D. D. (2011). "That sounded good!": Using Whole-Class Choral Reading to improve fluency. *Reading Teacher, 64*(6), 435–438.

Palincsar, A. S., & Brown, A. L. (1984). Reciprocal teaching of comprehension-fostering and comprehension-monitoring activities. *Cognition and Instruction, 1*(2), 117–175.

Palincsar, A. S., Marcum, M. B., Fitzgerald, M., & Sherwood, C. A. (2019). Braiding teacher practice and class-wide dialogue: An historical inquiry across three sociocultural interventions. *International Journal of Educational Research, 97*(1), 157–165.

Paris, S. G. (2005). Reinterpreting the development of reading skills. *Reading Research Quarterly, 40,* 184–202.

Pearson, P. D., Moje, E., & Greenleaf, C. (2010). Literacy and science: Each in the service of the other. *Science, 328*(5977), 459–463.

Pearson, P. D., & Tierney, R. (2021). *A history of literacy education: Waves of research and practice.* Guilford.

Pence Turnbull, K. L., Bowles R. P., Skibbe L. E., Justice L. M., & Wiggins A. K. (2010). Theoretical explanations for preschoolers' lowercase alphabet knowledge. *Journal of Speech, Language, and Hearing Research, 53*(6), 1757–1768.

Perfetti, C. A. (2011). Phonology is critical in reading: But a phonological deficit is not the only source of low reading skill. In S. A. Brady, D. Braze & C. A. Fowler (Eds.), *Explaining individual differences in reading: Theory and evidence* (pp. 153–171). Psychology Press.

Piasta, S. B. (2014). Moving to assessment-guided differentiated instruction to support young children's alphabet knowledge. *The Reading Teacher, 68*(3), 202–211.

Piasta, S. B., & Wagner, R. K. (2010). Learning letter names and sounds: Effects of instruction, letter type, and phonological processing skill. *Journal of Experimental Child Psychology, 105*(4), 324–344.

Pikulski, J. J., & Chard, D. J. (2005). Fluency: Bridge between decoding and reading comprehension. *Reading Teacher, 58*(6), 510–519.

Pinker, S. (1999). Foreword. In D. McGuinness (Ed.), *Why our children can't read and what we can do about it* (pp. ix–x). Touchstone/Simon & Schuster.

Portis, A. (2019). *Hey, water!* Neal Porter Books.

Pressley, M., Allington, R. L., Warton-McDonald, R., & Block, C. C. (2001). *Learning to read: Lessons from exemplary first-grade classrooms*. Guilford.

Quirk, M., Schwanenflugel, P. J., & Webb, M. (2009). A short-term longitudinal study of the relationship between motivation to read and reading fluency skill in second grade. *Journal of Literacy Research, 41*(2), 196–227.

Raphael, T. E., Highfield, K., & Au, K. H. (2006). *QAR now: A powerful and practical framework that develops comprehension and higher-level thinking in all students*. Scholastic.

Rasinski, T. V. (2003). *The fluent reader: Oral reading strategies for building word recognition, fluency, and comprehension*. Scholastic.

Rasinski, T. V. (2020). *The fluent reader: Oral & silent reading strategies for building fluency, word recognition, and comprehension* (2nd ed.). Scholastic.

Rasinski, T., Homan, S., & Biggs, M. (2009). Teaching reading fluency to struggling readers: Method, materials, and evidence. *Reading & Writing Quarterly, 25*(2/3), 192–204.

Rasinski, T., Padak, N., & Newton, J. (2017). The roots of comprehension. *Educational Leadership, 74*(5), 41–45.

Rauth, J., & Stuart, R. (2008). *Sound instruction: Phonemic awareness in kindergarten and first grade.* Fifth Annual National Reading First Conference.

Really Great Reading. (n.d.). *Heart word magic: Help students learn to read and spell high-frequency and sight words.* https://www.reallygreatreading.com/heart-word-magic

Recht, D. R., & Leslie, L. (1988). Effect of prior knowledge on good and poor readers' memory of text. *Journal of Educational Psychology, 80*(1), 16–20.

Reich, S. M., Yau. J. C., Xu, Y., Muskat, T., Uvalle, J., & Cannata, D. (2019). Digital or print? A comparison of preschoolers' comprehension, vocabulary, and engagement from a print book and an e-book. *AERA Open, 5*(3). https://doi.org/10.1177/2332858419878389

Reid, J., Forrestal, P., & Cook, J. (1989). *Small group learning in the classroom.* Heinemann.

Reutzel, D. R. (2015). Early literacy research: Findings primary-grade teachers will want to know. *The Reading Teacher, 69*(1), 14–24. https://doi.org/10.1002/trtr.1387

Reutzel, D. R., & Cooter, R. B. (1992). *Teaching children to read: From basals to books*. Merrill/ Prentice-Hall Publishing Company.

Rinaldi, L., Sells, D., & McLaughlin, T. F. (1997). The effect of reading racetracks on the sight word acquisition and fluency of elementary students. *Journal of Behavioral Education, 7*, 219–233. https://doi.org/10.1023/A:1022845209417

Rosenshine, B., & Meister, C. (1994). Reciprocal teaching: A review of the research. *Review of Educational Research, 64*(4), 479–530.

Ross, K. M., & Joseph, L. M. (2019). Effects of word boxes on improving students' basic literacy skills: A literature review. *Preventing School Failure: Alternative Education for Children and Youth, 63*(1), 43–51.

Ryan, P. M. (2002). *Esperanza rising.* Scholastic.

Saddler, B., & Graham, S. (2005). The effects of peer-assisted sentence-combining instruction on the writing performance of more and less skilled young writers. *Journal of Educational Psychology, 97*(1), 43–54.

Samuels, S. J. (1979). The method of repeated readings. *The Reading Teacher, 32*, 403–408.

Savage, R., & Carless, S. (2005). Learning support assistants can deliver effective reading interventions for "at-risk" children. *Educational Research, 47*(1), 45–61.

Scarborough, H. S. (2001). Connecting early language and literacy to later reading (dis)abilities: Evidence, theory, and practice. In S. Neuman & D. Dickinson (Eds.), *Handbook for research in early literacy* (pp. 97–110). Guilford Press.

Schmitt, M. C. (1990). A questionnaire to measure children's awareness of strategic reading processes. *The Reading Teacher, 43*, 454–461.

Scieszka, J. (1996). *The true story of the three little pigs.* Puffin Books.

Scott, C. (2009). A case for the sentence in reading comprehension. *Language, Speech, and Hearing Services in Schools, 43*, 184–191.

Segers, E., & Verhoeven, L. (2016). How logical reasoning mediates the relation between lexical quality and reading comprehension. *Reading & Writing, 29*(4), 577–590.

Seve, K. (2017). *National Geographic Little Kids first big book of weather.* National Geographic Kids.

Shanahan, T. (2019). *Which texts for teaching reading: Decodable, predictable, or controlled vocabulary?* https://shanahanonliteracy.com/blog/which-texts-for-teaching-reading-decodable-predictable-or-controlled-vocabulary

Shanahan, T. (2020, March 14). *Prior knowledge, or he isn't going to pick on the baseball study.* https://shanahanonliteracy.com/blog/prior-knowledge-or-he-isnt-going-to-pick-on-the-baseball-study

Shanahan, T. (2021). What does it take to teach inferencing? *Shanahan on Literacy.* https://www.shanahanonliteracy.com/blog/what-does-it-take-to-teach-inferencing#sthash.xZYY2omb.dpbs

Shanahan, T., Kamil, M. L., & Tobin, A. W. (1982). Cloze as a measure of intersentential comprehension. *Reading Research Quarterly, 17*, 229–255.

Sheets, W. (2013). *Developmental spelling stages* [Conference session]. 2014 National Reading Recovery & K-6 Classroom Literacy Conference. Literacy Collaborative, The Ohio State University.

Sheinkin, S. (2017). *Undefeated: Jim Thorpe and the Carlisle Indian school football team.* Roading Brook Press.

Shinn, M. R., & Shinn, M. M. (2002). *AIMSweb training notebook: Administration and scoring of reading maze for use in general outcome measures.* EDformation.

Silverman, R. D., Johnson, E., Keane, K., & Khanna, S. (2020). Beyond decoding: A meta-analysis of the effects of language comprehension interventions on K–5 students' language and literacy outcomes. *Reading Research Quarterly, 55*, S207–S233.

Smith, R., Snow, P., Serry, T., & Hammond, L. (2021). The role of background knowledge in reading comprehension: A critical review. *Reading Psychology, 42*(3), 214–240.

Snow, C. E., Burns, M. S., & Griffin, P. (1998). *Preventing reading difficulties in young children.* National Academy Press.

Solity, J., & Vousden, J. (2009). Real books vs. reading schemes. A new perspective for instructional psychology. *Educational Psychology, 29*(4), 469–511. https://doi.org/10.1080/01443410903103657

Stahl, K. A. (2011). Applying new visions of reading development in today's classrooms. *The Reading Teacher: A Journal of Research-Based Classroom Practice, 65*(1), 52–56. https://doi.org/10.1598/RT.65.1.7

Stahl, K. A. (2018). *Teaching academic vocabulary across all content areas.* NYS RTI TAC. https://nysrti.org/files/webinars/strand_21/1vocabassess.pdf

Stahl, K. A., & Bravo, M. A. (2010). Contemporary classroom vocabulary assessment for content areas. *The Reading Teacher, 63*(7), 566–578.

Stahl, K. A., Flanigan, K., & McKenna, M. C. (2008). *Assessment for reading instruction.* Guilford Press.

Stahl, S. A., & Heubach, K. M. (2005). Fluency-Oriented Reading Instruction. *Journal of Literacy Research, 37*(1), 25–60.

Stahl, S. A., & Miller, P. D. (1989). Whole language and language experience approaches for beginning reading: A quantitative research synthesis. *Review of Educational Research, 59,* 87–116.

Stanovich, K., & Cunningham, A. (1992). Studying the consequences of literacy within a literate society: The cognitive correlates of print exposure. *Memory & Cognition, 20,* 51–68.

Stanovich, K. E. (1986). Matthew effects in reading: Some consequences of individual differences in the acquisition of literacy. *Reading Research Quarterly, 21*, 360–406.

Stanovich, K. E. (1988). Explaining the differences between the dyslexic and the garden-variety poor reader: The phonological-core variable-difference model. *Journal of Learning Disabilities, 21*(10), 590–604, 612.

Stanovich, K. E., Nathan, R. G., West, R. F., & Vala-Rossi, M. (1985). Children's word recognition in context: Spreading activation, expectancy, and modularity. *Child Development, 56*(6), 1418–1428.

Stevenson, R. L. (1885). Bed in summer. *Poets.org*. https://poets.org/poem/bed-summer

Stigler, J. W., & Hiebert, J. (1999). *The teaching gap: Best ideas from the world's teachers for improving in the classroom.* The Free Press.

Student Achievement Partners. (n.d.). *Juicy sentence guidance.* https://achievethecore.org/content/upload/Juicy%20Sentence%20Guidance.pdf

Sullivan, M., Konrad, M., Joseph, L. M., & Luu, K. C. (2013). A comparison of two sight word reading fluency drill formats. *Preventing School Failure: Alternative Education for Children and Youth, 57,* 102–110. https://doi.org/10.1080/1045988x.2012.674575

Taba, H. (1967). *Teacher's handbook for middle school social studies.* Addison Wesley.

Tayback, S. (1999). *Joseph had a little overcoat.* Viking.

Tayback, S. (2007). *There was an old lady who swallowed a fly.* Child's Play International.

Taylor, M. D. (1976). *Roll of thunder, hear my cry.* Dial Press.

Taylor, W. (1953). Cloze procedure: A new tool for measuring readability. *Journalism Quarterly, 30*, 415–433.

Templeton, S. (2012). Teaching and learning morphology: A reflection on generative vocabulary instruction. *Journal of Education, 192*(2/3), 101–107.

Templeton, S. (2015). Learning, reading, and writing words closely and deeply: The archaeology of thought. In D. A. Sisk (Ed.), *Accelerating and extending literacy for diverse learners: Using culturally responsive teaching.* Rowman & Littlefield.

Tennyson, R. D., & Cocchiarella, M. J. (1986). An empirically based instructional design theory for teaching concepts. *Review of Educational Research, 56*(1), 40–71.

Thorndike, E. L. (1917). Reading as reasoning: A study of mistakes in paragraph reading. *Journal of Educational Psychology, 8*(6), 323–332.

Tierney, R. J., Readance, J., & Dishner, E. (1995). *Reading strategies and practices: A compendium.* Allyn & Bacon.

Tighe, E., & Schatschneider, C. (2014). A dominance analysis approach to determining predictor importance in third, seventh, and tenth grade reading comprehension skills. *Reading & Writing, 27*(1), 101–127.

TNTP. (2021). *Accelerate, don't remediate: New evidence from elementary math classrooms.* Author. https://tntp.org/publications/view/teacher-training-and-classroom-practice/accelerate-dont-remediate

Torgesen, J. K. (2004). Lessons learned from research on interventions for students who have difficulty learning to read. In P. McCardle & V. Chhabra (Eds.), *The Voice of Evidence in Reading Research* (pp. 355–382). Paul H Brookes Publishing Co.

Trabasso, T., & Magliano, J. P. (1996). Conscious understanding during comprehension. *Discourse Processes, 21*, 255–287.

University of Florida. [SoR-What I Should Have Learned in College]. (2020, August 15). *Q&A with Hollis Scarborough* [Video]. YouTube. https://youtu.be/83tfzOFpBak

Vacca, R., & Vacca, J. L. (2007). *Content area reading: Literacy and learning across the curriculum* (9th ed.). Allyn & Bacon.

Vadasy, P. F., & Sanders, E. A. (2021). Introducing phonics to learners who struggle: Content and embedded cognitive elements. *Reading and Writing, 34,* 2059–2080.

Van Cleave, W. (2019, April). *Morphology matters: Building vocabulary through word parts.* https://www.wvced.com/wp-content/uploads/2019/04/Morphology-Matters-4-1-19.pdf

Van den Broeck, W., & Geudens, A. (2012). Old and new ways to study characteristics of reading disability: The case of the nonword-reading deficit. *Cognitive Psychology, 65*(3), 414–456. https://doi.org/10.1016/j.cogpsych.2012.06.003

Vaughn, M., Premo, J., Sotirovska, V. V., & Erickson, D. (2020). Evaluating agency in literacy using the Student Agency Profile. *Reading Teacher, 73*(4), 427–441.

Vélez-Ibáñez, C. G., & Greenberg, J. B. (1992). Formation and transformation of funds of knowledge among U.S. Mexican households. *Anthropology & Education Quarterly, 23*(4), 313–335.

Vogel, J. (2018). *The science of magnets.* Lightbox.

Watkins, R. (2019). *Most marshmallows.* Chronicle.

Watkins Harper, F. E. (n.d.). *Learning to read.* Poets.org. https://poets.org/poem/learning-read

Wexler, N. (2022). Why 3 popular infographics on reading don't tell the whole story. *Forbes Magazine.* https://www.forbes.com/sites/nataliewexler/2022/07/12/why-3-popular-infographics-on-reading-dont-tell-the-whole-story/?sh=798af5d8b311

Wheeler, R., Cartwright, K. B., & Swords, R. (2012). Factoring AAVE into reading assessment and instruction. *The Reading Teacher, 65*(6), 416–425.

Wheeler, R. S., & Swords, R. (2006). *Code-switching: Teaching standard English in urban classrooms.* National Council of Teachers of English.

Wheeler, R. S., & Swords, R. (2010). *Code-switching lessons: Grammar strategies for linguistically diverse writers.* Heinemann.

Wiley, H. I., & Deno, S. L. (2005). Oral reading and maze measures as predictors of success for English learners on a state standards assessment. *Remedial and Special Education, 26*, 207–214.

Williams, J. P., Staggord, K. B., Lauer, K. D., Hall, K. M., & Pollini, S. (2009). Embedding reading comprehension training in content-area instruction. *Journal of Educational Psychology, 101*(1), 1–20.

Wiseman, R. Fisher, D., Frey, N., & Hattie, J. (2020). *The distance learning playbook for parents: How to support your child's academic, social, and emotional development in any setting.* Corwin.

Wissman, K. T., Rawson, K. A., & Pyc, M. A. (2012). How and when do students use flashcards? *Memory, 20*(6), 568–579. https://doi.org/10.1080/09658211.2012.687052

Wolf, M. (2009). *Proust and the squid: The story and science of the reading brain.* HarperCollins.

Wolf, M., Barzillai, M., Gottwald, S., Miller, L., Spencer, K., Norton, E., Lovett, M., & Morris, R. (2009). The RAVE-O intervention: Connecting neuroscience to the classroom. *Mind, Brain, and Education, 3*(2), 84–93.

Wolfe, M. B. W., & Goldman, S. R. (2005). Relations between adolescents, text processing and reasoning. *Cognition and Instruction, 23*(4), 467–502.

Wood, A. (2009). *The napping house.* Harcourt Brace.

Woodson, J. (2001). *The other side.* G.P. Putnam.

Worthy, J., & Broaddus, K. (2001/2002). Fluency beyond the primary grades: From group performance to silent, independent reading. *The Reading Teacher, 55*, 334–343.

Yaden, D. B., Smolkin, L. B., & Conlon, A. (1989). Preschoolers' questions about pictures, print conventions, and story text during reading aloud at home. *Reading Research Quarterly, 24*(2), 188–214.

Yamada, K. (2014). *What do you do with an idea?* Compendium.

Yopp, H. K. (1992). Developing phonemic awareness in young children. *The Reading Teacher, 45*(9), 696–703.

Zierer, K. (2021). Effects of pandemic-related school closures on pupils' performance and learning in selected countries: A rapid review. *Education Sciences, 11*, 252–264. https://doi.org/10.3390/educsci11060252

Zimmerman, B. S., Rasinski, T. V., & Was, C. A., Rawson, K. A., Dunlosky, J., Kruse, S. D., & Nikbakht, E. (2019). Enhancing outcomes for struggling readers: Empirical analysis of the fluency development lesson. *Reading Psychology, 40*(1), 70–94.

Zucker, T. A., Ward, A. E., & Justice, L. M. (2011). Print referencing during read-alouds: A technique for increasing emergent readers' print knowledge. *The Reading Teacher, 63*(1), 62–72.

Zutell, J. (1998). Word sorting: A developmental spelling approach to word study for delayed readers. *Reading and Writing Quarterly, 14*(2), 219–238.

Index